# Julio Cortázar

This anthology is an attempt to examine the works of the Argentine writer Julio Cortázar from a perspective informed by contemporary critical concerns. The articles gathered here investigate Cortázar's oeuvre from a variety of critical positions and focus on several of his multifarious writings: poems, short stories, novels, and miscellanea. The intention has been to create a context for a reappraisal of Cortázar that questions received notions and assumptions about his works and hence pave the way for a reevaluation of his contribution to and place in Latin American letters. Although significantly diverse in their theoretical approach, style, and their point of insertion in Cortázar's oeuvre, taken together these essays manage to configure a Cortázar whose contours will both surprise and enlighten the reader.

# Cambridge Studies in Latin American and Iberian Literature

# Julio Cortázar

## New Readings

*Edited by*

Carlos J. Alonso

**CAMBRIDGE**
UNIVERSITY PRESS

PUBLISHED BY THE PRESS SYNDICATE OF THE UNIVERSITY OF CAMBRIDGE
The Pitt Building, Trumpington Street, Cambridge CB2 1RP, United Kingdom

CAMBRIDGE UNIVERSITY PRESS
The Edinburgh Building, Cambridge CB2 2RU, United Kingdom
40 West 20th Street, New York, NY 10011-4211, USA
10 Stamford Road, Oakleigh, Melbourne 3166, Australia

First published 1998

Printed in the United States of America

Typeset in Baskerville

*Library of Congress Cataloging-in-Publication Data*
Alonso, Carlos J., ed.
Julio Cortázar: new readings / edited by Carlos J. Alonso.
p. cm. – (Cambridge studies in Latin American and Iberian
literature; 13)
Includes bibliographical references and index.
ISBN 0-521-45210-4 (hb)
1. Cortázar, Julio – Criticism and interpretation. I. Alonso,
Carlos J. II. Title. III. Series.
PQ7797.C7145Z6262 1998
863 – dc21
97-24282
CIP

*A catalog record for this book is available from the British Library.*

ISBN 0 521 45210 4 hardback

# Contents

# Illustrations

# Contributors

CARLOS J. ALONSO, professor and chair of the Department of Spanish at Emory University, is the author of *The Spanish American Regional Novel: Modernity and Autochthony* and *The Burden of Modernity: The Rhetoric of Cultural Discourse in Spanish America* (forthcoming).

ANA MARÍA AMAR SÁNCHEZ, associate professor of Romance languages at Harvard University, is the author of *El relato de los hechos: Rodolfo Walsh, testimonio y escritura* and has published an edition of *Los crepúsculos del jardín* by Leopoldo Lugones and a collection of short stories by Daniel Moyano.

ANDREW BUSH is associate professor of Hispanic studies at Vassar College. His publications include essays on Spanish and Spanish American authors such as Cervantes, Reinaldo Arenas, Ana María Moix, Juan Goytisolo, and Jorge Luis Borges.

JEAN FRANCO, emerita professor of Spanish and comparative literature at Columbia University, has authored and edited a number of books, among them *César Vallejo: The Dialectics of Poetry and Silence, Plotting Women: Gender and Representation in Mexico,* and *On Edge: The Crisis of Contemporary Latin American Culture* (with Juan Flores and George Yúdice).

ANÍBAL GONZÁLEZ, Edwin Earle Sparks Professor of Spanish and Portuguese at Pennsylvania State University, is the author of *La crónica modernista hispanoamericana, La novela modernista hispanoamericana,* and *Journalism and the Development of Spanish American Narrative.*

LUCILLE KERR is professor of Spanish at the University of Southern California. Her publications include *Suspended Fictions: Reading Novels by Manuel Puig* and *Reclaiming the Author: Figures and Fictions from Spanish America.*

NEIL LARSEN, professor of modern languages at Northeastern University, has published two books entitled *Reading North by South: On Latin American Literature, Culture, and Politics,* and *Modernism and Hegemony: A Materialist Critique of Aesthetic Agencies.*

FREDERICK LUCIANI is associate professor and chair of Romance languages at Colgate University. He has written articles on various colonial and contemporary Spanish American topics and has recently finished a manuscript on the works of sor Juana Inés de la Cruz.

ALBERTO MOREIRAS, associate professor of Romance studies at Duke University, is the author of *Interpretación y diferencia: análisis de estructuras interpretativas* and the editor of *La escritura política de José Hierro.*

GUSTAVO PELLÓN is associate professor of Spanish and Portuguese at the University of Virginia. He is the author of numerous articles on contemporary Spanish American literature and of *José Lezama Lima's Joyful Vision: A Study of* Paradiso *and Other Prose Works.*

RENÉ PRIETO is associate professor of foreign languages and literatures at Southern Methodist University. He has published *Miguel Angel Asturias's Archaeology of Return* and is the coauthor of *Michelangelo Antonioni: A Guide to Reference and Resources* (with Ted Parry).

DORIS SOMMER is professor of Romance languages at Harvard University. She is the author of *Foundational Fictions: The National Romances of Latin America* and of *One Master for Another: Populism as Patriarchal Rhetoric in Dominican Novels.*

# Introduction:
## "To burn like this without surcease . . . "
### *Carlos J. Alonso*

"The worst of it," Oliveira said to himself, "is that I want
to be an active onlooker and that's where the trouble
starts."

Julio Cortázar, *Hopscotch*

Just before his death in 1984, Julio Cortázar left two books ready for publication: a volume entitled *Salvo el crepúsculo* containing poems that had
never made it into print before, and another comprised of two previously
unpublished one-act plays: *Nada a Pehuajo* and *Adiós Robinson*. Subsequent to his passing Cortázar's legal heirs have released three other
books to press: *El examen* and *Divertimento* (both published in 1986) and
*Diario de Andrés Fava* (1995), all of them written during the years before
Cortázar had achieved literary prominence. The effect of this abundant
posthumous production has been to make the sort of closure one would
have expected to accompany the author's death difficult to achieve. But
the release of a number of works produced by Cortázar at the beginning
of his literary career in the late forties and early fifties is especially threatening, in that it points to the possibility of an endless regression of the
originary moment of writing – that avowed fountainhead required for
any attempt to arrive at a genetic understanding of a writer's oeuvre.
From this perspective, the body of texts that we customarily subsume
under the rubric "Cortázar" appears to be an opus still under construction even after the stark finality of his physical demise.

On the other hand, "Cortázar" the author-function is as much the
product of a way of reading that body of works as it is the totality composed by them, however unstable the latter may be. Indeed, one of the
concepts underlying this anthology of essays on Cortázar's oeuvre is that
the changes which have occurred in critical discourse during the last fif-
teen or twenty years have produced a different "Cortázar," whose contours begin to reveal themselves under the cumulative pressure of the
critical approaches brought together in this volume. That conviction is

1

reflected in the titles assigned the four parts into which the book is divided, all of which propose the activity of reading as the controlling and configuring operation.

There is a canonical image of Cortázar, a critical creation that has emerged from the accumulation of numerous acts of interpretation plied on his works and of countless scraps of biographical lore. This picture – which is also a plot of sorts – reads in its essential rendition something like this: Cortázar was a giant of a man (six feet four) who abandoned his native Argentina in his thirties for a life of permanent and voluntary exile in Paris. In his adulthood he suffered from a disease that, in Dorian Grayesque fashion, made him look substantially younger than he was. His stories – where his literary excellence truly resides according to this *récit* – are structured on the motif of the existence of two simultaneous orders that at privileged and unplanned moments touch one another in a way that allows for passage from one order to the other, leading to a reversal of the hierarchy that originally defined them. As a collection, Cortázar's stories are lighter, more playful versions of Borges's narratives. His novels, on the other hand, favor formal experimentation, are characterized by fragmentation and the incorporation of minimalia – press clippings, *faits divers,* and so on – and are imbued with an aesthetics that has more or less vague surrealist undertones. Cortázar was from the outset a strong supporter of the Cuban Revolution, but the Cuban bureaucracy's attempt to regulate artistic production (which culminated in the so-called Padilla affair) created a rift that never healed completely: In a series of articles and open letters he defended the possibility of engaging in revolutionary activity within the realm of the literary rather than in the political arena. His social commitment was rekindled by the Sandinista experiment in Nicaragua, which motivated Cortázar's late "conversion" or return to political engagement. Toward the end of his career, his works made increasing use of popular cultural forms, marking a turn in his production toward the recognition of "low" discourses as aesthetically viable vehicles.

In a number of ways, this collection of essays on Cortázar positions itself against the background provided by this received and well-established notion of the Argentine writer and his works. Its aim is to exploit the opportunity created by the two circumstances previously described: that is, the seeming open-endedness of Cortázar's oeuvre above and beyond his death, and the profound changes that have taken place in the critical scene in the last two decades. These essays, written by some of the most perspicacious and intelligent scholars in the field, offer a wide range of responses to the question of how Cortázar's relevance may be renegotiated from our critical present. Each contributor has managed to find a point of leverage for a reconsideration of Cortázar's oeuvre that ultimately calls into question the usefulness and accuracy of the conception of his works that we have inherited.

Part 1, "Reading Cortázar Today," groups essays in which the principal thrust lies in taking critical advantage of the chasm that has opened between a Cortázar that was and the one configured by a contemporary critical optics. They are guided by a desire to reframe Cortázar in order to shed light on aspects of his work that become noticeable only in a retrospective critical examination. For these critics, "Cortázar" is a fairly homogeneous textual entity whose ideological and literary underpinnings become clear when it is filtered through the interpretive interrogations put to it by the present critical moment.

In "Between Utopia and Inferno (Julio Cortázar's Version)," Ana María Amar Sánchez begins by positing the very question this anthology addresses: How indeed can one read Cortázar today? Her answer is to produce a novel reading of the Argentine author by placing him in the interpretive context of that long tradition of works which have sought to construct the entity referred to as Latin America. Amar Sánchez argues that the movement between binaries that is the typical situation depicted by Cortázar's stories serves to expose the fundamental contradiction at the heart of this textual tradition, one in which the encounter with Latin American essence is customarily represented as a displacement in time and/or space from a state of inauthenticity to one of plenitude that, paradoxically, becomes progressively more problematic as the protagonist draws closer to his avowed goal. Amar Sánchez sees in the structure of Cortázar's short stories, and especially in "Axolotl" and "Night Upside Down" (La noche boca arriba), a critique of that tradition – a critical positioning that makes visible a contestatory relationship between Cortázar and Spanish American literature in general which affords new insights regarding his place in that literary continuum.

Jean Franco's "Comic Stripping: Cortázar in the Age of Mechanical Reproduction" is a powerful meditation on Cortázar's place in the high–low culture divide in Latin America. Franco examines texts written by Cortázar in the early 1950s such as "The Gates of Heaven" ("Puertas al cielo") and the posthumously released El examen, a time in which Peronista populism had created mass movements that threatened bourgeois stability and norms. Franco sees in these early works a strategy that constitutes a response to this crisis, and that goes on to become a constant in

Cortázar's literary production: the postulation of an us–them division that is, in reality, the answer to the collapse of aesthetic value as an intrinsic quality of the art object and its replacement by a sense of taste that is an individual's subjective creation – namely, the sort of personal intervention that can create and valorize the most daring conjunctions of the popular and the classical. In this fashion, value becomes a function of a specific kind of consumption rather than an "objective," and therefore historically threatened, quality. Those individuals "in the know" then band together to form the various clubs ("La Serpiente," "La Joda," for instance) that reappear in Cortázar's works. Franco argues convincingly that this strategy is still at work even in later texts such as *Fantomas against the Multinational Vampires* (*Fantomas contra los vampiros multinacionales*), in which Cortázar appears to be relying heavily on elements of a mass aesthetics.

Neil Larsen's "Cortázar and Postmodernity: New Interpretive Liabilities" endeavors to describe and explain the experience of rereading Cortázar's *Hopscotch* from our postmodern vantage point. Larsen proposes that there is an eminently dated air to the novel that can be ascribed, first, to some of its formal and thematic qualities such as its conceptions of gender and its experimentation with form. But the core of the novel's archaism lies, according to him, in the changes that have occurred in what he calls the "ideology of reading" during the intervening thirty years. Larsen uses the various polemics in which Cortázar engaged concerning the question of the local versus the universal as it pertained to a political praxis for the Latin American author to explain Cortázar's caducity, but also to effect a critique of the ethnographically based critical localism that has finally gained the upper hand at the expense of a "universalist" Cortázar. His reading provides a firm historical foundation for the experience of reading Cortázar nowadays while simultaneously questioning the ideological investments of the background against which that complacent reading takes place. Hence Cortázar's "caducity" here functions as a paradigmatic instance that allows Larsen to expose the ideological underpinnings of contemporary Spanish American cultural criticism.

René Prieto engages in a classic psychoanalytic interpretation of Cortázar's short stories in "Cortázar's Closet." He skillfully assembles a catalogue of instances throughout Cortázar's short fiction in which characters are described as emerging from an enclosed space into a light-filled and threatening environment in which some version of death awaits. Prieto argues that this master story is fueled by an anxiety harking back to the violent separation from the mother that defines birth – what Freudian psychoanalysis refers to as "the wound that never heals." The desire to assuage that anxiety produces the repetitive appearance in Cortázar's work of motifs that are allusive to the birth situation: darkness, holes, tunnels, and experiences of suffocation, shortness of breath, and drowning. Out of this narrative crucible that typically signifies death for his characters, Cortázar manages, on the other hand, to abreact creatively his separation anxiety by means of the symbolic substitutions that Prieto carefully traces in his short fiction.

The part entitled "Cortázar Reads Cortázar," brings together contributions in which the schism that the essays in the previous section saw as a function of the difference between Cortázar's texts and the contemporary critical scene is projected instead onto Cortázar's oeuvre itself. All of the articles gathered here argue for the existence of a disjunction within Cortázar which they refigure metaphorically as a rereading and rewriting of Cortázar's previous work by himself. "Cortázar" here functions as a way to give a name and a location to that place in which reversals, contradictions, and fissures appear among the various strands that weave his texts, or between different moments of his literary production.

"Between Reading and Repetition (apropos of Cortázar's *62: A Model Kit*)" by Lucille Kerr considers the implications of the several statements on the poetics of the novel that appear frequently in Cortázar's works. Specifically, she addresses the relationship between *62: A Model Kit* (*62: modelo para armar*) and the pronouncements on the genre that are ascribed to the character Morelli in the text of Cortázar's *Hopscotch*. According to Kerr, there is an inescapable difficulty in the sort of theory-praxis connection that the prologue to *62: A Model Kit* establishes between the proposal for a new novel included in chapter 62 of *Hopscotch* and the novel that it introduces; for one of the explicit intentions of *Hopscotch* is to collapse the distinction between the novel and the poetics of the novel. She proceeds to perform a close reading of the opening pages of *62* that sees in them the introjection into the text of the reader's activity – of a technique for reading that thereby recuperates the author's regulatory role in the interpretive operation. This allows her to posit the existence in Cortázar of an inherently conservative perspective on interpretation that belies his repeated espousal of an avowedly liberatory reading practice.

Gustavo Pellón's "Cortázar and the Idolatry of Origins" is constructed around a series of rereadings and renegotiations of Cortázar by Cortázar himself. In his last published book, *Salvo el crepúsculo,* Cortázar collected a number of miscellaneous poetic texts from throughout his literary career, among them "Grecia 59," a poem in which he reevokes his youthful admiration for Greek culture in a moment of later maturity – a moment of recollection itself reread in the comments that serve as a preface to the poem now being published for the first time. Through a painstaking and intelligent close reading, Pellón follows the thread of Cortázar's fascination with origins as it manifested itself in his early mystification of Greek culture – the putative source of Western rationality – and his later questioning of that category. In the final embracing of Dionysian irrationality in a text that arises out of what Cortázar calls a "distracted" form of writing, Pellón sees an anticipation of the attack on rationalism and the serious yet goal-less playing that will be the cornerstones of *Hopscotch*.

Andrew Bush attempts to broach what is perhaps Cortázar's most haunting work, the photographic montage *Prose from the Observatory (Prosa del observatorio)*, in his essay "Supposing Morelli Had Meant to Go to Jaipur." In 1967 Cortázar visited and photographed the observatory built in Jaipur in the eighteenth century by Sultan Jai Singh. The photographs were then published alongside a meditation on the observatory by Cortázar, spurred by a scientific article on the life cycle of eels. Bush sees in the execution of this text a radical departure from Cortázar's literary figurations: rather than positing two conceptual poles to then propose a vehicle or avenue for achieving unity out of duality (a maneuver related to the will to interpretive power observable in scientific discourse), or engaging in formal actualizations of theoretical pronouncements about literature (such as we saw earlier in *62: A Model Kit*), Cortázar is content here with navigating discursively without final recourse to an enabling synthesis. The language and structure of Bush's essay bespeak a desire to allow his critical discourse the same free ranging through a field composed of a heterogeneous collection of texts as that evinced by Cortázar's work. The essay is thus held together in a rigorously playful fashion through the equally demanding displacement of the writing subject throughout works that are ultimately linked by the critic's readerly experience of them.

Cortázar's conflicted and complex concerns with the political are the subject of the two essays included under the part title "Reading Politics." The conventional critical plot reviewed earlier sees Cortázar as becoming progressively committed politically with time, from an early defense of a revolutionary praxis within the confines of literary form ("revolution in literature" rather than "literature in the revolution") to the later public statements and short stories that manifest solidarity with the Sandinista project in Nicaragua. And yet, the contributions included here attest to the fact that the presence of the political in Cortázar will not yield to easy formulas or commonplace assumptions.

Alberto Moreiras's "'Apocalypse at Solentiname' as Heterological Production" is a headlong plunge into the intricacies of what is perhaps Cortázar's most significant "statement" regarding the relationship between literature and politics. His intention is to move away from those readings of "Apocalipsis in Solentiname" that perceive it mainly as a document of denunciation against political violence. Moreiras sees the story as a series of attempts at representation or translation – from the painterly reproduction of a supposedly Arcadian peasant reality by Nicaraguan peasants in the island community of Solentiname, to the photographic appropriation of the latter by the protagonist of the story, to the subsequent projection of the photographs onto a screen in a Paris apartment. These operations are predicated on the existence of two kinds of "writing": one univocal and closed; the other multiple and disseminated. The ingenuous project of mimetic appropriation of the image – which parallels the utopian social experiment of the community in Solentiname – is put in check by what Moreiras calls the inescapable "loss of semiotic coincidence between model and copy." This creates a milieu for the return with a vengeance of that knowledge which has been repressed. Moreiras finally argues that it is in the midst of this theater of representation that any understanding of political solidarity on Cortázar's part must be properly understood.

Frederick Luciani's article, "The Man in the Car/in the Trees/behind the Fence: From Cortázar's 'Blow-up' to Oliver Stone's *JFK*," proposes to study the ambiguous presence of Cortázar's short story "Blow-Up" ("Las babas del diablo") in a collection of American films extending from the 1960s to the 1990s – what he refers to as "Cortázar's wayward and unrecognized Hollywood progeny": Brian De Palma's *Greetings* and *Blow Out,* Francis F. Coppola's *The Conversation,* and Oliver Stone's *JFK.* Luciani's genealogical investigation also includes Alfred Hitchcock's *Rear Window* as a "precursor" to "Blow-up," as well as the famous "Zapruder film," which accidentally captured the Kennedy assassination in Dallas. It also ends with a consideration of "Apocalypse in Solentiname," in which the author sees Cortázar again taking up the issues raised in his earlier text. Luciani reads in the American tradition "founded" by Cortázar's story an attempt to politicize the narrative through an emphasis on conspiracy theories rather than through engagement in a systematic ideological critique. He presents, as an alternative to this version of a political resemanticization of "Blow-Up," Cortázar's own subsequent reworking of that story in "Apocalypse in Solentiname."

The two essays in "The Ethics of Reading" are closely related to those in the previous part on the political in Cortázar, insofar as the political can never be cleanly separated from the question of ethics. In them the authors explore Cortázar's understanding of literature as a discourse that knows something about itself and about its own capacity to affect the world that produces it materially and to which it refers, directly or implicitly. What is – finally – the link between literature and truth, when is literature more truthful to its own nature, and how Cortázar's works are inscribed in this problematic are the essential concerns addressed by these essays.

In "Pursuing a Perfect Present" Doris Sommer sets her interpretive agenda against a possible deconstructive reading of Cortázar's story "The Pursuer" ("El perseguidor") – namely, an interpretation that would dismantle oppositions by showing the reducibility of the two terms of the ruling binary of the story (jazz performer versus music critic) to one another. She argues that such a reading would conceal the explicitly constructed nature of the difference on which the narrative is based, therefore endowing the latter with a homogeneity that would do violence to it. Instead, she proposes to read the story as a fable about the very refusal to overcome difference. In her view, there is in the narrative an ongoing struggle between the musician and his biographer for the mutual reduction of the Other that is significant precisely because of its undecidability. The similarities between the opponents that a deconstructive reading would emphasize entail the threat of the disappearance of those differences from which each character derives his particularity and identity. Hence, the story is seen by Sommer as acquiring its full significance in the context of intersubjective negotiations, an insight that she extends to Cortázar's awareness of the appropriating and fixating tendencies of writing.

Aníbal González's "'Press Clippings' and Cortázar's Ethics of Writing" is a trenchant exploration of Cortázar's understanding of the relationship between literature and evil. It takes as its point of departure the demand placed on Latin American writers to use literature as an instrument for the denunciation of social ills and argues that literature's effectiveness in such a task is bound to be compromised by the relationship to violence and negativity that is intrinsic to it. "Press Clippings" is the text in which Cortázar faces squarely the implications of this intuition for any programmatic assertion of solidarity asserted by a literary text. But according to González, Cortázar also eschews the facile association of literature with transgression that Georges Bataille's work would have made available to him as a form of personal consolation. In this regard, Cortázar's position – González argues – is a profoundly ethical one, as it precludes the possibility of letting him turn into a virtue what is clearly regarded by Cortázar as a failure. Furthermore, because the collagelike texture of the story is analogous to that of Cortázar's novelistic oeuvre after *Hopscotch,* one might perhaps read the story as a reconsideration by him of his earlier understanding of writing as an essentially playful activity.

As is perhaps evident even from these brief presentations, the essays gathered in this anthology intersect in a manner that will become increasingly obvious as the reader's itinerary advances. I would now like to try to identify some of the ways in which the individual pieces transcend their engagement with specific texts and problematics of Cortázar's oeuvre and, rather, point collectively to an alternative configuration of his writing.

I have already suggested that the articles which concern themselves with the question of the political in Cortázar are complemented by those which address the inscription of ethical considerations in his works. The essays grouped under both categories are arguing that there exists in Cortázar a desire to claim a space for ambiguity and suspension in the face of the commonly understood axiological demands of both politics and ethics. This is clearly the case in the essays by González, Sommer, and Moreiras, all of which propose to recognize in several of Cortázar's texts a compelling interrogation of comfortable notions regarding writing, ethics, and politics. In Luciani's essay, this dimension is identified in the reinscription of the political that, according to him, constitutes the rewriting of "Blow-Up" into "Apocalypse in Solentiname." This critical maneuver also serves as a point of connection with the essays grouped under the heading "Cortázar Reads Cortázar." For the articles by Kerr, Pellón, and Bush are intent on pointing out the existence of an internal reformulation and critique of the presuppositions that controlled Cortázar's ideology of writing at various points in his career. Each depicts a "moment" in which a self-critical operation obtains within Cortázar's oeuvre, a moment that has to be configured as integral to his writing on account of its repeated, continual occurrence throughout his literary career. This is the same critical operation that can be seen at work under various guises in the essays collected in the first part, "Reading Cortázar Today." Amar Sánchez locates it in Cortázar's dismantling of the long-standing Spanish American narrative of identity. Here, the critical regard is turned outward to confront the master narrative tropes of Spanish American cultural discourse rather than the presuppositions of Cortázar's own writing. In Prieto's essay the division is configured as a psychoanalytic splitting of the subject, whereas Franco's piece is built on the presumption of an internal chasm, as its purpose is to assert instead a continuity that belies the avowed transformations in Cortázar's oeuvre. Similarly, Larsen sees the difference between the past vitality of *Hopscotch* and its present caducity as an effect of the emergence of a new dominant reading optics, a proposal that projects that schism onto the history of the novel's reception.

One could argue, then, that the Cortázar who emerges from these essays is one who calls into question what has been traditionally regarded as the essential paradigm of his textual universe: the original positing of an oppositional duality whose effectiveness and viability are denied by depicting the passage from one term of the opposition to the other. Collectively, these essays alert us to the fact that the dynamics ruling Cortázar's works is not built on the dissolution of opposition by effecting a movement from one pole to the other, but rather on the displacement away from the dichotomy itself to a third "position" that defines a space in which those categories are suspended or rendered ineffectual. The cleavage created by this movement in each work, as well as in Cortázar's production as a whole, generates the internal difference that the essays gathered here have identified in their various ways. A brief examination of *Hopscotch* will prove illustrative of this procedure, which I argue is constitutive of Cortázar's literary discourse as a whole.

Traditionally, duality has been taken to be the structuring force behind the various levels of Cortázar's best-known novel: Paris versus Buenos Aires; the two texts of *Hopscotch* described by the famed "Table of Instructions" (Tablero de Dirección); Oliveira versus Traveler; La Maga versus Talita; the *lector hembra* versus the *lector cómplice;* the novel versus a poetics of the novel. And yet there is clearly another dimension of the text in which those structuring polarities are undermined by positing a third term that cannot be incorporated into either one of the two poles, or that results from a conflation of the two. The reader will remember the apparent division of *Hopscotch* into two large sections, "From This Side" and "From That Side," only to have yet a third section that negates their comprehensiveness and closure, entitled "From Diverse Sides." The same principle is at work in the novel's "Table of Instructions" and its attendant division of the readership into *lector hembra* and *lector cómplice*. For the arrangement of chapters that the table prescribes as the unorthodox reading incorporates the traditional order of reading, and opting for this supposedly more adventurous experience results, paradoxically, in the reader's final entrapment. This aspect of the novel must be highlighted, because it is this "experimental" quality of *Hopscotch* which is usually blamed for the dated feeling the novel is supposed to have for a contemporary reader.

Yet reading *Hopscotch* as an experimental novel misses the point that the text is profoundly derisive of its own experimentality. This is why the sort of active reading that is avowedly favored by the "Table of Instructions" ends up in an infinite loop in which the "creative" reader, in his or her hubris, is, at least metaphorically, lost forever. I think it has not been sufficiently understood that this self-thwarting "experimental" nature of *Hopscotch* is Cortázar's critique of the narrative characteristics of the French *nouveau roman* and its pretensions of nonclosure and ateleology. Cortázar's understanding of reading as an operation guided by an intense desire to impose meaning led him to question the ultimate radicalness of these novelistic experiments.[1] In keeping with the text's obliviousness to or even defiance of the dualities that it establishes, *Hopscotch* is a novel that argues for a prescriptive poetics on the novel to which it is manifestly not faithful (the Morelli chapters), a fact underscored by Cortázar's subsequent writing of another novel (*62: A Model Kit*) which is posited as the praxis to that theory, but which is equally and self-consciously far from fulfilling its stated aim.

This quality of the novel can also be seen at work in the six chapters that provide the points of articulation for the novel's plot: the Berthe Trépat episode (23), the death of Rocamadour (28), the incident with the *clocharde* Emmanuelle (36), the plank chapter (41), the morgue episode with Talita (54), and Oliveira's threshold experience at the window of his room in the insane asylum (56). The common thread in the narrative and epistemological function of all these events is the opportunity they appear to offer for the suspension of the dichotomic categories of knowledge, and the concomitant possibility of envisioning nondualistic experience. The novel is built on six such moments, each of which corresponds precisely to the concept of crisis as defined in the text by Oliveira:

Every time we enter a crisis the absurdity is total; understand that dialectics can only set our closet in order in moments of calm. You know very well that at the high point of a crisis we always work by impulse, just the opposite of foresight, doing the most unexpected and wildest sort of thing. And at that moment precisely it could be said that there was a sort of saturation of reality, don't you think? Reality comes on fast, it shows itself with all its strength, and precisely at that moment the only way of facing it is to renounce dialectics. (163)

Perhaps the most challenging of these chapters to the reader – because it almost seems to be consciously eliciting contempt for Oliveira – is the one that details the death of La Maga's child, Rocamadour. Oliveira has returned to the apartment after the encounter with Berthe Trépat and notices that the sick child has expired. He manages to tell surreptitiously all the other members of the group in the room what has happened, so that only the mother is unaware of the death of her child. While everyone is waiting for La Maga to discover the truth, the most intense philosophical discussion in the novel takes place, a dialogue about the nature of knowledge itself. What Oliveira creates by holding the dreadful information in abeyance is a moment of suspension that cannot be epistemologically recovered by either reason or emotion. He has learned his lesson well, just having returned to his apartment from his experience with Berthe Trépat, in which he had allowed his compassion for the pathetic woman to destroy an equivalent moment of epistemological and experiential suspension. Eventually La Maga will learn the truth, and then everything will proceed according to the conventions of mourning and sympathy. This interpretation is emphasized by the descent of the old neighbor from the apartment upstairs, who stomps down furiously to complain about noise, only to solemnly proffer his condolences in the most formulaic fashion after finding out about the infant's death. The rigor required of Oliveira in order to sustain the moment's duration is lost on all the members of the Serpent's Club – and on many of the novel's readers – whose reaction is to excoriate him on account of his lack of sympathy for La Maga's plight.

The six episodes that provide the text's narrative foundation are all similarly structured: They are moments of suspension – literally, in the case of Talita's "plank" episode – in which the dichotomous categories of knowledge are not sufficient to encompass what is transpiring. Hence, they represent not a gesture toward "another side" or a movement from one category to its opposite, but an attempt to define a space where the dyad itself is brought into question as a suitable epistemological instrument. This is the role of the narratively muted character of Pola in *Hopscotch* as well: to attenuate the La Maga/Talita affective pairing with Oliveira by suggesting the existence of a third possibility for Horacio's emotive and intellectual life.[2]

This maneuver is also evident in other works of Cortázar. Think, for instance, about the *Historias de cronopios y de famas,* with its suggestion of a universe divided between the two essential attitudes that *cronopios* and *famas* avowedly represent, and which goes on to posit yet a third being – the *esperanzas* – thereby invalidating the binary inscribed in the very title of the book. There are also works written from the far side of this knowledge, such as *A Certain Lucas,* in which the radical heterogeneity of the material presented makes irrelevant the essentialist definition of the individual whose experiences the text purports to chronicle.

My contention is that this deliberate and rigorous putting in check of the dichotomous structure of knowledge provides a perspective from which to renegotiate both the received notion of Cortázar and his relationship to Spanish American letters. When read in this vein, *Hopscotch* – published in 1963 – anticipates by a few years the radical questioning of structuralism that marked the end of the sixties in critical theory and has come to be identified with the works of Jacques Derrida. It is not my intent to claim some sort of precedence for Cortázar in this deconstructive enterprise, but to suggest a way in which to redefine the relationship that we maintain with his works from within our contemporary critical scene. In the specific Spanish American context, this interpretation of *Hopscotch* makes it very difficult to sustain the critical convention that includes this work among the texts of the so-called Boom, novels that exhibit a fetishistic and almost mathematical concern with structure and form which is expressive of their epistemological authority and certainty: Vargas Llosa's *La Casa Verde* and Fuentes's *La muerte de Artemio Cruz* come immediately to mind.

In fact, it could be argued that Cortázar's whole oeuvre is a challenge precisely to the sort of ethical and aesthetic assurances that were the ruling conceits of the literary ideology of the Boom. If critical orthodoxy insists on placing Cortázar squarely within the Boom, it is also obvious that Cortázar understood early on that the demand that literature be answerable to preoccupations of national or continental identity placed an impoverishing burden on cultural discourse in Latin America. In fact, his renewed shifting and questioning of the ground on which the ideological and philosophical category of identity rests aligns him more closely with the critique of that enterprise of ontological definition which is the hallmark – whether explicitly or not – of post-Boom literary production. This critique identifies him also with the philosophical preoccupations that have characterized the poststructuralist period as a whole: the exploration of the subject as problematically inscribed in language and the understanding of literature as a discourse whose existence discloses the precarious foundation of the other discourses with which it shares a social and cultural space.

From this perspective one begins to discern that perhaps Cortázar's search for a way out of the epistemological dichotomies of Western knowledge may not represent the author's debt to surrealism or paraphysics, as is commonly held, but rather a coeval and sui generis exploration of issues that preoccupied thinkers such as Derrida, Lacan, Serres, and several others. Timothy Reiss has said, for instance, that "the principal 'elements' of Derridean discourse: 'margin,' 'supplement,' '*différence*,' 'deferral,' 'athesis,' and so on can all be subsumed under a paradigm of 'between' (*entre*). . . . It is as though this discourse wished to expand the 'space' of the limits themselves. . . . 'Space' is of course the wrong term. 'Between' is a better indication of the attempt."[3]

Cortázar's swerve toward a third position in an attempt to effect a displacement away from the dichotomies of knowledge is clearly encompassed by this description. He seems to have understood that there was in fact no way out, no utopian other side from which to critique Western epistemology: As he has one of his characters say, in the philosophical dialogue alluded to earlier in *Hopscotch*, any critique of that system is like "the scorpion stabbing itself in the neck, tired of being a scorpion but having to have recourse to its own scorpionness in order to do away with itself as a scorpion" (158). Hence, the movement encompassed by Cortázar's oeuvre is neither an epiphany nor a solution, but rather a gesture toward an uncomfortable and unsettled "between." In this respect, the writing that we call "Cortázar" can be conceptualized as a discursive space that, precisely on account of its own internal dynamics, may never yield to the critical desire to establish its boundaries in a precise and rigorous fashion.

In diverse ways and to differing degrees, the essays gathered in this anthology point to that internal spatial dimension of Cortázar's writing which is opened up by the movement away from the very dichotomies that it establishes within itself. One can only hope that their collective interpretive force will provide the justification and the impetus for a comprehensive reexamination of Cortázar, however tenuous the prospect of any final critical mastery of his oeuvre may prove to be.

## Notes

1. Chapter 137, a "Morelli" fragment in *Hopscotch*, reads as follows: "If the volume or the tone of a work can lead one to believe that the author is attempting a sum, hasten to point out to him that he is face-to-face with the opposite attempt, that of an implacable *subtraction*" (526).
2. This becomes evident from the original sketchbook for the composition of *Hopscotch*. There Cortázar envisions a multiplication of affective pairings linking the various characters of the novel. See the *Cuaderno de Bitácora de Rayuela* (Buenos Aires: Sudamericana, 1981).
3. Timothy Reiss, *The Discourse of Modernism* (Ithaca, NY: Cornell University Press, 1982), 378.

# PART ONE

Reading Cortázar Today

# 1

## Between Utopia and Inferno
## (Julio Cortázar's Version)

*Ana María Amar Sánchez*

Translated by M. Elizabeth Ginway

> That time that can come sometimes outside of all
> time, a hole in the web of time,
> That way of being between, not above nor behind
> but between.
>
> Julio Cortázar, *Prosa del observatorio*

How can we read Cortázar today? What can we read in these works considered "sacred" by an entire generation? Cortázar's works have long received much attention from literary critics for their intertextuality and self-referentiality, as well as for their unique approach to the fantastic, to verbal play, and to narrative experimentation. Yet for many, some ten years after Cortázar's death, his texts bear the distinct marks of a "sixties ideology" that so typifies modern writing. The changes brought about by the 1980s have made one entire genre of his work – the novels – seem outdated. Thus, Cortázar ends up being pigeonholed into a certain type of narrative and time period: the "Boom." The loss of the beliefs – and hopes – of some twenty years ago has somewhat eroded Cortázar's validity. This comment often recurs in approaches to his texts, especially in his own country, Argentina. Because now everything possible seems to have been said about Cortázar, he is condemned to be the representative of an irremediably lost golden age of Latin American letters. His program of breaking with previous narrative tradition by reflecting on writing itself and experimenting with language makes Cortázar a paradigm of the literary innovators who came of age in the sixties. Yet, in hindsight, his rejection of realism is both parallel and alternative to another modality with strong ties to journalism and other popular genres that argued, perhaps, for an even more radical change in traditional forms. This latter current has enjoyed greater influence in the literature produced in the last few years, which may be one of the reasons for the premature aging that some critics attribute to such works as *Hopscotch*.

The binary play that Cortázar exploits in almost all of his work has been read as his own private system for exploring the relationship between two different settings, two worlds, two types of reality, and so on.[1] However, this condition of duality takes on a very distinct inflection when we separate it from the fantastic or the metaphysical. Although there can be no doubt that these elements constitute a good part of Cortázar's writing, I believe that this binary play, as set forth in his works, allows us to place at least part of his production within an entire body of Latin American texts, all of which share a similar problematic. Thus, Cortázar's work is not really about his own way of approaching the fantastic or a typical Argentine author's way of resolving the relationship between Buenos Aires and Paris, or even about the dilemmas of a *porteño;* rather, it belongs to a type of writing that debates, defines, and constructs the representation of the image that *is* "Latin America."

Moreover, this particular group of texts – which transcend differences of genre, era, and author – are tied to a system of representation that comprises an entire discourse on Latin America. These texts, in their choice of setting and narrative moment, construct the very subject, culture, and language of Latin America. It should be noted that these works, which appear to be very different on the surface, construct a fundamental problematic by creating an almost contradictory, if not ambiguous, representation of Latin America. This problematic becomes particularly acute when we consider that all of these texts are part of the canon of Latin American literature. More specifically, I am referring to works such as *La vorágine* by José Eustasio Rivera, *Los pasos perdidos* by Alejo Carpentier, and *Cien años de soledad* by Gabriel García Márquez, as well as *La Casa Verde* by Mario Vargas Llosa, *Pubis angelical* by Manuel Puig, *Plan de evasión* by Adolfo Bioy Casares, and finally, Cortázar's own stories "La noche boca arriba" and "Axolotl."[2] Despite their differences, all these texts constitute a particular discourse on Latin America, and they share a similar image. In the first place, they create contradictory representations of Latin America; and second, they all have been read as a type of "homage to the American soil." Thus they become representative of an entire literature, and of the continent itself.[3]

Given the multiple meanings of the word *representation,* we must define its use in this study. I think of it as having a distinct inflection that is in no way indebted to the concepts of mimesis or verisimilitude, both of which understand it as an attempt to imitate reality; on the contrary, I view representation as a principle that organizes meaning. Representations constitute the space of the imaginary, and as such are found in all types of discourse and even establish connections among various discourses. Representations also depend on the viewpoint of the subject, and thus become schemes for classification and valorization that construct meaning. The sheer variety of representation establishes multiple relationships among texts and generates a productive pattern of new meanings not previously assigned to the object. I understand representation as articulating a network of relations that construct meaning: It does not reflect the object correctly or incorrectly; rather, it interprets and orders by assigning meaning to reality. From this point of view, all "representations" propose a "political" reading of the world, in that a given reading involves taking a certain position – a stand or intervention – regarding the nature of things.

Our culture is made up of a complex system of representations, beliefs, myths, and fictions that conform to our social imagination and contribute to our idea of reality. Consequently, as Bourdieu has pointed out,[4] symbolic systems, as instruments of knowledge and communication, are present in all social practices and exert considerable power as ordering principles in the *construction of reality*.

We can conclude that representation, when understood as a discursive construction, produces (and does not reproduce) a reading of reality. Therefore, the textual representations of the selected group of this study, which concentrate on the depiction of a distinctly "Latin American" time and space, neither reflect nor reproduce an image that is closer or more distant from reality. When considered in this way, the difference between a fantastic and a realist text becomes irrelevant. All representations configure an imaginary system of Latin America and dramatize the tensions and contradictions among the multiplicity of discourses (literary and nonliterary) that have created and continue to create Latin America. At the same time, these texts, so very different from one another, still exhibit certain constants in their representation that allow them both to contribute to and to participate in the discourse of Latin America.

### *In Search of a Lost Space*

*Los pasos perdidos* by Alejo Carpentier is our point of departure and serves as a touchstone for the relations among the texts that constitute our study. Written in 1953, Carpentier's novel, even as it attempted to distance itself from or go beyond the regionalist novels of Latin America, nonetheless brought along with it a whole network of representations of Latin America, especially in its own concepts of time and space. *La vorágine*, written in 1924, can be taken as the starting point of the whole system, although clearly it is not the only novel we could use, as it is possible to construct a much longer list. Nevertheless, linking it to other works such as *Doña Bárbara* by R. Gallegos (1929) and *Don Segundo Sombra* by R. Güiraldes (1926) would allow us to pinpoint a key moment in what is traditionally thought of as a narrative deemed "celebratory" of Latin America, and therefore also a founding moment for the contradictory representations of Latin America referred to in this study.

Yet I am more interested in pointing out how another literary style such as Carpentier's, which thinks of itself as being so distant from and even opposed to these founding texts, cannot help but continue this very discourse on Latin America through notable points of contact with the earlier texts. *La vorágine* already lays the groundwork for the basic elements of representation that will be key in *Los pasos perdidos:* the trip to the country's interior as a flight from the codes and laws of civilization in search of a meaningful place of special significance; the idea of starting a new life faraway from European customs, which reverses the old opposition between civilization and barbarism by giving the latter positive connotations. This journey leads to the entrance into a "beautiful and impressive" natural world that quickly changes into an inferno; thus, this space becomes inhuman, impossible, and devouring, a space from which there is no possible escape and which implies death itself (remember the famous ending of *La vorágine:* "And they were swallowed by the jungle"). The tension between the descriptions of the jungle and the latter's devastating effects on the protagonists serves as a founding moment for the conflict that will continue in varying and contradictory forms in the other texts of this corpus.

*Los pasos perdidos* is the key work of this textual system. It develops and exaggerates the dichotomy between two locations (the negative "civilized" United States and the positive and "natural" South America). It is, in effect, an instance of travel literature, a novel of adventures, of passage, and it is defined by the conflict between two worlds, two languages, and two cultures, until it arrives at the ancestral nucleus of Santa María de los Venados. In this sense, it establishes the fundamental coordinates for many other textual representations of Latin American time and space. The story is about a journey toward a place that can be reached only by overcoming a series of borders, limits, and cities that protectively shield the privileged nucleus. Yet this journey implies a search back in time toward a lost geographical and temporal origin. The *traces* of this crossing are inscribed in the language, the meanings, and the culture of the protagonists' world.

This displacement slowly configures a space made up of differences in which nature (always described in a hyperbolic way) defines the "Latin

American zone" in opposition to a European or North American culture
that becomes synonymous with civilization. The point of contradiction or
conflict which develops throughout these narratives can be summed up
by the positions taken by the narrators and other characters in relation
to that world. If the text appears to be a paean, a gesture whose goal is
the return to nature and the American soil, then both plot and subject
begin to posit a series of contradictions: The traveler searches for a
desired lost space, but this is accompanied by a continuing descent into
a landscape that becomes ever more infernal.[5] This arrival at an anarchic
place where swamps and vegetation proliferate is parallel to the recovery
of the smells, language, and culture at the origin. This passage creates a
network of imagery and ideas that tie the text to *Cien años de soledad* and
*La Casa Verde.*[6]

Both the descent and the advance toward the past are linked by crossing various borders in *Los pasos perdidos.* However, Puerto Asunción
acquires particular meaning and becomes, along with the "city" of Santa
Mónica de los Venados, the privileged space that gives this text its central
position in relation to the entire network of representations of Latin
America. Puerto Asunción, the border town par excellence, is the point
of departure for the trip to that "other space," that mythic, unknown, and
desired place that calls for a guide. From this moment on, the journey
moves clearly toward the past, but actually represents a desirable future in
the mind of the protagonist. The "Virgil" that provides entrance into this
world is the Adelantado, whose name recalls the past (and alludes to a
remote history and occupation). We later learn that his name also means
"he who is ahead" – that is, he who goes faster – and in this way, he is a
builder of the future, particularly if we recall that he is the founder of an
absolutely archaic city which the narrator sees as his own space for the
future.

As representative of both past and future, the Adelantado does not
appear to have much to do with the present, and his encounter with the
narrator occurs in the most significant place in this border town halfway
through the story: the tavern called "Memories of the Future." This *space,*
is the key to the entrance into a utopian zone in the novel, but it is simultaneously the nexus that brings together and ties various texts through a
similar representational play. In sum, the tavern's name is shorthand for
all the time and space problems of the novel itself and leads us to other
texts of this group, especially to *Cien años de soledad* and the short stories
of Cortázar. On the border itself, just before the passage to the "other
side," the tavern, by its very name, indicates the relationship this space has
with time. "Memories of the Future" could very well be the title of *Cien*

*años de soledad,* if we go by its prophetic tone,[7] or that of "La noche boca arriba." But this is not just about titles, because "Memories of the Future" ties the past with the future and repeats the function of Santa Mónica de los Venados; and, just like it, necessarily leaves a *blank:* the present. In the space the novel constructs the present has no place, and there is nothing that refers to it. Existence in this strange land has to do with myth or utopia, while the present is reduced to a displacement, a crossing: it is this empty space which Cortázar's stories expose. In them, he makes explicit this elision at the center of *Los pasos perdidos,* and in other texts as well (perhaps because the fantastic allows one to "speak without risks"), and it becomes an essential narrative and structural device in his works.

At the same time, the other decisive space in *Los pasos perdidos,* Santa Mónica de los Venados, contains all the items that end up defining "Latin America." The narrator crosses a border that implies a transformation, almost a change of identity, and leaves "My shore, my people" to undertake a series of veritable rites of passage that will allow him entrance into "otherness." This is an unknown world whose accession implies initiation and a series of trials in the middle of an infernal natural world (i.e., the crossing of the swamps, the river, and the storms). This is a mysterious, fantastic, and unknown world, as is pointed out by the narrator himself, who is a stranger to this space. In any case, this very enunciation reveals the distance between the narrator and a place that is undoubtedly "other" to him.

On the other hand, his praise for Santa Mónica de los Venados, and his explicit idea to remain there, are contradicted by the facts. The narrator has already described the land as "the world of Genesis," before history and civilization, a world of temporal and spatial isolation marked by solitude, and thus by the absence of the flow of time.[8] Furthermore, a very fundamental contradiction arises in his decision to remain, because there are, among many others, two key elements that define his distance and his difference: writing and the law.[9] This instance reveals that the narrator belongs to another world and that it is impossible for him to remain, a fact that prepares us for his separation. Beyond the links between paper and the law (as González Echevarría has pointed out), the narrator proves that it is impossible for him to write music: in this land outside of time, there is not enough paper; but one cannot write oneself outside of history in any case (it is not by chance that he is thinking about setting the *Odyssey* to music, the text par excellence of the traveler who returns *home*). By the same token, when he needs to decide between two types of law, he refuses obedience to the codes of *that* land, because he cannot kill the leper. In this episode, he defines himself as a stranger and, from that point on, the one in charge of carrying out the law will take his place. There is nothing more for the narrator to do except depart for "the present," in search of paper, toward culture, toward history – that is, toward civilization itself.

The voyage and the return have created a series of representations that can be found in other texts, and which contribute to producing a particular discourse articulated around specific elements of this "network." The first of these are the oscillations in the narrator's perspective between his descriptions, decisions, and actions; other waverings include his position in regard to language, culture, and the customs of a land in which he does not know whether he belongs. In this sense, I believe that in almost all the texts in this group – and in this sense "Axolotl" will be especially apposite – the point of view of the narrating subjects will constitute a key element in their construction of representations. They assume mobile and ambiguous positions with respect to narratives that depict themselves as tales: *Los pasos perdidos* is a travel diary that is duplicated in the "innumerable lies" the narrator sells to a newspaper ("What I'm going to sell is a big lie. . . . I have a famous novel by a South American writer in my suitcase that includes the names of animals, trees, and a few references to indigenous legends and historical events, enough to give a semblance of veracity to my tale" (300). The clear allusion to *La vorágine* and *Canaima* by Rómulo Gallegos is meant to signal both filiations and differences: Those novels permitted the construction of false tales about these lands. On the other hand, the narrator reiterates that he is lying when he describes his relationship with Rosario, by "presenting this unexpected character . . . as someone remote, singular and incomprehensible . . . creating around her a backdrop of Earthly Paradise" (305). However, we can see that this description is really not so different from the one in the diary that we – the readers – have just read. In any case, the versions show themselves as fictions which are answerable to some vision of reality, to some expectations on the reader's part about that space. The text seems to be aware that it is constructing an imaginary space about Latin America which is closer to other discourses about the region than it is to any concrete geographical reality.

### Memories of the Future

In general, Cortázar's narratives rework the multiple forms of this representational network, but "La noche boca arriba" and "Axolotl" are the only stories that thematize the Latin American past. At the same time, these stories also transform this past into a basic component of Cortázar's famous binary system. Both stories are found in the third part of the collection *Final del juego,* and it is almost impossible not to see them as related to one another. They are particularly significant when considered as part of the group of works examined in this study because they condense and exhaust the contradictory play of Latin American "representations," so that both stories can be seen as a synthesis of the entire system.

Literary critics have devoted considerable attention to these two stories, particularly to "Axolotl," and have analyzed the use of the fantastic in both. Two articles deal with the tie between "Axolotl" and pre-Columbian myths: Fontmarty finds that these myths of creation "coincide with the story in their exact structure," and Ortega points out that the Aztec dualist concept of the world is present in "La noche boca arriba" as well.[10] Hence, the latter identifies the axolotl with Aztec reality and avers that the story "dramatizes the Latin American search for identity." Ortega interprets the story as a "metaphor" of the "inability to assimilate both the indigenous and the European in forging a unique identity." The stories are not read as part of an entire discourse, as a way of thinking about Latin America that is reflective of a conflicted, polarized, and irreconcilable imaginary, one constituted by a number of texts that debate and debate among themselves in their ambiguity. This discourse clearly discusses notions of identity, history, and the very idea of Latin America as a "nation" or specific space. Yet the discourse neither judges nor resolves anything; each text contributes to its development by making it more complex, by commenting on it, by attempting to project it as somehow "representative."

As mentioned earlier, the central locale of *Los pasos perdidos,* the tavern "Memories of the Future," points the way for us to connect Cortázar's stories with the group of texts considered here. The name of the tavern could well be that of "La noche boca arriba," to the extent that it takes the classical Cortazarian dichotomy and transforms it into a temporal as well as a spatial one. In an Aztec past – that of the *guerra florida* – someone belonging to a nonexistent indigenous group, the *motecas,* dreams of a future.[11] In the same way as in *Los pasos perdidos,* the absent and problematic time is that of the present. If in Carpentier's novel the journey concealed this absence, "La noche" is about "a void, an empty space he found impossible to fill. . . . this nothingness, had taken up an eternity. No, not even time, but rather as if he had passed through something or traveled great distances in this empty space" (176). This is a spatial-temporal void between two equally problematic worlds: a future that the reader confuses with his present (but which the text sets in the future) and the lost past of ancestral, indigenous peoples.

The first world is ambiguously situated in some Latin American country (although "Usté" and "amigazo" seem to give it some affiliation), and while it seems to be a menacing space where accidents, danger, and the possibility of death await him, it is also a safe world on account of its familiarity – it is described as a "protective ceiling" – in contrast with the world of the Aztec, the Latin American indigenous space par excellence, a world of darkness, war, blood, and night. The world of the past seems infinitely more dangerous and inescapable, where violent death becomes an inexorable force; it is "a cursed nightmare" that takes the protagonist "downwards" (toward an inferno of persecution and fear), from which he struggles to leave toward the future, the one of the story itself – the one described at the end of the story as a marvelous dream, as a utopia. Yet, at the same time, this utopia is an "infinite lie," because there too a man with a knife moves toward the protagonist. There is no actual time or space that has any true possibility, but the past is a nightmare without escape, a hostile zone that once again recalls *Los pasos perdidos*.

In the novel the narrator relates the encounter with the primitive tribes in terms of a journey back in time that takes him to "a remote world, whose light and time were unknown to me" (234). The temples of the Conquest are built on top of "the bloody base of the teocalli" (239), the sacrificial stone where the protagonist of "La noche boca arriba" dies. That world is equally hostile for the narrator of *Los pasos perdidos,* who feels like a stranger there: "We are intruders, ignorant outsiders – *metecos* of a short stay – in a city that is born *at the dawn of History"* (240; my emphasis).[12] This world is uninhabitable, a zone of constant danger, a land from which no one returns: exactly the predicament of the protagonist in "La noche boca arriba." Each time the nameless protagonist[13] passes to the "other side," he encounters a land with the smell of marshlands: "no one returns from the place where marshes and quakes begin"; from there he must flee from war toward the jungle and through the bog. Hence the text repeats the gesture begun in *La vorágine;* the flight toward the land's interior only brings destruction in the middle of a Nature whose destructive qualities are described time and again (*La vorágine, Los pasos perdidos, Cien años de soledad,* and *La Casa Verde*).

"Compared to the night from which he had just returned, the warm shadows of the ward appeared delicious to him" (175). These words will define the relationship betwen the two spaces: "this side" seems tolerable and secure by comparison; the "other" – the "true" side – offers no escape.

The "escape plan" from the latter space cannot succeed, and the only hope is to remain on this side. But to the extent that this should become impossible and one cannot get back (as the contact between the two worlds runs this risk), the nightmare is confirmed, and in that sacred time the only present possible is that of death: "Now sleep returned to overtake him," "Now they were taking him away . . . it was the end," and "now he knew that he was not going to awake."

The irreversible and dangerous aspect of the passage from one world to the next was already present in other texts of the group: *Los pasos perdidos, La Casa Verde, Plan de evasión,* and *Cien años de soledad* (in which the last Buendías that remain in Macondo are wiped out in the only moment that unites the past and the future of prophecy: the present of death). "Axolotl" is possibly the story that exposes this dangerous impossibility most openly by playing with one of the categories that best synthesizes the contradictory nature of these representations: the speaking subject, the narrator, the ambiguous perspective that can never be certain of the position from which it speaks. "Axolotl" disturbs the whole representational system, by placing it at the core of the story, by turning it into its theme.

The narrator of "Axolotl," a story that has been the object of many studies focusing on the problem of the fantastic, represents and dramatizes the passage into the Latin American space as a dead end. The narrator's attraction and link to the world of the axolotl's aquarium is shown to be an impossibility. The process of becoming closer implies a transition ("every morning the recognition was greater"), as in allowing "himself to penetrate," "eat them with his eyes," and "be devoured." Yet despite his proximity, contact is impossible. It is pointless to tap against the glass or press one's face against it, because the glass is the border. And to understand this one must go to the other side, to make oneself other; but in that case there is no return; rather, the acceptance of belonging to that world. This is a world and a condition (that of the axolotl) which is easily associated with pre-Columbian America, primitive and outside of time. It is the object of utopian desire throughout the texts of the corpus and the obsession of the narrator (once again, a man without a name), but its image is constituted by an assemblage of negative representations. The aquarium is not only "wet and dark," "petty and narrow," but is also an enclosed space without a way out, in which all axolotls are defined as having "small Aztec faces"; as larval shapes, masks; as phantoms with a will to "abolish *time and space* with their indifferent immobility" (163; my emphasis).

This appealing and remote world in which the narrator recognizes himself is at the same time an impossible space that "produces the horror of someone who is buried alive and suddenly awakens to his fate" (167). The story relates again, now in a fantastic mode, the lot of the other protagonists in this group of texts (i.e., *Los pasos perdidos, La vorágine, Plan de evasión*). All of them feel connected to and recognize themselves in that other space – but assimilation remains impossible: they return to "this side" (as in *Los pasos perdidos*) or they die (as in *La vorágine, Cien años de soledad, Plan de evasión,* and "La noche boca arriba"). In "Axolotl" the tension between the two worlds (which is as clear as the contradictions of the narrator in *Los pasos perdidos*) is resolved in the doubling of the narrator/character. Crossing the glass and the borders between the two worlds implies becoming "other" in an irreversible way. Yet, in this separation, the axolotl remains in a world of silence and enclosure ("the bridges between us have been cut off"), whereas the man can extricate himself from this obsession (his historical past, this "other" space, and the "axolotl" part of his identity) through writing. Ultimately, he is the one charged with writing about the axolotl.

In this final movement, the story condenses another of the fundamental elements of this network of representations. Indeed, the story opens with an "I" that exists in a given time frame – "I used to think a lot about the axolotl" – and closes when a part of this "I" is excised – the part that has remained on "this side," the side of history and culture, and decides to "perhaps write about us." The story uncovers, with the paradoxical transparency of the fantastic, the trait repeated by the corpus and which has already been mentioned: Most of them present themselves as forms of writing (diaries, prophecies, or reports) in which the enunciation is handled from the point of view of the "excised" subject, or from a position close to him. Those able to speak of this "other" world as they construct it, and with which they entertain an ambiguous link, are already outside of it – they have already ceased to belong. Writing is possible only in the space of "civilization," in a historical time which is precisely lacking in that "other" world. This is why the narrator of *Los pasos* returns to New York, and why in "Axolotl" he stops visiting the aquarium: One can only write about that "other space," can only construct and sustain the utopia, after having distanced oneself from that inferno.

These texts seem to recognize two fundamental principles for their constitutive representations. First, they often present themselves as unreliable texts or are themselves copied by others who may be telling lies (*El arpa y la sombra,* another Carpentier narrative, is paradigmatic in this sense). Second, the narrator, placed in the contradictory position of being distant and seduced by this world to which he cannot fully belong, is nevertheless charged to speak of it; therefore, at the center of his writing is a fundamental tension between the desire for this other world (utopia) and his rejection of it (inferno).

In this sense "Axolotl" is a key text, because the narrator's oscillation makes this irreconcilable difference explicit and depicts it as a difference that cannot be overcome: Even if he recognizes that the axolotl represents "a different life, another way of looking," on the other hand, the "I, which is an axolotl" knows that no understanding is possible from the outside, that the man was "outside the aquarium, his thought was a thought outside the aquarium" (167). In this perpetual state of "metecos," the narrators establish an ambiguous tie with language, culture, and the knowledge represented by the two spaces; hence the permanent confrontation between the European and the Latin American worlds (as well as its traditional dichotomy between nature and culture). For this reason the human narrator at the beginning of "Axolotl" claims to understand by consulting dictionaries in a library in Paris; but *recognition,* fascination, and danger can only be experienced through contact, the ambiguous closeness made possible through the looking glass.

Among the works that compose this corpus, "Axolotl" is one that places the issue of "truth" in the foreground. Indeed, what is this text that we the readers read? Is it a story the human narrator imagined? or what the axolotl managed to "communicate" to him in the first days of his transformation? In any event, the story as recounted on "this side" loses much of its reliability; it seems impossible to know for sure how things are in the world of the aquarium. The possibility of representing that world from within the story is called into question, and Cortázar's story has worked this very problem into the center of its construction (the way he did with the category of time in "La noche boca arriba"). Yet the majority of the texts of this group also depict complex relationships among several unreliable versions of their narratives (recall my earlier comment on *Los pasos perdidos*): *La vorágine* is the protagonist's diary framed by a letter/prologue that plays on the tension between the fictiveness and possible veracity of the story. One can find echoes of *La Casa Verde* in various later texts by Vargas Llosa that actually function as recastings of the novel.[14] The truthfulness of the protagonist's letters in *Plan de evasión* is doubted by the narrator, who finds in them "the proportion of truth and error that the best prophecies aspire to." This takes us back to the story of Melquíades in *Cien años de soledad,* on the one hand, and to the tension within these texts regarding the position(s) of their enunciation, on the other. The struggle of knowing and being able to talk about this "other" place that we saw in "Axolotl" is replayed in *Plan de evasión* between the narrator who is "imprisoned" in the Devil's island and the narrator who finds himself on "this side," the side of civilization. The question is who can construct and imagine that other space. *El arpa y la sombra* can also be considered a key text in many ways, because Columbus confesses, in his story (framed by that of another narrator), that his own diary is nothing but a pack of lies, a forged tale. It is not coincidental that Columbus's diary, truly the founding text of this whole discursive system, is represented by one of the texts belonging to it as an interested account, as a series of falsehoods destined to construct a (politically) convenient image appropriate to Columbus's interests. *El arpa y la sombra* appears to narrate the origin and cause of these fictions, created by a "meteco" hopelessly "shipwrecked between two worlds," who replaced a "country never found" with a utopia, an imaginary earthly paradise that was soon turned into an inferno where he was awaited by "the devil, who would try to make me fall into his traps" (183).[15]

Carpentier's text gathers up all the terms of the representations of this group of texts and establishes an origin for them, particularly the contradictory opposition between utopia/inferno, which dominates and organizes the entire system and acquires different inflections in each text. Perhaps fantastic texts like Cortázar's stories and *Plan de evasión* by Bioy Casares may be the ones that best capture this dichotomy. The island of *Plan de evasión* is the Devil's island, yet it is also part of the Islands of Salvation, a space to escape to, and one from which, very quickly, the protagonist hopes to escape. The utopian island paradise is actually a prison where death can be met.[16] Through this inversion, the text explores the very meaning of the word "utopia," the *no place* that is beyond all reach, an idealized place impossible to attain and which can easily change into its very opposite.

In *Plan de evasión* and Cortázar's stories, this representational system seems to generate the story itself and to become fully visible. It is possible that the ambiguities of the fantastic somehow allow for the open development of contradictions in a world that is both desired and rejected, a world where one belongs but in which one is also a foreigner, a world described as a paradise yet where one lives and dies as in a type of hell. The doubling of the narrator in "Axolotl" defines the place of writing: For the "axolotl," there is only enclosure and immobility, since language and freedom are in the civilized world, Europe. The text appears to outline another utopian space that results from the dichotomies it manipulates and from the impossibility of real communication (as the glass of the aquarium is the very definition of separation). On the other hand, "La noche boca arriba" warns of the dangers of this passage through time and space: the *void* that the protagonist falls through toward the bottom cannot be traversed. From that perspective, the well-known scene of the plank in *Hopscotch* acquires new interpretive possibilities: It is not just the Buenos Aires–Paris dichotomy or a metaphysical exercise. The failure to cross, the impossibility of crossing, also reminds us that there is no *way* across, that there is no *between* to stand on.

In this oscillation the texts construct a set of imaginary representations about a land which is their own yet also foreign, wished for and rejected. And the result is their contribution to a discourse that has been developing since the beginnings of reflection on the identity of Latin America. This discourse, articulated through multiple formulas and voices, is modulated in the most varied registers, and its traces can be found in historical, legal, and political writing as well. This discourse, this long story, has created Latin America, or rather an imaginary constructed out of an assemblage of representations that make up our culture and can be found in a great variety of distinct textualities.[17] The character of these representations is intrinsically political, and their power and strategic force are connected to subject positions which cannot be other than ethical and political and which determine ways of thinking about the real. In this sense, the notions of identity and nationhood, and the ways of thinking about oneself and the world, are linked to a struggle between representations for the power to "make visible and make believe."[18]

Latin American literature contributes to this discourse and finds itself permeated by it, and a great number of its texts use this representational system. Literary texts cannot escape it and are themselves shaped by this imaginary so powerful as to purport to "define and describe what Latin America is." This entire collection of works is characterized by the painful ambiguity of a discourse in which Latin America is read from a variety of superimposed positions and through a multiplicity of dichotomies. The characters who enunciate this discourse are mired in these contradictions and thereby construct an impossible space: heaven and hell at once; a no-place without a present and without history; an enclosed space in which one can only plan for escape.

Cortázar's stories find themselves at the center of this struggle and are part of the unresolved tension generated by thinking and thinking oneself from within a dominant discourse, one always already constituted and from which there is no escape. The terrible paradox of these texts is that they expose the conflict and construct themselves out of it, but they cannot escape it, because writing – even for them – comes from this side. And, as we know well, the "axolotl" stayed in his dark and silent world, a world without time, waiting perhaps for "that time that may come sometime," for that plank that destroys the dichotomy; or simply for another discourse that makes the chasm disappear and in which death does not await on the other side.

*Notes*

1. For a number of studies in this vein, see the collection of essays in *Lo lúdico y lo fantástico en la obra de J. Cortázar* (Madrid: Fundamentos, 1986). For a very different critical position, see D. Viñas, *Literatura argentina y realidad política* (Buenos Aires: Siglo XX, 1971), which deals with the binary play between Buenos Aires and Paris.
2. These two stories are both in *Final del juego* (Buenos Aires: Sudamericana, 1973), 169–79 and 161–8. The quotations cited are from this edition. Besides sharing many similar elements, these two stories are most clearly linked to the works cited above. At the same time, however, their defining characteristics, dealt with at length in the present study, can also be found in many of Cortázar's other works.
3. Considered in this way, these texts are most commonly read as an exploration of the search for national identity.
4. P. Bourdieu, *O poder do simbólico* (Lisbon: Difel, 1989). Also B. Backzo in *La imaginación social* (Buenos Aires: Nueva Visión, 1991). Backzo considers representation as the articulation of ideas, rites, and means of acting: "The understanding of the intelligible structures of social activities undergoes a necessary reconstruction by the intervening system of representation and in the analysis of its disposition and functions" (23). In the same vein, see R. Chartier, *A história cultural: entre prática e representações* (Rio de Janeiro: Difel, 1990).
5. The arrival of the narrator in his land of origin is narrated in the following manner in *Los pasos perdidos* (Madrid: Cátedra, 1985): "Our ears warned us that we were descending . . . ," "a war of centuries against the marshes, yellow fever, the insects . . . ," "there was something in the air like an evil grain of pollen, a bewitching pollen, an untouchable woodworm, flying mildew – which starting acting up. . . . It's the Worm!" (67–9).
6. The tie with *Cien años de soledad* is particularly close. The treatment of space and time, and the similarities between Macondo and Santa Mónica de los Venados, establish a very complex relationship between the two works which is beyond the scope of the present study.
7. For the examination of temporal relations in *Cien años de soledad*, see Noé Jitrik's "La perifrástica productiva en *Cien años de soledad*," in his *Producción literaria y producción social* (Buenos Aires: Sudamericana, 1975), 19–47.
8. There is an immediate relationship to *Cien años de soledad*: the same spatial-temporal isolation, a time outside of history. It is necessary to recall the

words of the founder of the lineage: "we will rot away without receiving the benefits of science" and "we will never get anywhere." Macondo, a new version of Santa Mónica de los Venados, uses the same modes of representation of an "uninhabitable" place, an infernal space without a present.

9. R. González Echevarría, *Myth and Archive: A Theory of Latin American Narrative* (Cambridge University Press, 1990). He considers *Los pasos perdidos* as a founding text that prefigures *Cien años de soledad* and analyzes the relationships between writing and the law in the text. His reflections on Carpentier's novel as a founding text were fundamental to the present study.

10. F. Fontmarty, "Xolotl, mexoltl, axolotl: Una metamorfosis recreativa," *Coloquio Internacional. Lo lúdico y lo fantástico en la obra de Cortázar* (Madrid: Fundamentos, 1986), 79–88, and B. Ortega, "Cortázar: 'Axolotl' y la cinta de Moebius," *Nuevo Texto Crítico* 2, no. 3 (1989): 135–40.

11. Cortázar himself humorously suggested that the *motecas* were an indigenous people who rode around on motorcycles. Nonetheless, this does not prevent us from establishing ties with a fragment from *Los pasos perdidos* related to the Cortázar story, which I will cite later on. Interestingly enough, in Carpentier's text the narrator considers himself a *meteco,* that is, a stranger, an intruder, an "other," in the world of the past.

12. The *Diccionario de la lengua* defines *meteco* as a foreigner in ancient Greece who established himself in Athens but did not enjoy the rights of citizenship. *Advenedizo,* "outsider"; opposite: "native of, aborigine." The narrator considers himself a stranger in the utopian land he seeks, and which he also chooses to leave. The same thing happens to the *moteca* in "La noche boca arriba," because the natives of the land are others, the Aztecs; he is the only one hunted down in a hostile country where death awaits him.

13. The problem of a name and of naming recurs in all the texts of the corpus. We do not know the narrator of *Los pasos perdidos* or of "La noche boca arriba": "for himself, to go along thinking, he had no name. . . ." In "Axolotl" the same problem is broached by translation: "I found its name in Spanish, *ajolote* . . . ," but throughout the story the indigenous word is used. Names change or become confused in *La Casa Verde* and *Cien años de soledad;* as in *Los pasos* and *Cien años de soledad* it is necessary to find names for new things. This is not only a problem of identity but also of representation: Naming implies an intervention in the world, an establishment of a new discourse about how to represent it. This becomes the conflict that these texts discuss and dramatize. S. Fischer's "Geography and Representation" (Ph.D. diss., Columbia University, 1995) analyzes the distinct tie between representation and naming.

14. The stories of *La Casa Verde,* or parts of them, are reiterated in *El hablador,* in "Crónica de un viaje a la selva," and "Cómo se hace una novela." Beyond differences in genre, the texts work the same issues of representation cited in the group of texts studied here.

15. A. Carpentier, *El arpa y la sombra* (Mexico City: Siglo XXI, 1989). All references are to this edition.

16. Suzanne J. Levine's *Guía de Adolfo Bioy Casares* (Madrid: Fundamentos, 1982), analyzes this text in the tradition of utopian literature and science fiction, and considers it as failed utopia. This observation opens up a new series

of connections with another text in our group, *Pubis angelical*, which unfortunately exceed the dimensions of the present study.

17. We could apply this to what Timothy Brennan points out in the concept of "nation" in his "The National Longing for Form," in *Nation and Narration*, ed. H. Bhabha (New York: Routledge, 1990): "The 'nation' is precisely what Foucault has called a 'discursive formation' – not simply an allegory or imaginative vision, but a gestational political structure" (46). And he later adds: "Nations, then, are imaginary constructs that depend for their existence on an apparatus of cultural fictions in which imaginative literature plays a decisive role" (49).

18. P. Bourdieu, *O poder simbólico*, 113.

## References

Backzo, B. *La imaginación social*. Buenos Aires: Nueva Visión, 1991.

Bourdieu, P. *O poder do simbólico*. Lisbon: Difel, 1989.

Brennan, Timothy. "The National Longing for Form." In *Nation and Narration*, ed. H. Bhabha, 44–70. New York: Routledge, 1990.

Carpentier, Alejo. *Los pasos perdidos*. Madrid: Cátedra, 1985.

*El arpa y la sombra*. Mexico City: Siglo XXI, 1989.

Chartier, Roger. *A história cultural: Entre prática e representações*. Rio de Janeiro: Difel, 1990.

*Coloquio Internacional: Lo lúdico y lo fantástico en la obra de J. Cortázar*. Madrid: Editorial Fundamentos, 1986.

Cortázar, Julio. *Final del juego*. Buenos Aires: Sudamericana, 1973.

*Prosa del observatorio*. Barcelona: Lumen, 1983.

Fontmarty, F. "Xolotl, mexoltl, axolotl: Una metamorfosis recreativa." *Coloquio Internacional: Lo lúdico y lo fantástico en la obra de Cortázar*, 79–88. Madrid: Fundamentos, 1986.

González Echevarría, Roberto. *Myth and Archive: A Theory of Latin American Narrative*. Cambridge University Press, 1990.

Jitrik, Noé. "La perifrástica productiva en *Cien años de soledad*." In *Producción literaria y producción social*, 19–47. Buenos Aires: Sudamericana, 1975.

Levine, Suzanne J. *Guía de Adolfo Bioy Casares*. Madrid: Fundamentos, 1982.

Ortega, B. "Cortázar: 'Axolotl' y la cinta de Moebius." *Nuevo Texto Crítico* 2, no. 3 (1989): 135–40.

Viñas, David. *Literatura argentina y realidad política*. Buenos Aires: Siglo XX, 1971.

# 2

## Comic Stripping:
### Cortázar in the Age of
### Mechanical Reproduction

*Jean Franco*

Ricardo Piglia's *Argentina in Fragments (La Argentina en pedazos)* is a compilation of essays and comic strips originally published in the mid-1980s in *Fierro,* a magazine aimed at young readers. The format was a brief critical digest followed by comic-strip versions of well-known Argentine literary texts by Esteban Echeverría ("El matadero"), David Viñas, Discépolo, Lugones (*Las fuerzas extrañas*), Borges, and Cortázar.[1] Although there is a long tradition of comic-book classics, this is the first comic-book literary criticism, as far as I know, to have been written and edited by a well-known Latin American novelist. García Márquez, Vargas Llosa, Luis Rafael Sánchez, and Manuel Puig have all, in their different ways, made their overtures to mass culture – García Márquez in his telenovelas, Vargas Llosa in *Aunt Julia and the Script Writer,* Manuel Puig beginning with his first novel, *Betrayed by Rita Hayworth.* It was not only the prospect of reaching bigger audiences that induced García Márquez to write telenovelas and Vargas Llosa, Octavio Paz, and Juan José Arreola to anchor cultural programs on television, but also the need to hold on to the slipping hegemony of the intelligentsia.[2] Piglia's comic-strip criticism marks a more advanced stage in the long and complex two-step, the moment when the book itself has become an adaptable and transient commodity and the author a brand name.

I am here using the term *mass culture* not to refer to the imagined degradation that sullies the purity of "true" or "authentic culture," but to the "assembly-line" culture targeted through market techniques to particular consumers. So-called pulp literature, cinema, animation, and comic strips provided new media for narrative, altering by the very method of production received notions of author (there is often no single author), reception, and originality. The violent rejection of mass culture as anti-art by many modernists was, in fact, only the initial stage in a long and intricate relationship marked by denunciation, appropriation, and, finally, celebration. "Mechanical reproduction" opened up the possibility of destroying the hierarchical structures underpinning artistic institutions. Not only did new media allow the intensification of shock effects by means of collage, photomontage, cinematic montage, and mixed media, but they also encouraged the persistence and resurrection of older forms of narrative such as melodrama and romance; indeed, in some contemporary writing, mass culture is associated with nostalgia for affect at a time when romantic love and passion seem anachronistic.[3] Older subgenres revitalized through pastiche act as reminders of the time when emotional expression (exiled from literature by irony) was still believed to be the common currency in the "low" sphere of popular urban culture.

Walter Benjamin was, as is well known, one of the first to understand the revolutionary potential of the new technologies. His essay "The Work of Art in the Age of Mechanical Reproduction" first appeared in 1936 in the *Zeitschrift für Sozialforschung*. The now familiar argument on which Benjamin's essay was based is that "the technique of reproduction detaches the reproduced object from the domain of tradition. By making many reproductions it substitutes a plurality of copies for a unique existence. And in permitting the reproduction to meet the beholder or listener in his own particular situation, it reactivates the object reproduced."[4] One consequence of this is that what will now be considered to be "culture" spills out of the confines of the concert hall, the museum, the theater, and the book. The modest range of mechanical reproduction Benjamin takes into account – primarily photography and cinema – must now be extended to include photocopying, electronic mail, the screening of film "versions" of novels before the printer's ink is even dry, the travels of genres such as melodrama from stage to screen to telenovella and back to "real life," the universal use of pastiche, and even virtual reality. Yet what was and remains innovative in Benjamin's essay is that, while arguing that mechanical production would result in the tarnishing of that uniqueness or aura of the work of art, he embraced the liberatory possibilities opened up by that very loss. The work of art potentially comes to inhabit new and unsanctified environments, rubbing shoulders with the commodity, while appropriating technology in order to create dialectic images.

Benjamin foresaw that techniques of reproduction that bypassed hierarchy and tradition had explosive and revolutionary possibilities and thus inevitably annihilated older cultural institutions. Writing of the filmmaker Abel Gance, whose methods imply a "liquidation of the traditional value of the cultural heritage," he quotes the latter's belief that "all legends, all mythologies and all myths, all founders of religion, and the very religions . . . await their exposed resurrection" (224). Benjamin believed that this was an invitation to the funeral of what had formerly been considered high art and, while shedding no tears, he saw that the changes in reception and sensibility were irrevocable.[5]

There are analogies between the German situation that motivated Benjamin's essays and Peronist Argentina. Mass consensus was achieved in Peronist Argentina as in Fascist Germany through ritual – Benjamin would call it the aestheticization of politics – and also through the ruling elite's speedy grasp of the importance of the media in securing consent. Although in his own personal mythology Cortázar liked to attribute his politicization to the Cuban revolution, his rejection of nationalism, his assertion of solidarities based on personal sympathies, were attitudes shaped by Peronist Argentina. This helps to explain why, even when Cuba was embracing "patria o muerte" (fatherland or death) politics and when the director of Casa de Las Américas was arguing that writers could not write effectively outside their own national boundaries, Cortázar refused to be drawn into this particular guilt trip:[6] "The fact that my books have been available for years in Latin America does not invalidate the deliberate and irreversible fact that I left Argentina in 1951, and that I continue to reside in a European country that I chose for no other reason than my sovereign will to live and write in the form that seemed the fullest and most satisfying to me" (29).[7] He goes on to argue that, not only does his engagement with Latin American politics spring from "a much more European than Latin American and a more ethical than intellectual perspective" (30), but also that writing outside a national context gains in breadth what it loses in local detail: "it becomes so to speak more global, it operates by means of assemblages and synthesis, and loses the energy that is concentrated in an immediate context; on the other hand, it achieves a lucidity that is sometimes unbearable but always enlightening" (31).

National identity was never a priority for Cortázar: "I am very much of a mimic. I am sure that if I were to live for five years in the United States, I would feel identified with what I like in the United States which is less than what I don't like. But I would identify myself deeply with what I liked."[8] The final phrase epitomizes what will afterwards constitute, for Cortázar, the grounds for sociability and identity – namely, taste. Because, in the contemporary world, taste can no longer be grounded in firmly established values or universal criteria, it becomes a matter either of market classification or of elective affinities. The arbitrariness of these affinities in Cortázar's work – the bond may be forged just as effectively through the mediation of Louis Armstrong, or of Gesualdo, or a shared project such as traveling slowly along the freeway from Paris to Marseille –

destroys "distinctions" on the grounds of nationality, class, or gender (let us overlook for the moment the notorious "lector hembra").[9] These social groups may form short-lived heterotopias like the motorists in "Weekend" ("Autopista del sur"). However, group cohesion also depends on the exclusion of those who do not understand, of those who are bound by routine, are lacking in imagination and emotionally crippled.

Considered in this light, Piglia seems to have hit the target when he calls Cortázar's writing "an epic of consumption," "the adventure of a seasoned and cunning explorer who tries to leave his footprint in the indiscriminate jungle of the capitalist marketplace" (40). For Piglia, this epic of consumption encompasses two seemingly incompatible regimes: "on the one hand, there is the search for some exclusive and secret object whose value derives from its scarcity and originality: on the other hand, it is a question of discovering and salvaging certain popular artifacts that are selected for their authenticity and for the dignity that derives from a slight anachronism: Xenakis and Rosita Quiroga, Hermann Broch and Cesar Bruto, gulash and bitter mate, hashish and a touch of eccentricity. Whereas one series is private and refined and is constituted by collecting, the other series is mass-mediated, 'natural' and is constituted by means of selection and exclusion" (40).[10]

The implications of this are far-reaching. Because Cortázar repeatedly constitutes ephemeral groups on the basis of arbitrary and unmarketable taste, it follows that value, once thought to be intrinsic in the work of art, has migrated to the aesthetic experience itself. Cortázar's focus on reception (which critics too often identify *only* with the reader) involves far more than literature in the conventional sense, for the "conjuntos y síntesis" (assemblages and syntheses) which produce profane illumination are unpredictable, unclassifiable, and can be motivated by almost any change in a pattern.

As I suggested above, Peronist Buenos Aires was instrumental in the shaping of this aesthetic. The novel *The Examination,* written in 1950 and published in 1987, already sketches in the recurring incidents and characters of Cortázar's later writing – the apocalyptic cityscape shrouded in fog, a routinized populace, traces of a decayed high culture (books rotting in the humidity, the concert in which the soloist fails to perform as planned), a small group of students, and a "chronicler" wandering through this city and united by affect and by taste. Groups are bonded by a shared or idiosyncratic repertoire of cultural references drawn from popular music, literature, painting, or simply everyday objects.[11]

It is not only the political circumstances of the writing that makes *The*

*Examination* interesting, however, but the fact that the art object already seems to have been contaminated; one of the characters has the following confrontation with a recording of Beethoven's Seventh: "I entered my darkened room and picked up an album of the Seventh Symphony, subtitled the apotheosis of dance. As I picked it up in pitch darkness, I felt it moving in my hand. You can imagine my reaction; The Seventh flew to the other end of the room with me groping like a madman for the light switch. Then I saw on my hand the hairs of a still-wriggling centipede" (197). The contact with the insect obviously ends any prospect of aesthetic pleasure, but in any case this has already been sullied by the commercial renaming of the symphony as "the apotheosis of the dance." The auratic work seems to have undergone an unpleasant metamorphosis as well as having been turned into a commodity: the novel is replete with references to the *Reader's Digest,* the yellow press, and Peronist rhetoric. Still there remains the possibility of redemption; music can be resacralized – for instance, the chronicler of *The Examination* treats the corny "London calling" by Eric Coates with religious respect. The group in *The Examination* anticipates the Serpent Club of *Hopscotch* and La Joda of *A Manual for Manuel,* whose members are bound by private codes and references that often depend on a ritualistic object.

But if any object can be resacralized, then there is no basis, other than a voluntaristic one, for discrimination. It also follows that traditional class stratification or "distinction" no longer coincides with the distinction between high and mass culture.[12] The implications of this are explored in "Las puertas del cielo" ("The Gates of Heaven"), the story originally included in *Bestiary* (1951) and comic-stripped in Piglia's *La Argentina en pedazos.*

In his later years, "The Gates of Heaven" would embarrass Cortázar because of its grotesque and racist portrayal of the masses. It is the story of the narrator Hardoy's fascination with the "low" Mauro and his girlfriend, Celina. From the vantage point of the early seventies and the revived if transient hopes in left-wing Peronism, Cortázar would feel called upon to apologize for the political implications of the narrative. It expressed, he said, "a lot of friction, a lot of tension for political reasons, in Argentina, between ourselves, the petty bourgeoisie and those we called 'little black heads,' the low-class Peronists who, according to us, had invaded Buenos Aires."[13] Looking back on this period of his life, he describes his anti-Peronism as a political mistake but argues, "I was exasperated by this type of invasion of the lower classes of the population of the capital and of what I call the monsters who were called at that time the 'little black heads.'" (97).

His attempt to immerse himself in the underclass was initially inspired by literature, by reading Roberto Arlt, and by wanting to see "what we called 'el bajo'." "El bajo" in Buenos Aires was the waterfront, but it also means the low life of the brothel and prostitution. The dance hall gave him entry into this world: "So I was at this dance hall, I saw the women and men, saw them dancing. I saw that scene in which one of them slapped his woman around, because she was dancing with someone else and he didn't like it and he gave her a blow that knocked her sideways. And no-one stepped between them, because if anyone had done so it would have been a fight to the death and nobody thought it was worth the trouble. If he wanted to hit her, let him hit her. Nobody interfered. And I think that at that moment at that dance, I was Hardoy? What was his first name?" (97).

"I was Hardoy" is not a surprising admission given that Hardoy is the avatar of a whole series of Cortázar narrators and protagonists, from Bruno of "The Pursuer" through Oliveira of *Hopscotch* and Michel of "Blow-up." What is surprising is Cortázar's apparent attribution of Hardoy's views to himself when, in the narrative, irony seems to intervene to prevent such an identification. (In this respect, it is significant that in the interview he could not remember Hardoy's first name.)

Cortázar's opinion of the Peronists had undergone a radical change by the early seventies so that he came to believe that "The Gates of Heaven" reflected a mistaken view of things, forgetting perhaps that the viewpoint in the story is supposedly Hardoy's. However, it can also be argued that the caricaturesque descriptions of "the monsters" as seen by the fastidious chronicler, Hardoy, are functional to the narrative, as the resolution of the story depends on maintaining this very distinction between intellectual and mass. It is, after all, not Hardoy who enters the gates of heaven, but the vulgar Celina. Aesthetic rapture is not the exclusive domain of the lettered but can be experienced just as well in the dance hall as in the private reading. That the representation is grotesque hardly needs emphasis. Hardoy confesses:

"It seems right for me to say here that I come to this dance hall to see the monsters, I know of no other place where you get so many of them at one time. They heave into sight around eleven in the evening, coming down from obscure sections of the city, deliberate and sure, by ones and by twos, the women almost dwarves and very dark, the guys like Javanese or Indians from the north bound into tight black suits or suits with checks, the hard hair painfully plastered down, little drops of brilliantine catching blue and pink reflections, the women with enormously high hairdos which make them look even more like dwarves, tough, laborious hairdos of the sort that let you know there's nothing left but weariness and pride." (129)[14]

"The Gates of Heaven" faithfully (perhaps too faithfully for an older Cortázar) translates the official discourse of the thirties and early forties which had associated the immigrant population with contamination. Celina dies of tuberculosis at the beginning of the story. Puig's *Boquitas pintadas,* set in the 1940s, would pick up this same association between immigration and sickness. However, Celina is contaminated not only because of her disease but because of her association with the dance halls. With the closing of the Buenos Aires brothels in the 1930s, the dance halls had become marketplaces for prostitutes and pimps,[15] and in Cortázar's narrative they metonymically link Celina to the degeneration of society as a whole. In fact, Perón's attempts to reopen the brothels met with opposition precisely because this discourse of degeneration and contamination was so deeply rooted among the "gente decente."[16]

In Piglia's version of "The Gates of Heaven," the comic strip drawn by Carlos Nine exaggerates the grotesque features of the lower classes. The drawings of Mauro often focus on one facial feature: his aggressively curly black hair, his uneven teeth, his large, thick-lipped mouth. In one close-up there is only a protruding eye shedding giant tears over a huge hooked nose. Celina has thick lips, bushy hair, and a wide mouth. The sweating masses are shown cheering on fighters in the boxing ring and slurping their drinks. In contrast, Marcelo's face is never fragmented. His features conform to the conventions of comic-strip handsomeness but reveal nothing of his feelings. The comic strip also reaffirms the "Hardoy soy yo" theme, though in ironic fashion, since at the end Cortázar is seen beside a microscope, holding a cigarette whose smoke roughly reproduces Latin America as a monster being tweaked by Donald Duck. The concluding sentences of the comic and the story are almost identical: "he knew that he was wasting his time, that he would come back, tired and thirsty, not having found the gates of heaven among all that smoke and all those people" (51).

What the comic "digests" to the point of disappearance, however, is the subtler aspect of the dénouement, in other words, the difference that Hardoy establishes between his own experience of the sublime and Mauro's inferior search for Celina's copy.[17] A reference in "Gates of Heaven" to Ortega y Gasset provides the clue to this difference. Ortega's dissection of "el hombre mesa" in *The Rebellion of the Masses* (1924) was of course part of the intellectual baggage of the period. Thus it is not surprising that one of Hardoy's "fichas" (file cards) specifically identifies Mauro with Ortega y Gasset's scathing description of those who use technology without contributing to its invention or understanding its underlying scientific principles. Echoing Ortega, Hardoy comments: "Exactly where one would imagine a cultural shock, there is, on the contrary, a violent assimilation and enjoyment of the progress. Mauro talks about refrigeration units and audio-frequency amplification with the self-sufficiency of the Buenos Aires inhabitant who firmly believes he has everything coming to him" (51).

Yet if Mauro represents Ortega's mass man, Hardoy himself reminds us of the "disinterested" artist in *The Dehumanization of Art* (1925). It will be recalled that, at the beginning of his essay, Ortega had described the different attitudes toward death experienced by the dying man's wife, the doctor, a reporter (who feigns emotional involvement while keeping a professional distance) and the artist, the latter being the most detached from emotional or intellectual involvement and concerned primarily with the visual scene.[18] Cortázar's story includes the same cast of characters: the emotionally involved family, the doctor, and Hardoy, who doubles as artist and reporter/recorder with his card file ("Las fichas"), absorbed in registering reality and distanced from the emotional scenes at the wake and the funeral – "I hardly heard the old women crying and the commotion in the courtyard, but on the other hand I remember that the taxi cost two pesos sixty, and that the driver had a shiny cap" (118). Hardoy is transformed into the artist when at the end of the story Celina's face, in his imagination, becomes dehumanized, "all her face changed and muddied by the yellow light of the smoke" (136).[19]

Piglia argues that the fascination with the low and the feminine, as well as with those who "incarnate the elemental and monstrous world of passion and feeling," is a recurrent feature of Cortazar's writing: "That world of the others, of the monsters who invade and destroy order, contaminates all reality; the fascination with this contamination is one of the great themes of Julio Cortázar's fiction" (40).

But there is another aspect to this fascination. Andreas Huyssens has shown that modernist writing tended to exclude women and mass culture from the aesthetic on similar grounds. Both were identified with the indiscriminate, the chaotic, unbridled emotion, the loss of boundaries.[20] "The Gates of Heaven" is interesting because, although it seems to exaggerate this modernist position (Celina is identified not only with mass culture but also with sexuality and contamination), the conclusion nevertheless suggests, in the manner of certain poststructuralists, that feminine "jouissance" is beyond the limits of patriarchal discourse. Cortázar would seem to be taking both an ironic stance against older modernist notions that excluded mass culture and woman from the aesthetic and against Adorno's negative dialectic that places mass culture entirely on the side of the routinized and the systemic.[21] His "gates of heaven" (and of course the references to Dante in the story), rather, evoke the profane illumination of Walter Benjamin and the surrealists.[22]

*Only* Celina can enter the gates of heaven (albeit in Hardoy's vision), for woman embodies what is unrepresentable. Yet the story is perhaps less about Celina who is the pre-text than about the difference between the two men. For whereas Mauro goes to the Santa Fe palace in search of a copy of Celina (he is, after all, mass man), Marcelo experiences the "sublime" through the impossible and visionary resurrection of the dehumanized original. As Lyotard suggests, there is a distinction in Kantian aesthetics between the sublime and taste, for the sublime is the Idea "of which no presentation is possible" and "modern aesthetics is an aesthetic of the sublime, though a nostalgic one. It allows the unpresentable to be put forward only as the missing contents; but the form, because of its recognizable consistency, continues to offer to the reader or viewer matter for solace and pleasure" (81). The postmodern, in this account, is "that which, in the modern, puts forward the unpresentable in presentation itself; that which denies itself the solace of good forms, the consensus of a taste which would make it possible to share collectively the nostalgia for the unattainable; that which searches for new presentations, not in order to enjoy them but in order to impart a stronger sense of the unpresentable."[23] What is significant in Cortázar's story is that the difference between Mauro and Hardoy has now (ironically) become a difference between the secondary and unsatisfactory but perhaps attainable copy and the unrepeatable and unpresentable sublime. As for Celina, like the Lacanian mystic, she experiences jouissance "but doesn't know anything about it."[24] Benjamin wrote that "The reader, the thinker, the loiterer, the flâneur, are types of illuminati just as much as the opium eater, the dreamer, the ecstatic. And more profane."[25] Interestingly, however, Hardoy is not quite redeemed in "The Gates of Heaven." Starting out as Ortega's "disinterested" artist, his voyeuristic experience of sublimity is, in reality, no more authentic or satisfying than Mauro's search for the copy.

Cortázar's description of a different experience of the sublime – "Louis, enormísimo cronopio" – included in *Around the Day in Eighty Worlds*,[26] was written shortly after Armstrong's Paris concert of 9 November 1952 and thus belongs roughly to the same period as *The Examination* and "The Gates of Heaven." Jazz is, of course, not to be equated with mass culture; its roots are popular and collective, the antithesis of commodification. Nevertheless, by becoming the first great solo performer, Louis

Armstrong "moved jazz into another era: the ascendancy of the soloist began."[27] Collective improvisation was replaced by "individual expressiveness." And jazz recordings subverted the one-time-only improvisation that is crucial to the very essence of jazz. When Armstrong visited Paris in 1952, his style was already considered passé by those for whom jazz had become identified with the cool and "highbrow" style of Miles Davis.

Although Cortázar's essay describes a moment when the boundaries between self and other erode, in this essay, the erosion has strong connections to male sexuality. The male musicians get their high by playing on female instruments. "Arvel Shaw who plays bass as if holding a naked shadowy woman in his arms and Cozy Cole who arches over the drums like the Marquis de Sade over the backsides of eight whipped and naked women" (122). Louis, on the other hand, is described in terms that remind us of the mystics:

From Louis' trumpet the music emerges like the ribbons of speech from the mouths of primitive saints, a hot yellow writing is inscribed on the air, and after this first signal *Muskrat Ramble* is unleashed and those of us in the stalls, hanging on to anything that can be hung on to, and our neighbors do the same, so that the auditorium seems like a vast gathering of crazed octopus and in the midst of everything is Louis with the whites of his eyes behind the trumpet, with his handkerchief waving in a continuous farewell to something that we can't identify, as if Louis had to continually say goodbye to that music that creates and disintegrates in the instant, as if he knew the terrible cost of that marvelous liberty of his. (123)

The turned-up whites of the eyes recall those of the (female) mystic ("elle" jouit). But the jouissance is transmitted to an audience and binds those who are participants. As for those members of the audience who are not "cronopios," "naturally they didn't understand anything."[28]

To follow the thread of this particular discrimination between those who are "in" and those who are "out" as it runs through Cortázar's work would be an interminable and probably superfluous exercise. One has only to recall the reiteration in his work of different forms of discrimination (the separation between *cronopios* and *fames,* for instance). From *The Winners* to his final *Autonauts of the Cosmoroute: An Atemporal Trip from Paris to Marseille,*[29] there are constantly shifting boundaries separating the two: for instance, the levels of complicity that divide the readers of *Hopscotch* into *cómplices* (accomplices) and *hembras* (females), the "insider's" vision of Latin America experienced by the narrator of "Apocalypse in Solentiname" and the outsider and surface vision of his girlfriend, Claudine, and so on and so forth. What I am emphasizing here is not only the drawing of boundaries, but rather an aspect of Cortázar's writing that made it so exemplary of the zeitgeist of the 1960s, when the "advanced" position included both a liberation from the tyranny of proletarian consciousness (and realism) and from the political ascesis of high modernism. Put in another way, "us" and "them" were now configured by new social actors – on the one hand, classless, uprooted visionaries and, on the other, the entire body of those who had bought into consumer society, ranging from workers to the haute bourgeoisie.

Interestingly, two films inspired by Cortázar stories – Antonioni's *Blow-up* (1966), described as a "hypnotic pop-culture parable of a photographer caught in a passive life-style," and Godard's *Weekend* (1967), "an essential sixties time-capsule"[30] – register this new divide. Neither film is, in reality, a true adaptation; indeed, Godard's film is in many ways its antithesis, but they reflect the "holy madness" of the time.

Antonioni's *Blow-up* was "inspired" (according to the credits) by Cortázar's story "Las babas del diablo."[31] However, in the film, Cortázar's amateur photographer and translator is transformed into a trendy narcissist living in swinging London. Antonioni's film is based on a fairly conventional contrast between imagination and routine, between a "real" woman, Vanessa Redgrave, and the conveyor-belt women who work as models for the photographer. The "blow-up" becomes a lesson in imagination ("L'Imagination au pouvoir") that culminates in the famous finale – a tennis game played by carnavalesque figures without racquets or balls. There are of course huge differences between film and story. For one thing, Antonioni allows the Vanessa Redgrave character to be a participant rather than simply an object focused by the camera tense ("l'objectif"), and the boy of Cortázar's story has become an older man. Yet the topics of the film – consumer culture, loss of affect, simulation and redemption through imagination – belong to a shared zeitgeist. The carnivalesque crowd in Antonioni's film resembles one of Cortázar's "clubs" formed without any reference to anterior ties of class identity.

*Weekend,* on the other hand, is closer to Buñuel than to Cortázar. Godard would say about his film *One Plus One,* which featured the Rolling Stones and was made just after *Weekend,* "what I want above all is to destroy the idea of culture. Culture is an alibi of imperialism. There is a Ministry of War. There is also a Ministry of Culture. Therefore, culture is war."[32] Apart from the prolonged tracking shot of cars jammed on a highway, *Weekend,* which Godard described as "a film adrift in the cosmos" and "found on the scrap heap," has only a tenuous link to Cortázar's "La autopista del sur."[33] If anything, the film resembles the end of the orgy as described by Baudrillard: "We live amid the interminable reproduction of ideals, phantasies, images and dreams which are now behind us, yet which we must continue to reproduce in a sort of inescapable indifference."[34]

Godard's and Antonioni's films both identify the common enemy as a "consumer culture" that provokes violence and encourages conspiracy. This cold war zeitgeist was shared by Cortázar, who began to explore the possibility of political intervention through literature, notably in *A Manual for Manuel* and *Fantomas*. It is clear that in these two texts the air of the faux naif which had served Cortázar well in much of his fiction becomes strained under the pressure of documentation on torture and disappearance.

The attempt in *A Manual for Manuel* to bridge the political and the literary caused Cortázar a great deal of anguish. The novel marks the moment when he (like his "alter ego," Andrés) connects the avant-garde and vanguard.[35] The effectiveness of the move, however, depends on the reader's acceptance of conspiracy and violence as overriding political realities that can only be opposed by conspiracy and violence. In other words, such an analysis presupposes the nonexistence or the fragility of the public sphere of democratic debate. This is reflected in the entangled codes, puzzles, and private languages of the novel. At the same time, the reappearance in different forms of the "club," "la Joda," the telephone community, suggests that Cortázar needs to envisage these heterotopias as substitutes for a public sphere which no longer has any material existence.[36] It is in this light that I wish to examine Cortázar's anachronistic choice of *Fantomas* as a bridge between the intelligentsia and mass culture which he saw as having coopted the public sphere.

*Anachronism* is hardly an innocent word in dealing with Cortázar. In *A Manual for Manuel* he introduces a long meditation on the archaic piano that Stockhausen uses in his music along with electronic and aleatory devices. Even though (following the logic of the avant-garde) the piano should be destroyed, Andrés suggests that these anachronistic references are needed as bridges that extend toward the unknown. The familiar sound of the piano may well induce automatic responses, thus interfering with the creation of the new; however, Andrés "understands" why Stockhausen feels the need to retain the instrument: "You've got the bridge problem too, you have to find the way of speaking intelligibly . . ." (27).

In *Around the Day in Eighty Worlds,* on the other hand, anachronism is clearly nostalgic, for the Pannemaker engravings from the first edition of Verne's collected works not only refer the reader back to "innocent" adventure stories, but also to a moment when there was a shared popular culture.

*Fantomas and the Multinational Corporations* (1975) bridges high and popular culture in a different way, for it takes us back not to childhood but to a more sinister and violent world that heralded modernity. The first *Fantomas* novel, published in 1911 and coauthored by Pierre Souvestre and Marcel Allain, ushered in a new stage of mass culture – new, at least, in France. The novels were read, writes John Ashbery, by "Countesses and concierges: poets and proletarians; cubists, nascent Dadaists, soon-to-be surrealists. Everyone who could read, and even those who could not, shivered at posters of a masked man in impeccable evening clothes, dagger in hand, looming over Paris like a somber Gulliver, contemplating hideous misdeeds from which no citizen was safe."[37] This popularity, however, reflected a social imagery of urban violence and conspiracy.

The authors were journalists who drew on the popularity of the yellow press and possibly on the sensational accounts of anarchist groups, active around 1911 and 1912, whose deeds were not very different from those of la Joda in *A Manual for Manuel*.[38] The popularity of the series was secured both by slick advertising and by the five Fantomas films that were screened between 1913 and 1915 and directed by Louis Feuillade Allain who, in particular, had calculated consumer need (carefully): "The public of popular fiction is essentially a public that wants to know 'how it ends.' If the author allows their curiosity to be aroused between one book and the next, the series is assured of a growing success." Allain, who survived Souvestre and continued the series as sole author, was quick to grasp the importance of adapting *Fantomas* for radio, the comic strip, and even eventually television.[39]

The first Fantomas adventure, modestly priced at 65 centimes, was so popular that there were thirty-one sequels, each sequel being motivated by the villain's miraculous escape from imminent capture by the police chief, Juve, and his increasingly violent and improbable escapades, which often involved the destruction of sacred Paris monuments. Fantomas robs the gold from the dome of the Invalides, brings about the crash of the Simplon–Paris express, robs the Banque de France, and blows up the Montmartre reservoirs. In the cat-and-mouse game of the novels, the police chief Juve is often outwitted. His sidekick, Bertram/Fayard, who comes from an aristocratic family, works as a police informer and journalist on a newspaper appropriately named *La Capitale*. The capital city, Paris (la capitale), is not only the preferred scene of the Fantomas adventure but also provides productive capital (le capitale) on which the novels can draw.

Although these popular novels have antecedents in the nineteenth-century master-criminal novels (of which Balzac's *Comédie humaine* surely holds pride of place), they ushered in a new era of mass-marketed fiction. Image and legend rapidly outstripped the confines of the book. The covers of Fantomas novels illustrated by Gino Starace were luridly gripping and designed to glamorize the villain. It was this, no doubt, that inspired the interest of the avant-garde. Soon after the publication of the first *Fantomas,* Guillaume Apollinaire founded the Society of the Friends of Fantomas. The mystery man inspired poems by Max Jacob and verses by Neruda, and was admired by Aragon, Colette, Raymond Queneau, and Cocteau;[40] in 1933, Robert Desnos wrote a Fantomas "Complainte," or Lament, that was set to music by Kurt Weill and sung by a chorus conducted by Antonin Artaud.[41] The Belgian poet Ernst Moerman referred to him as a "world lost in space" and invited him to "save poetry" long before Cortázar invited him to save books.[42]

The avant-garde and the surrealists were drawn to Fantomas novels because of their antisocial violence. As an enemy of the established order, and especially of the police, he was compared to Maldoror because he blatantly defied the moral code as it was defined by bourgeois society. More significantly, Fantomas was a symptom of the dark side of modernity. Like their predecessors (Eugene Sue and Balzac), Allain and Souvestre depicted an urban world in which "identity" had become a matter of performance and acting a significant trope. In the first Fantomas, Gant (Fantomas) is caught and condemned to the guillotine. When the blade falls, however, it is not on Fantomas but on an actor who unknowingly has been trapped into impersonating him. In these novels nobody retains his or her original identity for very long. Fantomas's mistress, Lady Bertram, doubles as head of a convent; Juve appears in many disguises, as a man in a wheelchair, as a "pale man with a greenish complexion," and as a "mysterious tramp."[43] In the *Secret Executioner,* Fantomas is both a doctor and a lowlife thief.[44] Anticipating the stakeouts of the drug era, the police themselves engage in elaborate charades, constantly appearing in disguise as gang members and criminals. In the world in which Fantomas has the power of ubiquity (just as in Conan Doyle's Sherlock Holmes mysteries, this is helped by railway timetables), nobody is safe, locked doors are no protection, and the most innocent-looking bystander is either a criminal or a police spy.

For Cortázar, Fantomas as popular villain and avant-garde hero provided a useful bridge. In an earlier story, "The Other Heaven" ("El otro cielo"), he had explored the ominous urban cityscape, conflating the arcades of nineteenth-century Paris with Peronist Buenos Aires.[45] *Fan-*

*tomas,* on the other hand, was published in 1975,[46] at a time when the *conspiracy* of the multinational corporations in Chile was still on people's minds, and he gave it the subtitle *A Realizable Utopia.*

Cortázar's *Fantomas* was published by *Excelsior,* the Mexican newspaper which at the time, under Julio Scherer, was showing some independence from government control; the royalties went to the Russell Tribunal, which was investigating torture in Latin America. In Cortázar's text, the Fantomas comic is a Mexican adaptation.[47] The narrative begins with Cortázar-as-narrator picking up a Mexican comic at the railway station. In the opening episode, Fantomas, disguised as a young theatergoer, emerges from *The Threepenny Opera* and is shown explaining to his female companion that Brecht used criminals to parody the customs of the bourgeoisie as he realized that there was hardly any difference between the gangster and the financier.

Cortázar's *Fantomas* combines the comic strip with the narrative of Cortázar's train journey from Brussels to Paris after a session of the Russell Tribunal.[48] It also includes serial views of Wall Street, Washington, the IBM logo, the Paris police, and automatic weapons, as well as nineteenth-century illustrations from popular literature, a photomontage of a knife cutting an eye (a reference to Buñuel, it goes without saying), newspaper reports, and an appendix that includes the Russell Tribunal report. "Mechanical reproduction" (the multiple photographs of Capitol Hill), like the "hormigas" ("ants" – a term that refers to the enemy) in A *Manual for Manuel,* illustrate the reproduction of U.S. hegemony, while the multiple disguises of Fantomas (even though as a lone ranger his tactics are anachronistic) anticipate the heterogeneity of "the people," whose cause is taken up, among others, by that cult figure Susan Sontag (seemingly the only woman intellectual whose word counted for anything). The story culminates in a miracle of communication when the silent masses are heard on the telephone, a feat apparently accomplished by Fantomas who, as it were, creates a network of solidarity. The text thus pits the monumentalism of the hegemonic power against a civil society that is truly heterogeneous and seems to prefigure the as yet nonexistent global public sphere.

Toward the end of his life, Cortázar tended to explore literature as a form of political intervention and came to see mass culture as a bridge that would have to be seized by "la avanzada" (the advance column). Indeed, he often speaks in apparently contradictory ways, sometimes using the traditional language of class struggle (the bourgeoisie and the petit bourgeois), while at the same time also evoking a culture in which such class terms no longer seem relevant. After his visit to Sandinista Nicaragua, he would refer to cultural workers[49] and urge his colleagues not only to become actively engaged in alternative politics but also to use video, cartoons, photonovels, and comic strips, citing Luis Britto Garcia on the need to gain access to the mass media. His goal was still the utopian one of liberating the creative potential of Latin America, which he now envisaged as "that immense book that we can write all together and for us all" (97). But Cortázar never repeated the *Fantomas* experiment. When, in the eighties, Piglia followed Cortázar's injunction to use mass culture in order to reach new publics, the latter were already way ahead of the intelligentsia in their reading of images and their speedy adoption of new musical styles. Is it high culture's representation of Argentina that has left it in fragments? Piglia's comic-stripping of Argentine literature seems to underscore the fact that "the immense book" (whether of the nation or of Latin America as a whole) can no longer be bodied forth from high culture and that, since the wall between high and mass culture has come down, the former may now simply have become the repertoire for the latter.[50]

### Notes

1. Ricardo Piglia, *La Argentina en pedazos* (Buenos Aires: Ediciones Urraca, 1993).
2. Nestor García Canclini, "De las utopías al mercado," in *Culturas híbridas: Estrategias para entrar y salir de la modernidad* (Mexico City: Grijalbo, 1989), 31–63.
3. A good example of this is Luis Rafael Sánchez's deployment of bolero lyrics in *La importancia de llamarse Daniel Sánchez* (Hanover: Ediciones del Norte, 1988) and, in a rather different mode, Manuel Puig's use of melodrama and sentimental radio novel in *Boquitas pintadas* (Buenos Aires: Sudamericana, 1969).
4. Walter Benjamin, "The Work of Art in the Age of Mechanical Reproduction," in *Illuminations: Essays and Reflections* (London: Jonathan Cape, 1970), 233.
5. In the epigrammatic conclusion of the essay, Benjamin sets communism's "politicization of art" against fascism's "aestheticization of politics." What he could not foresee was the virtual disappearance of politics in a global culture.
6. This was the position advanced by Haydée Santamaría to the jury of the Casa de Las Américas prize in 1969, and it was reiterated by Oscar Collazos in his essay, included in *Literatura y revolución,* to which both Cortázar and Vargas Llosa wrote replies.
7. Julio Cortázar, "Acerca de la situación del intelectual latinoamericano." The essay was published in *Casa de Las Américas* (Havana, 1967) and is included in the collection *Textos políticos* (Barcelona: Plaza y Janes, 1984), 27–44; see especially 29.

8. Evelyn Picón Garfield, *Cortázar por Cortázar* (Mexico City: Universidad Vera-cruzana, 1978), 50. Cortázar would maintain this position until the end of his life. In a speech, "El escritor y su quehacer en América Latina," *Nicaragua tan violentamente dulce* (Managua: Editorial Nueva Nicaragua, 1983), 86–98, he would reaffirm that exile was an enrichment.

9. In a personal conversation in 1981, Cortázar once told me that was a phrase he came to regret. Even so, I don't think his perceptions of gender difference underwent any radical change. This is evident from his replies to Evelyn Picón Garfield in *Cortázar por Cortázar* and in his articles on Nicaragua, *Nicaragua tan violentamente dulce,* in one of which he says he has no information on the Sandinistas' policy on birth control – something that would hardly have been difficult to discover. In fact church pressure prevented any measures on abortion from being passed.

10. Rosita Quiroga was a popular singer, César Bruto a comic-strip artist. Thanks to Josefina Ludmer for clarifying these references.

11. Julio Cortázar, *El examen* (Madrid: Alfaguara, 1986). Nicolás Rosa discusses aspects of Cortázar's groups in the preface to *El perseguidor y otros cuentos: Antología* (Buenos Aires: Centro Editor de America Latina, 1981).

12. The thesis of "distinction" or social stratification that is constituted by "habitus" and as taste was advanced by Pierre Bourdieu, *Distinction: Critique of the Social Judgement of Taste* (Cambridge, MA: Harvard University Press, 1986).

13. Picón Garfield, *Cortázar por Cortázar,* 17.

14. Julio Cortázar, "Las puertas del cielo," in *Bestiario* (Buenos Aires: Sudamericana, 1978), 117–37.

15. Donna Guy, "Tango, Gender, and Politics," *Sex and Danger in Buenos Aires: Prostitution, Family, and Nation in Argentina* (Lincoln: University of Nebraska Press, 1990), 144–74.

16. "Patriotic Prostitutes and Dangerous Men," in Donna Guy, *Sex and Danger,* 180–204.

17. For the intellectual atmosphere of this period, see John King, *Sur: A Study of the Argentine Literary Journal and Its Role in the Development of a Culture 1931–1970* (Cambridge University Press, 1986).

18. José Ortega y Gasset, *La deshumanización del arte,* 11th ed. (Madrid: Ediciones Revista de Occidente, 1976).

19. *Desdecía* is here translated as "muddied," but though the Spanish word means "degenerated," it is formed from *decir* ("to speak") and so vividly suggests a discursive construct that is dissolving into smoke.

20. Andreas Huyssens, "Mass Culture as Woman, Modernism's Other," in *Beyond the Great Divide: Modernism. Mass Culture. Postmodernism* (Bloomington: Indiana University Press, 1986), 44–62.

21. Theodor Adorno, *Aesthetic Theory,* trans. C. Lenhardt (London: Routledge and Kegan Paul, 1984); see especially 336–7 for the dilemma of art as commodity.

22. Walter Benjamin, "Surrealism," in *Reflections: Essays, Aphorisms, Autobiographical Writings,* trans. Edmund Jephcott (New York: Harcourt Brace Jovanovich, 1978), 177–92.

23. Jean-François Lyotard, *The Postmodern Condition: A Report on Knowledge,* trans. Geoff Bennington and Brian Massumi (Minneapolis: University of Minnesota Press, 1984).
24. For a discussion of woman as unrepresented in discourse, see Alice A. Jardine, *Gynesis: Configurations of Woman and Modernity* (Ithaca, NY: Cornell University Press, 1985), especially 167.
25. Walter Benjamin, "Surrealism," 90.
26. "Louis enormísimo cronopio," *La vuelta al día en ochenta mundos* (Mexico City: Siglo XXI, 1967), 121–5.
27. Leroi Jones (later Amiri Baraka), *Blues People: Negro Music in White America* (London: MacGibbon & Kee, 1965), 155.
28. *Cronopios and Fames,* trans. P. Blackburn (New York: Pantheon, 1969), introduces a classification based not so much on taste as on attitudes to life. The *cronopios* are spontaneous enthusiasts who are not quite synchronized with "real life."
29. Carol Dunlop and Julio Cortázar, *Los autonautas de la cosmopista. Un viaje atemporal Paris–Marsella* (Mexico City: Nueva Imagen, 1984). This book, written in collaboration and completed just before the death of his companion, Carol Dunlop, constitutes a heterotopia within the freeway system.
30. The digests are from the updated edition of Leonard Maltin, *TV Movies and Video Guide* (Winnipeg, 1989).
31. The literal translation would be "devil's spit," which apparently refers to a kind of wispy cloud formation.
32. Quoted by James Miller in *The New York Times,* Sunday, 25 July 1989, 20.
33. "La autopista del sur," *Todos los fuegos el fuego* (Buenos Aires: Sudamericana, 1966).
34. Jean Baudrillard, *The Transparency of Evil,* trans. James Benedict (London: Verso, 1993), 4
35. *Cortázar por Cortázar,* 61.
36. Julio Cortázar, *Libro de Manuel* (Buenos Aires: Sudamericana, 1973). "Heterotopia" is a word used by Foucault to account for the existence of antisystemic groups within the system, though he never really develops this concept. D. Emily Hicks has a Deleuzian interpretation of *Libro de Manuel* which interprets the book as "border writing." See her *Border Writing: The Multidimensional Text* (Minneapolis: University of Minnesota Press, 1991). She also tries to read the structure of the novel in terms of Stockhausen's music.
37. Marcel Allain and Pierre Souvestre, *Fantomas,* introduction by John Ashbery (New York: William Morrow, 1986), 1.
38. Louis Chavance notes the coincidence of the publication of the first volume and the first reported activities of the anarchist Bonnot gang; see "La morale de Fantomas" in the special issue on Fantomas of *Europe,* nos. 590–2 (juin–juillet 1978): 64–8, esp. 67.
39. Marcel Allain, "Du roman populaire et de ses possibilités commerciales," *Europe,* nos. 590–2 (juin–juillet 1978): 23; my translation.
40. The *Europe* bibliography includes the novels, plays, comic strips, and photonovels. See "Bibliographie de Fantomas," *Europe,* nos. 590–2 (juin–juillet 1978): 141–61.

41. Fantomas is mentioned in Neruda's poem "Las Pacheco," in *Memorial de Isla Negra. Obras completas* (Buenos Aires: Losada, 1968), 2:510. For the various avant-garde admirers of Fantomas, see Roland Stragliati, "'Fantomas'? oui, mais . . . ," *Europe,* nos. 590–2 (juin–juillet 1978): 72–8.

42. Hubert Juin, "Pour éveiller nos joies un beau crime est bien fort," *Europe,* nos. 590–2 (juin–juillet 1978): 11.

43. Cited by Juin, ibid., 14–16.

44. Marcel Allain and Pierre Souvestre, *The Silent Executioner* (New York: William Morrow & Company, 1987).

45. In "Homenaje a una joven bruja," written in 1975, he says that he discovered Valentina comic strips thanks to Heinz van Cramer; see *Territorios* (Mexico City: Siglo XXI, 1978), 19. "The Other Heaven" ("El otro cielo"), with its allusions to Lautréaumont, and possibly to Benjamin of the *Passagenwerk,* includes a guillotining episode that could well have been lifted out of a Fantomas novel. "El otro cielo" is included in the collection *Todos los fuegos el fuego* (Buenos Aires: Sudamericana, 1966).

46. Julio Cortázar, *Fantomas contra los vampiros multinacionales: Una utopía realizable* (Mexico City: Excelsior, 1975). See Ellen M. McCracken, "*Libro de Manuel* and *Fantomas contra los vampiros multinacionales,*" in *Literature and Popular Culture in the Hispanic World* (Gaithersburg, MD: Hispamérica, 1981), 69–77. It is interesting that it was written before Cortázar came up against the wilder claims of certain guerrilla movements to be initiating a nationwide revolution; see n. 48 below.

47. Fantomas comics began to be published in Mexico in the 1930s by *Paguín* comics. In the 1970s they were published by Editorial Novaro. See Irene Herner's exhaustive history of the comic strip in Mexico, *Mitos y monitos: Historietas y fotonovelas en México,* written with the collaboration of Maria Eugenia Chellet (Mexico City: Nueva Imagen, 1979); see especially 22 and 172.

48. The Russell Tribunal was initiated by the Bertrand Russell Foundation during the Vietnam War. The Russell Tribunal II dealt with Latin America and met twice, in Rome (1974) and Brussels (1975). It has to be remembered that in the early seventies "human rights" were not yet incorporated into U.S. official policy. Because it had no government backing either in Europe or the U.S.A., the Tribunal was not able to put into effect recommendations or even effectively publicize its work, which is why its recommendations were included in *Fantomas.* For a comment on Cortázar's position vis-à-vis the ERP guerrilla movement and his activity in the Tribunal, it is interesting to read María Seoane, *Todo o nada: La historia secreta y la historia pública del jefe guerrillero Mario Roberto Santucho* (Buenos Aires: Planeta, 1992). Santucho interviewed Cortázar, and Jaime Petras wanted the Tribunal to make a public declaration in favor of the guerrillas movement. Both Cortázar and Petras doubted the realism of their war tactics and argued that their request was not within the Tribunal's competence. But reportedly Cortázar was deeply disturbed by the hostility of the guerrilla to this response.

49. "El escritor y su quehacer en America Latina," in *Nicaragua tan violentamente dulce* (Managua: Editorial Nueva Nicaragua, 1983), especially 95.
50. On the city as a figure for the utopian, see Jean Franco, "Paris, ciudad fabulosa," in *Novelistas hispanoamericanos de hoy,* Juan Loveluck, ed. (Madrid: Taurus, 1976) 271–90.

## References

Adorno, Theodor. *Aesthetic Theory.* Trans. C. Lenhardt. London: Routledge & Kegan Paul, 1984.

Allain, Marcel. "Du roman populaire et de ses possibilités commerciales." *Europe,* nos. 590–2 (juin–juillet 1978): 18–29.

Allain, Marcel, and Pierre Souvestre. *Fantomas.* Introduction by John Ashbery. New York: William Morrow, 1986.

*The Silent Executioner.* New York: Wiliam Morrow, 1987.

Baudrillard, Jean. *The Transparency of Evil.* Trans. James Benedict. London: Verso, 1993.

Benjamin, Walter. "Surrealism." In *Reflections, Essays, Aphorisms. Autobiographical Writings,* trans. Edmund Jephcott. New York: Harcourt Brace Jovanovich, 1978.

"The Work of Art in the Age of Mechanical Reproduction." In *Illuminations: Essays and Reflections.* London: Jonathan Cape, 1970.

Bourdieu, Pierre. *Distinction: Critique of the Social Judgement of Taste.* Cambridge, MA: Harvard University Press, 1986.

Chavance, Louis. "La Morale de Fantomas." *Europe,* nos. 590–2 (juin–juillet 1978): 64–8.

Cortázar, Julio. "Acerca de la situación del intelectual latinoamericano." In *Casa de las Américas* (Havana, 1967) and in *Textos políticos,* 27–44 (Barcelona: Plaza y Janes, 1984).

"La autopista del sur." *Todos los fuegos el fuego.* Buenos Aires: Sudamericana, 1966.

*Cronopios and Famas.* Trans. P. Blackburn. New York: Pantheon, 1969.

"El escritor y su quehacer en América Latina." In *Nicaragua tan violentamente dulce,* 86–98. Managua: Editorial Nueva Nicaragua, 1983.

*El examen.* Madrid: Alfaguara, 1986.

*Fantomas contra los vampiros multinacionales: Una utopía realizable.* Mexico City: Excelsior, 1975.

"Homenaje a una joven bruja." In *Territorios,* p. 19. Mexico City: Siglo XXI, 1978.

*Libro de Manuel.* Buenos Aires: Sudamericana, 1973.

"Louis enormísimo cronopio." In *La vuelta al día en ochenta mundos.* Mexico City: Siglo XXI, 1967.

"The Other Heaven." In *Todos los fuegos el fuego.* Buenos Aires: Sudamericana, 1966.

"Las puertas del cielo." *Bestiario,* 117–37. Buenos Aires: Sudamericana, 1978.

Dunlop, Carol, and Julio Cortázar. *Los autonautas de la cosmopista. Un viaje atemporal Paris–Marsella.* Mexico City: Nueva Imagen, 1984.

Franco, Jean. "Paris, ciudad fabulosa." In *Novelistas hispanoamericanos de hoy,* ed. Juan Loveluck, Madrid: Taurus, 1976.

García Canclini, Nestor. "De las utopías al mercado." In *Culturas híbridas: Estrategias para entrar y salir de la modernidad,* 31–63. Mexico City: Grijalbo, 1989.

Guy, Donna. "Tango, Gender, and Politics." In *Sex and Danger in Buenos Aires: Prostitution, Family, and Nation in Argentina,* 144–74. Lincoln: University of Nebraska Press, 1994.

Herner, Irene, and Maria Eugenia Chellet. *Mitos y monitos: Historietas y fotonovelas en México.* Mexico City: Nueva Imagen, 1979.

Hicks, Emily. *Border Writing: The Multidimensional Text.* Minneapolis: University of Minnesota Press, 1991.

Huyssens, Andreas. "Mass Culture as Woman, Modernism's Other." In *Beyond the Great Divide: Modernism. Mass Culture. Postmodernism,* 44–62. Bloomington: Indiana University Press, 1986.

Jardine, Alice A. *Gynesis: Configurations of Woman and Modernity.* Ithaca NY: Cornell University Press, 1985.

Jones, Leroi (later Amiri Baraka). *Blues People: Negro Music in White America.* London: MacGibbon & Kee, 1965.

Juin, Hubert. "Pour eveiller nos joies un beau crime est bien fort." *Europe,* nos. 590–2 (juin–juillet 1978): 9–17.

King, John. *Sur: A Study of the Argentine Literary Journal and Its Role in the Development of a Culture 1931–1970.* Cambridge University Press, 1986.

Lyotard, Jean-François. *The Postmodern Condition: A Report on Knowledge.* Trans. Geoff Bennington and Brian Massumi. Minneapolis: University of Minnesota Press, 1984.

McCracken, Ellen. *Literature and Popular Culture in the Hispanic World.* Gaithersburg, MD: Hispamérica, 1981.

Maltin, Leonard. *TV Movies and Video Guide.* Winnipeg, 1989.

Miller, James. *The New York Times.* Sunday, 25 July 1989, 20.

Neruda, Pablo. "Las Pacheco." *Memorial de Isla Negra.* In *Obras completas,* 2:510. Buenos Aires: Losada, 1968.

Ortega y Gasset, José. *La deshumanización del arte.* 11th ed. Madrid: Ediciones Revista de Occidente, 1976.

Picón Garfield, Evelyn. *Cortázar por Cortázar.* Mexico City: Universidad Veracruzana, 1978.

Piglia, Ricardo. *La Argentina en pedazos.* Buenos Aires: Ediciones Urraca, 1993.

Puig, Manuel. *Boquitas pintadas.* Buenos Aires: Sudamericana, 1969.

Rosa, Nicolás. *El perseguidor y otros cuentos: Antología.* Buenos Aires: Centro Editor de América Latina, 1981.

Sánchez, Luis Rafael. *La importancia de llamarse Daniel Santos.* Hanover: Ediciones del Norte, 1988.

Seoane, María. *Todo o nada: La historia secreta y la historia pública del jefe guerrillero Mario Roberto Santucho.* Buenos Aires: Planeta, 1992.

Stragliati, Roland. "'Fantomas'? oui, mais. . . ." *Europe,* nos. 590–2 (juin–juillet 1978): 72–8.

# 3

## Cortázar and Postmodernity: New Interpretive Liabilities

### Neil Larsen

### *Revenge of the "lector hembra"*

> But he had ended up without words, without people, without things, and, potentially, of course, without readers.
> (*Hopscotch,* 502)

To write about Julio Cortázar requires, it seems, that one first reread him – a commonplace, no doubt, but one that already says a good deal about the intellectual nature of the task itself. In one obvious sense, this necessity to reread is unavoidable, as the Cortazarian opus has now become a finite one – barring the appearance of previously unpublished material. But having to reread, for me at least, is a consequence of *not having read* Cortázar for a considerable length of time. I cannot state this as a fact per se, but I would guess that this preparatory need to "dust off" Cortázar is not just my peculiarity, but is shared by students, critics, and general readers of Latin American literature in the 1990s. Left out of this group, perhaps, are those who "specialize" in Cortázar and, of course, those reading him for the first time. But am I wrong in sensing that this latter cohort comprises a steadily dwindling number?

Where, then, to start this rereading? *Hopscotch:* there could be no hesitation here. Other works – the short stories, in particular – scarcely bear excluding, but to reread Cortázar without rereading *Hopscotch* would clearly be self-defeating. This is not necessarily because *Hopscotch* is, or is deemed, Cortázar's best or most important work. Although this has tended to become the accepted wisdom among critics and literary historians, there is certainly a sizable minority of Cortázar's readers who might dispute it.[1] But magnum opus or not, it was *Hopscotch* – published, now, some three decades ago – that gained Cortázar entry into what is still that most exclusive and exalted of chambers in the modern Latin American literary canon: not just the "boom" but, as it were, its path-breaking and inaugural texts. Although perhaps less and less frequently read over the years, *Hopscotch* – along, of course, with *One Hundred Years of Solitude* – has lost nothing of its glamour as an *event* in what is still the dominant *grand récit* of Latin American literary history. *Hopscotch* has become a literary monument that one may be forgiven for having to reread but that must never be omitted when conducting the guided tour of canonical points of interest. Indeed – as sometimes has a way of happening in the course of negotiating the canon – the very habit of speaking of *Hopscotch* as a "classic" appears, somehow, to vouchsafe its nonreading.

Having now reread it, I think I know why this is: *Hopscotch* has a profoundly dated quality. It *reads* like the literary equivalent of, say, a rock-and-roll album cover from the same period: the sixties are written all over it, but in a way that produces (at least for a reader of my generation) embarrassment rather than nostalgia – much less an illumination. Through page after page of Cortázar's great *succès de scandale* I found it impossible to suppress the sensation that I was in the presence of a relic. The past was not in it; rather, this text *was* the past itself – that irrecoverable, irredeemable pastness of something that once marched at the vanguard of fashion and taste, but that now, having been rapidly overtaken, forfeits the dignity of what is merely "old" – say, a table or even a radio from the same period. *Hopscotch* has become, to quote the novel itself, "like those objects, those boxes, those utensils that sometimes would turn up in storerooms . . . and whose use no one can explain anymore" (468).

To admit to such a reaction may be considered out of place here and will very possibly anger Cortázar specialists and connoisseurs, who might just as easily counter that this is not at all *their* experience when reading *Hopscotch*. Perhaps I am giving too much importance to my own literary idiosyncrasies, but, again without having proof of the fact, I would wager that the impression I have described of extreme datedness – almost of archaism – is more than just an accident of personal taste. Indeed, in its own particular way, the experience afforded by rereading *Hopscotch* now, thirty or more years after its first appearance, may qualify as "postmodern." Without necessarily assuming new literary identities as postmodern textual or cultural specimens themselves, *Hopscotch* in particular – and the Cortazarian opus in general – become highly discreet, readerly sites for the production of what might be termed the postmodern *affect:* the unmistakable sensation of coming *after* what was *already* the hypermodern – or what Roberto Schwarz has described as "that slightly passé air which surrounds the modernist desire to change everything with distance and nostalgia" (Schwarz, 190). *Hopscotch* would have to have been, effectively, the last book in order to be read as seriously as it plainly desires us, in all its emphatic self-projection as "écriture," to read it. I would like to understand better why that is, and thus it is with an analysis and exploration of this, as yet, strictly spontaneous and intuitive sense of the postmodern that I propose to begin.

Where, then, to start? It seems to me that this can only be with *Hopscotch*'s particular narrative approach to sexuality and gender – what we might term its gender heroics. Even if the novel were, in every other respect, free of the more embarrassing marks of its late-modernist pretentiousness, this feature alone, I think, would be sufficient to unmask it as an archaism. I refer, here, not merely to the obvious ways in which it confines its female characters (La Maga and Talita, principally, but including the more peripheral characters of Babs and Gekrepten) within a symbolic narrative of masculine agency and feminine passivity – Cortázar's "bourgeois-romantic vision of women" (Concha, 137; my translation). The fact that Oliveira, despite all his desperate longing for both a present and an absent La Maga, can never conceive of her as anything but an objectification of his own mock-heroic soul-searchings, does not, after all, do much to set apart Cortázar's novel from what is, obviously enough, a long-standing literary and cultural-psychological norm. What makes the aggressive masculinism of *Hopscotch* really egregious, I suggest, is not that it tacitly legitimates such a gender(ed) heroics, but that it regards itself as being, for this very reason, at the vanguard of philosophical consciousness: "To rape is to explain"; "Otherness lasts only as long as a woman lasts" (45, 103). Betokened in charming maxims such as these (and there are many more) is not only a perpetuation of a patronizing and degrading view of women – which Cortázar shares with the general culture – but its conscious, pseudophilosophical apology. I leave aside as spurious the possible defense of Cortázar here on the grounds that these are only the views of his protagonist Oliveira and that the author surely meant them to be condemned.[2] Surely *nothing* in the novel is *meant*, in this blatant sense, to be condemned or praised. But one does not have to read Oliveira as a public-school role model to understand that the spontaneous sympathies evoked, as a rule, in all heroic literature will have the effect of granting such a "philosophy" a legitimacy it might not otherwise be able to claim. I think it is bad faith on the reader's (and critic's) part to deny the obvious here: that Oliveira's idea of women is presented to us, his readers, as a reason to take him seriously, even as a reason to find him sexy. His "tragedy" – if it is one – is not that he regards La Maga (and, in a wider sense, all women) as his own self-objectification in the form of the "other," but rather that he must inevitably fail to merge with this object (see, especially, Oliveira's outpourings in chapters 21 and 48). The full reality of how women are made to live as a result of such gender heroics (or antiheroics) does not enter into the symbolic universe of *Hopscotch*.

If it did, the novel might be centered instead on La Maga, whom we would then follow on her flight back to Montevideo, or accompany in what might also be her suicide, failed or successful. Speculating on such a would-be "feminist," *Hopscotch* may, in the end, be a pointless exercise, but it is hard, as one rereads it, not to sense that this sort of narrative unfolding would have made for a much more compelling novel. I suggest that there is something about us as readers now – something, perhaps, that subtends our more or less vague identity as "postmoderns" – that makes the protagonism of an Oliveira seem increasingly unimportant, not to say irritating. By the same token, the thought of La Maga as heroine kindles a certain sympathetic interest that, as I read it, Cortázar fails to project or to anticipate within the novel. And this failure points, in my view, to one of the great failings of the novel itself, when read in light of the demands placed on any work of literature by contemporary events themselves: Cortázar, writing in the late 1950s and early 1960s, simply did not perceive the real import or developing energy of the women's movement – arguably one of the most signal of modern "cultural revolutions." Cortázar's "modernity" plainly did not include feminism – which is part of the reason why, reading it now, it seems almost intolerably obsolete.

The second mark of *Hopscotch*'s archaism I wish to remark on here is its purportedly nonlinear structure, or the hopscotch itself. If *Hopscotch*'s sexist gender heroics produce its *ethical* embarrassment for the reader, then it is the gimmick of the hopscotch – of the novel which is really two, or an infinite number, of novels – that seems the most unmistakable signature of its *aesthetic* obsolescence. To be honest, I have forgotten whether in my first encounter with the novel in the early 1970s I read "hopscotch" or "lector hembra" fashion, only that it was the excited talk of a novel that could be read in a nonlinear order that had originally caught my interest. But in either case, rereading *Hopscotch* in Cortázar's recommended, nonsequential order now produces (for me, at any rate) only a persistent sense of impatience and irritation. The much anticipated moment of, to use Benjamin's apt phrase, "profane illumination" (Benjamin, 179) simply never arrives.

In the early 1970s the sheer will to have such an "experience" was perhaps great enough to overcome, or at least put off, this disappointment. But not now, I think. For the hopscotch turns out to be really just a conventionally linear experience of reading, broken up by a miscellany of clips and "morelliana" of widely varying interest but never formally any-thing more than *interruptions*. Perhaps the only saving grace of the hop-scotch is that it draws attention away from the schematism and poverty of the linear plot itself – the fact that so remarkably little actually happens in the novel of fifty-six chapters, much less in the 155-chapter version. As Boldy writes – with a critical aim opposite to mine, of course – "historical and political action has been excluded from *Rayuela* and, indeed, there is little action of any sort in the novel" (Boldy, 74). Of course, Cortázar, in his bid to produce a *nouveau roman* that would be the envy of his French contemporaries, is in good company here. My guess is that if peo-ple read *Hopscotch* little these days, they read the novels of Robbe-Grillet, Butor, Simon, Sollers, and so on even less. (Marguerite Duras may be the single important exception, at least insofar as the breathless, pseudopro-fundity of the *nouveau roman* still echoes faintly in narratives such as *The Lover.*) But even a casual browse through, say, Robbe-Grillet's *Jealousy* is sufficient to experience what has become, now that the novelty has faded, the utter boredom of the aleatory, nonsequential narrative, the great, arid myth of the *coupage,* or, in the then oncoming structuralist enthusiasm, of the *combinatoire.* One appreciates more than ever, from this perspective, the fine poetic sagacity of Borges who, exhilarated by essentially the same dream of an infinite and labyrinthine narrative, understood its formal impossibility from the standpoint of the reader and chose instead to tell, repeatedly, only the *story* of this dream – and to tell it *briefly* and through carefully crafted, Poe-like plots that could not possibly be *less* aleatory or *more* linear. Cortázar's great blunder was thus, so to speak, not to have tried to imitate Borges but to have written as though the Borgesian utopia could be consciously enacted.

What, if anything, salvages *Hopscotch* from the wreck of its own formal conception are the sporadic occasions on which it treats this aesthetic ironically. The supreme instance of this, for me, is chapter 23, or the Berthe Trépat episode – although one may wonder whether in this case the irony is unintentional. Recall how Oliveira, in order to get out of the rain – or is it to get out of the pastiche of Sartre's *Nausea* with which the chapter begins? – ducks into the "Salle de la Géographie," where the pianist and composer Berthe Trépat is about to perform a triple bill con-sisting of the "*Three Discontinuous Movements* of Rose Bob (première), the *Pavan for General Leclerc* by Alix Alix (first time for a civilian audience), and the *Délibes–Saint-Saëns Synthesis,* by Délibes, Saint-Saëns and Berthe Trépat" (112). This latter piece Trépat has composed – as Valentin, the master of ceremonies and Trépat's elderly, gay housemate informs the audience – according to the principle of "prophetic syncretism." Cortázar's account of the concert, culminating in the performance of the *Synthesis,* and over the course of which the already sparse and ragtag audience dwindles down to one – Oliveira – is a minor tour de force of black comedy. "It was," writes Cortázar, "almost like a chapter out of Céline, and Oliveira felt himself incapable of thinking beyond the general atmosphere, beyond the useless and defeatist survival of such artistic activities among groups of people equally defeated and useless" (117). And the "prophetic syncretism," Cortázar continues, "was not long in revealing its secret": "three measures of *Le Rouet d'Omphale* were followed by four more from *Les Filles de Cadix,* then her left hand offered *Mon coeur s'ouvre à ta voix,* while the right one spasmodically interspersed the theme of the bells from *Lakmé,*" and so on (ibid.). There follows the incident this chapter is best known for, as Oliveira, stricken with an inexplicable surge of affection for the aged, masculinized, and grotesquely attired Trépat – a truly Célinesque rapture that will consummate itself erotically with the *clocharde* Emmanuelle at the close of the novel's first part – offers to accompany her home and is physically rebuffed when she takes his solicitations to be sexual. But is not the most striking aspect of this musical interlude the manner in which, for us as "postmodern" readers, it perfectly mimics the experience of reading *Hopscotch?* What better term than "prophetic syncretism" to describe the literary "theory" of Cortázar's novel itself? And has not the reader ideally constructed by such prophetic syncretism become, like Trépat's audience, defeated and useless?

Perhaps this is a conscious self-parody on Cortázar's part. I am inclined to doubt this, but then neither, I admit, can it be considered purely fortuitous. For if Berthe Trépat becomes, here, an unexpected comic heroine of the "linear" novel, do we not find in Morelli her counterpart as concerns the "expendable" chapters of *Hopscotch?* It has long been a commonplace of *Hopscotch* interpretation that the character of Morelli serves Cortázar as a mouthpiece for his literary philosophy, especially as it touches on *Hopscotch* itself. But the crucial and perhaps overlooked point here is that, as Morelli's conception, this philosophy is ultimately unable to take itself seriously and becomes, like the *Délibes–Saint-Saëns Synthesis,* the object of a certain postmodern laughter.

How so? The Morelli chapters are of three basic sorts: (1) those in which Morelli's metaphysical and literary dicta are presented directly to the reader; these generally bear the heading of "Morelliana" and are not marked as citations; (2) those in which some member of the Serpent

Club cites a fragment of Morelli; and (3) chapters in which the members of the club directly propose various readings, interpretations, and evaluations of Morelli's "works" (among these, evidently, his "novels," which do not appear in *Hopscotch* – unless, of course, *Hopscotch* is to be read as one of them). This latter set of chapters climaxes in the full-scale *disputatio* of chapter 99, as the disciples meet in Morelli's apartment after his death. (A possible fourth group here is the one chapter, 154, in which Oliveira and Etienne visit Morelli himself in the hospital.) Read together, the first two series of chapters present us – in addition to a miscellany of metaphysical speculations that could just as well be Oliveira's – with the "theory" of a "new" novel, of which *Hopscotch* is perhaps the prototype. (Chapter 62, of course, is to give us *62: a Model Kit*.) This new novel is one in which, simply put, representation itself has been reduced to an absolute minimum, forcing the reader to step into the "narrative" (as its "one true character," according to Wong's reading of Morelli in chapter 97) but promising him a transcendant experience of pure, unmediated being. Thus, in chapter 79, Morelli 'writes' of a "text that would not clutch the reader, but which would oblige him to become an accomplice ('lector cómplice') . . ." (406). As against the conventional, or "female" reader ("lector hembra"), the "lector cómplice" "would be able to become a co-participant and co-sufferer of the experience through which the novel is passing, *at the same moment and in the same form* . . ." (407). And such a novel, Morelli pompously declares, implies "a rejection of literature" itself; its mission is "to take from literature that part which is a living bridge from man to man . . ." (406).

It is clearly this "lector cómplice" – this reader that, in theory, comes before or leaps instantaneously beyond all representational mediacy – who must read *Hopscotch* for it to succeed as a novel, or indeed as a work of art *tout court*. The evident fact that such a reader does not – indeed, cannot – exist, given the very representational mediacy of all verbal processes, even those which postulate a leap beyond representation, is what often makes reading *Hopscotch,* in practice, so enervating. Indeed, as Concha, in what remains the most thoughtful of the Marxist critiques of *Hopscotch,* observes: "nowhere is this theory [of the "lector cómplice"] less valid than in the actual text of [Cortázar's] novel itself" (140; my translation). This, however, is not the fundamental point at issue here. Rather, it is to take note of a historical and cultural shift: Whereas circa 1963 one could still perhaps *desire* to *be* such a reader and therefore take on *Hopscotch*'s aesthetic failures as one's own readerly shortcomings, over the last thirty years this desire has effectively petered out. One no longer

wants to read the "last book" to, as Oliveira demands, "destroy literature." One wants to read, if I can put it this way, *another* book, not the
book that was to bring modernism, finally, to its teleological climax of
autonegation, but a book – or, indeed, multiple books – that high modernism could not have allowed for or imagined. Some time after *Hopscotch*'s appearance it gradually began to dawn on readers such as myself
that modernism had developed a suspicious habit of producing a new
"last book" at regular intervals. And as one of the latest of these last
books, *Hopscotch*'s grace period seems fated to have been relatively short.
It is now the "lector hembra" – not the novel – that seems entitled to
demand "accomplices."

To make matters more complex, however, the alternative or expendable *Hopscotch*, with Morelli as its effective hero, seems almost to anticipate this development. Morelli, after all, unlike Oliveira, must face his
actual flesh-and-blood readers in the members of the Serpent Club. And
for all their strenuously orthodox, almost monastic pledge to become
Morelli's reader-accomplices, Oliveira, Gregorovious, Wong, Etienne –
not to mention the camp-following La Maga and Babs – show rather
telling signs of impatience with this task. Or so, at least, is suggested by a
selective rereading of the chapters (124, 141, 60, 109, 95, and 99) in
which the club not only trades citations but engages in outright *disputatio*. In chapter 109, for example, the narrator – unidentified, but who,
one senses, speaks for the club as a collective subject – describes Morelli's
plan for a narrative analogous to a set of photographic stills rather than
to a movie. It is to be left to the "lector cómplice" to set the pictures into
motion, thereby "participating, almost, in the destiny of the characters"
(477). "The book would have to be something like those sketches proposed by Gestalt psychology, and therefore certain lines would induce
the observer to trace imaginatively the ones that would complete the picture" (478). There is a pause, however – graphically marked by an extra
space between paragraphs – which is then followed by this evidently less
than gratified observation: "Reading this book [for Morelli has, evidently, written this 'would-be' narrative] one had the impression for a
while that Morelli had hoped that the accumulation of fragments would
quickly crystallize into a total reality" (ibid.). "Had hoped" – but, clearly
enough, had hoped in vain. And, in any case, such a crystallization, even
if it were possible, would be only the image of a "world that was taking on
coherence." Thus "there was no cause for confidence," the narrative
voice continues, "because coherence meant basically assimilation in
space and time, an ordering to the taste of the female reader" (ibid.).

Thus the "lector cómplice," although he does exactly what is required, will somehow always end up as "lector hembra." And even Morelli himself, as the directly discoursing subject of the "Morelliana," lapses occasionally into similar moments of melancholic self-irony. In chapter 112, for example, he soliloquizes on the "deliberate poverty" of his narratives (483). Perhaps, after all, it is "preferable to renounce all writing," as there is "no hope of dialogue with the reader" (484). And chapter 94 begins with a dictum that, for all its evident grotesque humor as fictionalized self-deprecation, comes uncomfortably close to describing the fate of *Hopscotch* itself: "A piece of prose can turn rotten like a side of beef" (438).

Not only, that is, does Morelli's reception by his disciples prefigure the "postmodern" reading of *Hopscotch;* the very sequence of affect in which the supreme instant of "prophetic syncretism" is promised, only in the next moment to be sheepishly dismissed as whimsical nonsense, assumes concrete, dramatic configuration in the character of Morelli himself. In this way, one might argue, Morelli takes on the rough outlines of what might, or indeed, what *ought* to have been the true, *comic* hero of *Hopscotch.* (The novel aimed at by Morelli, remember, is the "roman comique.") So emerges *this* hero, as against Oliveira, in whom this same quest for a transcendent experience of pure, unmediated being becomes something we, as readers, are urged to take with complete seriousness. But, whereas Morelli's comic enactment of this quest, although banal, achieves a certain degree of artistic integrity, in Oliveira's story it becomes both merely silly and unbearably tedious. Held up against Morelli, Oliveira is exposed as the *mock-tragic* hero of *Hopscotch* – or at least of the *Hopscotch* that, above all others, Cortázar seems to have meant us to read.

### Authenticating Circumstances

> . . . the ethical torture of knowing one is tied to a race or to
> a people . . . (*Hopscotch,* 302)

I would like to turn away, now, from *Hopscotch* and pose the question of a postmodern Cortázar on a more general, literary-historical plane. For, if my intuition is right and Cortázar is less and less read these days, this cannot be solely the fault of one novel. Let me begin, again, by stating things bluntly: The same, generally prevalent standard of literary taste – or "canonicity" – that awards *Hopscotch* honorific status as a boom-inaugurating text has also gradually affixed to Cortázar the stigma of his seeming *inauthenticity.* Doubts persist as to whether, in fact, Cortázar can be considered a genuinely "Latin American" writer – whether classifying him as "European" or perhaps simply as "cosmopolitan" might not be a better fit. In its crudest form, the case for Cortázar's inauthenticity rests on literary geography: his decision to remain Paris-based rather than to stay in Buenos Aires. Despite his frequent visits to Latin America (Cuba and Nicaragua included), Cortázar's voluntary exile is somehow felt to foreground his writing in a way that, for example, the cosmopolitan location of a García Márquez or a Vargas Llosa (both of whom have maintained legal residences in Europe) does not. Yet even if this residency requirement is waived, questions remain about Cortázar's Latin American "identity" as they do not in the case of practically any other major figure of twentieth-century Latin American literature, Borges included. Why is this?

Part of the answer clearly lies in a more global shift within what we might call the ideology of reading, a shift toward what, grosso modo, has come to be termed the postmodern and which has condemned not only Cortázar but entire generations of authors to relative neglect. Concerning Latin American literature in particular, this shift has coincided with a progressive loss of enthusiasm for the "boom" and corresponding gains for more heterodox genres, most notably the "testimonial" narrative. Underlying this shift, especially as it pertains to readers in the metropolitan north, is, I think, a complex political and cultural realignment. Whereas an earlier ideology of reading, swayed by an upsurge in decolonizing and anti-imperialist struggles in the 1960s and early 1970s, welcomed the boom in a spirit of what I have elsewhere termed "canonical decolonization," the more recent trend, reflecting a general panorama of imperialist "reflux," has been to question whether this initial utopianism may not have concealed a certain overdetermining drive to recolonize Latin America (and the third world generally) through a subtle "voicing-over" of the "subaltern." Enter, then, the testimonial, not so much as a "postmodern" genre in its own right (although some have argued for this), but as a kind of cultural marker for Latin America – that is, as a new "ideology of reading" – within the overall postmodern scene.[3] In fact, this same readerly tendency to escalate the demand for the authentic seems to have operated within the boom itself, as the earlier hunt for – so to speak – the Latin American *Ulysses* (with *Hopscotch* as the main contender) shifted its sights onto the texts of "magical realism" (enter *One Hundred Years of Solitude*). Now, of course, even a Rulfo or a Guimarães Rosa may arouse suspicions insofar as they still appear to be speaking *for* the subaltern, while in the case of a Rigoberta Menchú or a Guaman Poma true subalternity or alterity is somehow sensed as certified. But in any case, the point is that Cortázar has, by this time, long since dropped out of the picture.

Thinking more locally, the key intellectual and literary event to consider here is probably the famous journalistic debate between Cortázar and Arguedas as rehearsed in the pages of the Cuban literary journal *Casa de las Américas* in 1969. Cortázar, of course, had begun to draw fire from various quarters of the Latin American left soon after publication of *Hopscotch,* often entering the fray himself in defense of his own "revolutionary" credentials. The interchange with Oscar Collazos, later published as *Literatura en la revolución o revolución en la literatura* is perhaps the most frequently cited of these. But my guess is that the bitter dispute with Arguedas – terminated, of course, by the latter's tragic suicide – has, over the years, done the most to inaugurate, as concerns Cortázar, the new ideology of reading of which I have spoken. A full recapitulation would be impossible here, but the essential facts are these: Cortázar had, in 1967, published a long open letter to Roberto Fernández Retamar in *Casa de las Américas* (it later appeared in the second volume of *Ultimo Round* as "Acerca de la situación del intelectual latinoamericano") in which he sought to justify his decision to remain in Europe as necessary for someone who aspired to the condition of a universal or "planetary" intellectual:

On the margins of local circumstances, set apart from the unavoidable dialectic of daily challenge and response that grows out of the political, economic, and social problems of a country and that demands the immediate commitment of every conscious intellectual, one's sense of the human process becomes, so to speak, more planetary, operating through aggregations and syntheses, and if it loses the concentrated force of an immediate context, it gains, on the other hand, a lucidity that is sometimes unbearable but always clarifying. (Cortázar, *Ultimo Round,* 267; my translation)

This prompted an angry response from Arguedas, which first appeared in 1968 in a species of prologue to *El zorro de arriba y el zorro de abajo* known as the "Primer Diario" ("First Journal"). Arguedas complains of

this Cortázar who goads us with his "geniality," with his solemn convictions that the national essence is better understood from the upper spheres of the supranational. As if I, raised among the people of don Felipe Maywa and thrust, for some years of my childhood, into the very *oqllo* [breast] of the Indians, only to return to the "supra-Indian" sphere from which I had descended among the quechuas, were to propose myself as a better, more essential interpreter of the spirit of don Felipe than don Felipe himself. What a lack of respect and due consideration! (Arguedas, *El zorro,* 22; my translation)

Arguedas contrasts Cortázar to García Márquez and Guimarães Rosa, who, purportedly like Arguedas himself, had descended to the "the very root [*cuajo*] of their people" (23). Cortázar becomes, for Arguedas, the typical "professional writer," as against Arguedas et al. (Rulfo is added to the list at this point) who embody, as a positive virtue of course, the writer as "provincial" (25).

Writing in *Life en Español* in April of 1969, Cortázar then retorted by asking Arguedas to consider the case of Vargas Llosa, who, says Cortázar, had "disclosed a Peruvian reality in no way inferior" to that depicted in Arguedas, but had done so from Europe. "As always," Cortázar continues, "the error lies in generalizing a problem whose solutions are exclusively particular: what matters is that . . . 'exiles' cease to be 'exiles' as far as those who read them are concerned, that their books keep, exalt, and perfect the most profound contact with their native soil and people" (quoted in *Casa de las Américas;* my translation). To this, finally, Arguedas replied (in a letter originally published in *Marcha*) that, be this as it may, exile for Cortázar was still not the same as exile for, say, a Vallejo, since in Cortázar's case exile was not only willed but implied a patronizing contempt for "those of us who work in situ" (quoted in *Casa de las Américas;* my translation).

As I have said, Cortázar is historically the loser in this debate, in that it makes painfully obvious what we would now label his "Eurocentrism." As in the case of feminism, Cortázar here again exhibited a curious incapacity, despite his "planetary" perch in Paris, to see which way the political-intellectual edge was cutting. Arguedas, on the other hand, clearly anticipated here (as in the text of *El zorro* itself) what was to become a new "ideology of reading" epitomized in the metropolitan reception of testimonial narrative. And yet, as one rereads this exchange *post festum,* a number of "postmodern" ironies become apparent. One is that, on "debate points," Cortázar seems the clear winner here: For even if we assume that a genuine criterion for a Latin American literary "authenticity" exists, this can hardly be reduced to a question of whether the writer writes "in situ." Even Rigoberta Menchú, after all, gives her testimony in Paris. "What matters is that . . . 'exiles' cease to be 'exiles' as far as those who read them are concerned." Precisely so. And yet, with these very words, Cortázar furnishes the argument for an unfavorable judgment of his *own* literary practice – an argument, moreover, to which Arguedas himself remains insensible, oblivious, as he seems to be, to the problem of the reader. For is it not precisely "as far as those who read him are concerned" that Cortázar cannot elude his image as a self-willed and opportunistic "exile"? Writing in "Acerca de la situación del intelectual latinoamericano," Cortázar openly espouses the ideal of a universal standpoint or "mental ubiquity" from which it would, in theory, be possible to "proceed in the gradual discovery of the radical truths of Latin America without losing, for that reason, a global vision of history and of man" (*Ultimo Round*, 270; my translation). "From my country," he writes, "there departed a writer for whom reality, as Mallarmé imagined, ought to culminate in a book; in Paris there was born a writer for whom books ought to culminate in reality" (272; my translation). One can only admire such sentiments. But the problem – and perhaps it is here that the Cortazarian tragedy *is* finally enacted – is that Cortázar's books do not, in the final analysis, discover those "radical truths," do not "culminate in reality."

The further irony of this debate over authenticity has to do with what its two sides have in common. For, as becomes readily apparent to anyone who rereads it now, *both* Cortázar and Arguedas take as given a kind of conceptual or allegorical map in which Europe automatically has assigned to it the category of the universal, while Latin America occupies the site of the particular. Cortázar, it is true, envisions an ideal location from which the universal would encompass all possible coordinates; and perhaps an analogous urge to synthesis is latent in the Arguedian principle of transculturation. But both initially concur in locating authenticity on the side of the particular. The only question is *how best to situate oneself in relation to this particular* – whether as "provincial" or as "planetary" intellectual. Thus, if Cortázar's thinking remains entrapped in Eurocentrism, then Arguedas, by merely reversing the initial polarity of values, offers no real means of escape here either. Arguedas's defense of the provincial restricts itself to the logic of what Samir Amin has termed "inverted Eurocentrism": in repudiating Europe, one leaves unchallenged its prior conceptual mapping as the universal.[4]

In this regard, it is instructive to recall another of the more polemical left-wing critiques elicited by Cortázar in the late 1960s. I am thinking of David Viñas's *De Sarmiento a Cortázar*. Viñas here locates Cortázar within a tradition of Argentine intellectuals for whom the inevitable "viaje a Europa" is both rationalized and experienced by the subject as a flight from a violent and aggressive "body" (Viñas's precise word is *escisión* or "schism") and a quest for "espíritu." Cortázar, however, represents a novel complication of this, as Viñas terms it, "metáfora mayor" – a "new way of being a writer" ("una nueva manera de ser escritor") (125) – which would seem to go beyond that of the mere "escritor profesional." Having once realized the spiritual quest, Cortázar nevertheless senses the continual absence of the body, of *materia,* as a threat to the maintenance of his new, purified writerly self. It becomes necessary to bring this body – which, as Peronism, prompts the original act of flight from violation – into some new relationship of proximity to the writing subject. Cortázar finds this new, spiritually safe and "universalized" body, argues Viñas, in revolutionary Cuba. And yet "this latching on to Cuba is already sensed as an effort of generosity (understood as a recognition of the 'others') and as a way of resolving, somewhere else, local impossibilities. For Cortázar, [Cuba becomes] the 'purification' of what here [i.e., in Argentina] occurred as something confused and intolerable. Cuba – in essence – was an American situation refined . . . through its Europeanization" (124–5; my translation).

Cuba, that is, can satisfy Cortázar's need for a Latin American body – his universalizing need for an authenticating particular – primarily because of the body – Argentina – that it is not. Viñas does not, it should be stressed, disdain Cortázar's publicly pro-Cuban stance as somehow insincere because of this. In fact, he discerns, with remarkable insight and critical integrity, a curious parallelism between Cortázar's abstract-universalist "Cuba" and the philosophy of *foquismo* itself: Cortázar is likened to Debray[5] but also, in answer to Cortázar's allusion to "the future Ernesto Guevaras of Latin American literature," to Che himself:

Here we have an exemplary case of texts inseparable from their body; a body that at no time lags behind the theory of the revolution being advanced. Or at least, not until Bolivia, because, if anything is to be posed for frank criticism now it is the space that opens up for the first and only time between the final Guevara and a people – as the prolongation of his body – that, alloying itself to him, might have sustained him. It's not easy to write this; but, for now, the niceties are for others: through this space there appears among other things an image of failure and schism [*escisión*] a falling back into an individualized omnipotence as all that was finally left of a man who desired himself to be a socialist but who, in that conjuncture, found himself separated from the body of the masses. (131–2; my translation)

What Cortázar finds so attractive in the *foco*, then – to follow Viñas – is principally the manner in which it seems to replicate, qua politics, the vanguard writer's own heroic isolation: his "revolución en la literatura." And so it is that we are left with a Cortázar who, despite adopting all the political opinions demanded of him by his critics on the Latin American left, still cannot quite seem to transmute personal solidarity into literary authenticity.

Yet this is not quite the end of the story, I think. For if the new ideology of reading prefigured in Arguedas's defense of the "escritor provincial" has condemned Cortázar to increasing marginality, it nevertheless seems to me that we can find in Cortázar certain vantage points from which to see through, if not beyond, this ideology itself. I have in mind here one of his later short stories, "Apocalypse at Solentiname." As the reader will recall, the story recounts, in a quasi-autobiographical mode, a trip taken by Cortázar to Solentiname, the Nicaraguan island community of radical Christians founded by Ernesto Cardenal. While there, the narrator, impressed by their vivid colors and visionary energy, takes a number of photographs of paintings by peasant residents of Solentiname. Later, on his return to Paris, he has the film developed and sits down for a private slide show, only to discover that the images of the paintings have been mysteriously replaced by photographed scenes of torture and political repression, among them the execution of Roque Dalton. Terrified, the narrator arranges to have his companion, Claudine, view the slides as well; she, however, sees only the paintings. He decides to say nothing to her.

Given its open (although somewhat vexed) allusions to the authenticity issue – "Why don't you live in your country?" (119), the narrator is asked on arrival in Costa Rica – it is hard not to read "Apocalypse at Solentiname" as a gesture of self-criticism and rectification. The hero behaves like the stereotypical progressive "cultural" tourist, filled with enthusiasm for popular causes in Latin America but ultimately driven by the affluent cosmopolite's will to *collect* such causes in the form of its cultural artifacts – artifacts which, especially when made by peasants, effectively become the *fetishized* tokens of a hypothetical and abstract political commitment. In fact, the hero of "Apocalypse at Solentiname" doesn't even deign to *buy* any of the paintings, preferring the cheaper and more efficient method of making photographic copies. (The character of Cardenal laughingly accuses him of being an "art thief" and "image smuggler") (123). But divine – or supernatural – retribution is not long in coming, as the comfortable apartment back in Paris in which the collection is to be housed and enjoyed, turns out to be insecure against the "return of the repressed." The "cultural" coach has turned back into the "political" pumpkin.

However, it seems to me possible to go further here and read "Apocalypse at Solentiname" as a parable intended to dramatize not only the foibles of progressive cultural tourism but also the latent ideological distortions of the provincial writer-as-committed-ethnographer celebrated by Arguedas. Is this writer – Cortázar seems to be asking – any less implicated, finally, in the practice of cultural fetishism than the character of

Cortázar himself in "Apocalypse at Solentiname"? Take the case of Rulfo, one of the central figures of Arguedas's "provincial" canon. As I have argued elsewhere,[6] the fact that the reader of Rulfian fictions can have the vicarious experience of "descent," along with the author, into the very *cuajo* of the Jaliscan peasantry, seemingly without the need for the discursive markers of ethnographic reason, is proof of these fictions' deep embeddedness in ideology, not in authenticity.[7] Suppression of these markers only makes the cultural fetish itself less detectable. Rulfo's narratives – especially the short stories of *El llano en llamas* – become, like the photographed paintings in "Apocalypse at Solentiname," the portable souvenirs of Latin American rural-popular culture, souvenirs that the reader, in whom the ethnorational frame has become implicit, even a kind of unconscious, can all the more easily pocket.

The word *fetish* is, to be sure, a provocative one, but I think it is the exact concept required to bring into full view the ideology of reading under critical examination here. For, if I may state things abstractly, what but a fetish form of the object can be the result when the desire for its authenticity is overdetermined by the more powerful and provincial aversion for the planetary? Should not the goal of a provincial literature, as Arguedas initially conceives of it in his repudiation of Cortázar, be the authentic, not as against the universal, but as against the *abstract* – the authentic, that is, as the *concrete*? But the concrete, as we learn from Marx, "is the concrete because it is the concentration of many determinations, hence of unity in the diverse" (Marx, 101). The concrete, that is, only becomes fully concrete as the concrete *universal*. In flight from universals, however, the "provincial" desire for authenticity must satisfy itself with a mere abstract particular – with a fragment falsely magnified into totality – that is, with a reification, a fetish.

To speak of this abstract particular as "culture" may be true enough in its way. And certainly Arguedas's provincial writer (and reader) is as sincere in his or her quest for the cultural truth of Latin America as anyone could wish. But the point is that the interest in culture is itself a symptom of entrapment within the reified categories of what might be termed the ethnographic reduction: Culture as the rationalized object of the ethnographer does not progress *beyond* but merely substitutes itself *for* the disdained categories of an abstract, universal reason. The provincial writer may, to be sure, reject the ethnographer's claim to objectivity or neutrality, but the world he or she depicts through fiction falls within the same narrow, reified conceptual limits. In the case of Rulfo, this is a world of pure ethnoscapes, a world immune to historicization. That Arguedas, especially in *Todas las sangres* and *El zorro*, struggled to break through this reified frame is evident. But one must be skeptical of his success here. By seeking to make indigenous culture the active, form-giving principle of his poetics, Arguedas nevertheless could not, it seems to me, cease to frame this culture itself as ethnographic.[8] Thus the ethnographic fetish is opposed, but only within the framework of a thinking generated by the fetish itself.

Much less, of course, does "Apocalypse at Solentiname" free itself of such fetishism, for all of Cortázar's allegorizing cleverness in pointing to its existence. "Apocalypse at Solentiname" is essentially a variation on the standard, fantastic plot device to which Cortázar resorted over and over again, and which, as one of his admiring students is candid enough to admit,[9] has its popular-cultural equivalent in any *Twilight Zone* episode. The difference is simply that Cortázar has here used it to thematize his own "authenticity" problem in relation to the question of fetishism. At the setting prompt he pulls down the "Latin America" menu before making his selection. We meet authentic Latin Americans such as Ernesto Cardenal, Roque Dalton, and Sergio Ramírez in authentic Latin American locales such as Costa Rica, Los Chiles, and Solentiname. So in what sense is this any less "authentically" Latin American a piece of fiction than, say, Rulfo's "Es que somos muy pobres" or even a contemporary testimonial narrative? For, to give Cortázar his due here, the fact that we still tend spontaneously to read the latter sorts of texts as authentic while remaining doubtful of Cortázar suggests, to my thinking, not any fundamental difference qua literary content, but rather how completely we, as readers, have internalized the ethnographic reduction, how adept we have become at recognizing and attempting to suppress any discursive or poetic reminders of our postmodern cultural fetishism. Again, the fact that "Apocalypse at Solentiname" is able to thematize this ideology of reading does not mean that Cortázar succeeds in breaking with it – merely that he has caught a glimpse of how fungible a substance "authenticity" has become, and exploits this knowledge to ironic and purely formal effect.

To gain some insight into what a radical, progressive break with cultural fetishism entails in objectively aesthetic terms would, to my mind, mean leaving behind *both* the "planetary" and modernist Cortázar *and* his "provincial," postmodern opposites and looking to other Latin American narratives entirely. I have in mind here a species of "suppressed lineage" of modern realism that would, in particular, include the great Latin American feature films made over the last three decades, from *Blood of the Condor* and *The Last Supper* to *The Official Story*. And with respect to the novel itself, I am thinking – not without trepidation and a heightened sense of ethical and political irony, I must confess – of Vargas Llosa. In a work such as *The Storyteller,* it seems to me, the latter realizes in practice an authentic – because both richly concrete and *non*provincial – portrayal of certain "radical truths of Latin America" – truths that Arguedas, although for far better political motives, reduced in practice to ethnography, and that Cortázar, with his heart similarly well placed, could only contemplate as theoretical abstractions. An enigma, to be sure. But that, as the saying goes, is a subject for future discussion.

*Notes*

1. Jaime Concha, for example, pointedly refers to Cortázar as "el gran cuentista argentino," ("great Argentine short-story writer;" Concha, 131).
2. See, e.g., Stephen Boldy's comment that "Cortázar excels at the subtle depiction of bad faith in his characters and, indeed, it is on this aptitude that much of the density and ambiguity of his prose depends" (Boldy, 74).
3. For a fuller account of this shift, see the introduction to my own recent work, *Reading North by South: On Latin American Literature, Culture, and Politics* (Minneapolis: University of Minnesota Press, 1995).
4. See Samir Amin, *Eurocentrism,* trans. Russell Moore (New York: Monthly Review Press, 1989).
5. ". . . the graduate of the Mariano Acosta Normal School for Teachers goes in search of his 'spirit' in Paris, and, in fact, crosses paths with the graduate of the Ecole Normale Supérieure, on his way to America in search of the concrete embodiment of the theories he has learned . . ." (Viñas, 122; my translation).
6. See Neil Larsen, *Modernism and Hegemony: A Materialist Critique of Aesthetic Agencies* (Minneapolis: University of Minnesota Press, 1990), chap. 3.
7. On this score I find useful González Echevarría's theory of twentieth-century Latin American literature as largely governed by the "masterstory" of anthropology. See *Myth Archive: A Theory of Latin American Narrative* (Cambridge University Press, 1990). Unlike González Echevarría, however, who regards this as a relation internal to the radically fictional character of all discursive practices, I see both the dominance of this "masterstory" as well as the conditions for its transcendence – in keeping with the theory of ideology – as lying with the social and historical reality reflected in all fictive discourse.
8. For further discussion, see "Indigenism, Cultural Nationalism and the Problem of Universality," in Larsen, *Reading North by South* (n. 3). See also Silverio Muñoz, *José María Arguedas y el mito de la salvación por la cultura* (Minneapolis: Instituto para el Estudio de Ideologías y Literatura, 1980).
9. See Terry Peavler, *Julio Cortázar* (Boston: Twayne Publishers, 1990), 20.

*References*

Arguedas, José María. *El zorro de arriba y el zorro de abajo.* Lima: Editorial Horizonte, 1984.

Benjamin, Walter. "Surrealism: The Last Snapshot of the European Intelligentsia." In *Reflections*, trans. Edmund Jephcott. New York: Schocken, 1979.

Boldy, Stephen. *The Novels of Julio Cortázar.* Cambridge University Press, 1980.

*Casa de las Américas,* no. 57 (November–December 1969), Año X, 136–8.

Concha, Jaime. "Criticando *Rayuela.*" *Hispamérica* 4, no. 1 (August 1975): 131–51.

Cortázar, Julio. "Acerca de la situación del intelectual latinoamericano." In *Ultimo Round,* vol. 2. (Mexico City: Siglo XXI, 1974).

"Apocalypse at Solentiname." In *A Change of Light and Other Stories,* trans. Gregory Rabassa, 119–28. New York: Knopf, 1980.

*Hopscotch.* Trans. Gregory Rabassa. New York: Avon/Bard, 1971.

Marx, Karl. *Grundrisse.* Trans. Martin Nicolaus. New York: Vintage, 1973.

Schwarz, Roberto. *Misplaced Ideas: Essays on Brazilian Culture.* Ed. John Gledson. London: Verso, 1992.

Viñas, David. *De Sarmiento a Cortázar.* Buenos Aires: Ediciones Siglo Veinte, 1971.

# 4

## Cortázar's Closet

*René Prieto*

Cortázar never failed to recognize that his lavish obsessions were more guardian demons than avenging angels, purveyors of a torment that was as cherished as it was useful. He viewed the creative act as a way to bring to the fore and ultimately exorcize the incubus that tormented him, and himself as a transmitter of messages, not an "author" conscious of what he was creating. As far as he was concerned, writing was a way of "settling the bill with something that pesters us" (quoted by Prego, 34).

Ana Hernández del Castillo points out, in her illuminating book *Keats, Poe, and the Shaping of Cortázar's Mythopoesis*, how, very early in his career, and primarily through his reading of Keats, "Cortázar defined his concept of the poet as one who is 'possessed' by the magnetic forces of the collective unconscious and thus manifests in his writing, 'archetypal themes and figures'" (4). By the time the budding author started to publish his first stories, he was thoroughly convinced that the thematic obsessions that pestered him stemmed "neither from a conscious nor a rational plane," but rather, "from down under . . . from within" (Prego, 40). Recognizing that literature reveals an author's deep-seated preoccupations and is also a means to channel anxiety, he came to regard his own writing and, most particularly, the short stories in *Bestiario,* as a sort of remedial treatment. These, he told Omar Prego in 1983, "were, without my knowing it (I would only realize this later), a kind of psychoanalytic self-therapy" (Prego, 182).

When discussing his approach to writing, Cortázar also liked to emphasize the *figuras* or recurrent constellations of symbols that haunted him. Although the following list is by no means complete, in his work, hands, breathing disorders, fear of darkness, claustrophobia, animals, bridges, and tunnels represent a repressed complex through unconscious association; in other words, these figures are used to divert the expression of an instinctual desire or impulse from its primitive form to one that is considered more culturally acceptable.

Many critics have studied Cortázar's obsessive themes but few have approached them other than as isolated entities; to my knowledge, no one has investigated how they dovetail into one another to create a patchwork of perfectly orchestrated parts. Cortázar's master plan remains enigmatic because, to put it in his own words, the "central point in which every discordant element can finally become visible as a spoke in a wheel" is still unfathomed (*Libro de Manuel*, 8). In other words, we know he was obsessed with hands and tunnels, but we don't know why. We know the symptoms of his trauma but not its origin.

And yet this origin is not beyond our purview. After all, if certain themes are said to be sublimated symptoms aired while putting pen to paper, isn't there a way we might reach the sore spot, the center of the problem by looking at the manifest content of a story, at the connecting medium that binds together the "spokes of the wheel"? Studying the recurrent obsessions figured by Cortázar as independent entities obstructs from view the source from which they originate. What we need to do is search for the way in which they hinge upon one another in order to form clusters of meaning. And wouldn't finding such clusters be tantamount to discovering a kind of Rosetta Stone, the as yet uncharted fountainhead from which Cortázar's fictional universe springs?

With a great deal of candor and no less humor, the author of *Bestiario* unraveled the little worm of his obsessions to Evelyn Picón Garfield during their now famous 1973 interview. "Hands have always been an obsession of mine," he told Picón at the time, "from the time I was young, in the first pages I ever wrote, hands play an extremely important part" (110). One thinks immediately of "Dg," the hand with a life of its own that flies in through the window and keeps the narrator company in "Estación de la mano" (from *La vuelta al día en ochenta mundos*). Other stories come readily to mind. "Cuello de gatito negro" from *Octaedro*, for example, in which the unbridled and seemingly autonomous hands of a woman come close to castrating a stranger she picks up in the Paris Metro. Or "No se culpe a nadie," one of the most bewildering dressing scenes in the history of fiction.

Hurriedly donning a sweater to be on time for a date, the ill-starred protagonist of "No se culpe a nadie" gets stuck in what is probably the wrong opening and begins to suffocate under the clinging pressure of the wool over his nose and mouth. Mounting anxiety leads to utter confusion; the by then half-smothered hero continues to struggle in a futile effort to pull the sweater down over his head, but only succeeds in getting deeper and deeper into the engulfing wool. Short of breath, practically unable to see, and confined in the narrow tunnel of what is likely the sleeve and not the turtleneck, he tosses, swerves, comes out only to be attacked by his own right hand, cowers back into the possessive embrace of the sweater, and *falls* out of a twelfth-floor window. (This, at least, is what we are given to understand, although Cortázar pointedly avoids using this verb. What the last sentence literally says is that the man "redresses himself" after cowering back into the sweater in order to "arrive at last somewhere with neither hand nor sweater, a place [where] there would only be a tumultuous air that would envelop and accompany him, and twelve stories," 289.)

In her article on the ambivalence of the hand in Cortázar's fiction, Malva Filer explains that the antagonism of the hands in "No se culpe a nadie" is another instance of the schizoid condition present in "Estación de la mano" and wonders "what kind of inner conflict could be represented by the nightmare of having a part of the character's own body attack and destroy him?" (131). Filer suggests that the man with the blue pullover may have been suffering from the restrictions of a very conventional life-style, and the split between the hand and the body could be "a rebellion against that part of the self that had submitted to the tyranny of domestic and social duties" (131). Filer could be hitting the nail on the head; a sort of inner rebellion might be the cause of the accident. But why restrict ourselves to speculation when concrete clues are so liberally strewn across the pages of this short story? It is these we need to examine in order to get to the bottom of what this same critic refers to as the "inner conflict . . . represented by this nightmare" (131).

Filer goes on to report that in "No se culpe a nadie" the protagonist's head finally "emerges from the asphyxiating pullover, only to face five black nails striking against his eyes and pushing him into death" (131). Like "Dg," in "Estación de la mano," the right hand in this story behaves of its own accord: it "pinches" the narrator's thigh and then "scratches him . . . through the layers of clothing" (288–9). The ensuing struggle which, anatomically speaking, splits the protagonist in two is conspicuously linked with a sense of claustrophobia and difficulties in breathing. After the protagonist feels "as if his face were flushed," the blue wool "clings . . . with an almost irritating pressure to his nose and mouth, it stifles him more than he could have imagined, forcing him to take deep breaths" until finally "the blue envelops the wet mouth, the nostrils . . . and all that fills him with anxiety" (285–6). Later on in the action, the sweater becomes so firmly stuck to his face that when his right hand "pulls upward he feels a pain as if his ears were being yanked off " (287–8).

A lot of ink has flowed on the subject of confinement and alienation in "No se culpe a nadie"; not enough has been said about the more dubious business of entrances and exits. The first point that needs to be made in this regard is that, in spite of the countless difficulties which the stifling sweater brings with it, the hero does manage to emerge from his woolly prison: "all of a sudden, the cold air on his eyebrows and forehead" (289). "Absurdly," the narrator goes on to say, "he refuses to open his eyes, but he knows he has come out, that cold substance, that delight is the outside air, and he doesn't want to open his eyes, and . . . he lets himself live in a cold and different realm, the world outside the sweater" (289). By now, the protagonist is down on his knees, declaring, "it's great to be this way until little by little, gratefully, he begins to open his eyes free from the blue spittle" (289). It is then, in that first open-eyed moment, that one-half of the divided self turns openly murderous, and his right hand attacks him. Pulling away from it in the nick of time, he covers his eyes with his left hand and cowers back into the safe embrace of the sweater, which the helpful left hand is hurriedly pulling back up over his neck, letting the "blue spittle" (*baba azul*) "envelop his face once again" (289). Only then, in an effort to arrive somewhere "where there would only be a tumultuous air that would envelop and accompany him" does he fall prey to the beckoning abyss represented by the open window (289).

The same ambivalent dread of confining spaces and of stifling darkness resurfaces in "Cuello de gatito negro" eighteen years later. As Lucho makes love to Dina in this story, the lighted tableside lamp falls to the floor with a thundering crash; Dina "had bolted upright as if terrified, refusing to succumb to darkness" (159). However, after reaching a climax together later in the action, they are both temporarily safeguarded from fear by the "great womb of night" (161). In total darkness, where one is "clumsy like an infant," Lucho blindly searches for matches (161). On his hands and knees, letting his hands do the work his eyes are unable to carry out, it was "even darker, it smelled of time and seclusion" (162). At this point, Dina makes a lunge for Lucho's sex organs, and "the jerk on his genitals made him scream more out of fear than out of pain" (162). Trying to avoid her next attack, he drags himself away from the sound of her voice while doing his best to control "an asphyxiating hiccough that went on and on" (163). Adroitly, Cortázar adds to the pervasive sense of confinement by eliminating paragraphs altogether from "No se culpe a nadie," and from the beginning of the attempted castration scene until the end of "Cuello de gatito negro." Visually speaking, the pages of both stories read as a solid textual mass that has no breaks, no visual breathing space of any kind.

Despite the ever-encroaching darkness, confinement, and pain, there *is* a way out of the threatening world portrayed in "No se culpe a nadie" and "Cuello de gatito negro," however. In the latter story, the window that had been featured in the sweater saga has been substituted for a door Lucho succeeds in reaching after skirting countless obstacles. He opens it to face "a frozen air that blended with the blood covering his lips" (163). As he comes out naked into the light, Lucho feels so cold and forlorn that he is ready to turn around and go back inside. He repeatedly begs Dina, "Open up . . . open up, it's already light out" (164). But to no avail; he is out and remains out. Sitting on the steps, "removing the blood from his mouth and eyes," he thinks, "she probably passed out from the blow," and adds regretfully, she "won't open up, always the same, it's cold, its cold" (164). Naked and covered with blood in the story's last scene, Lucho goes on pleading with Dina to open up and let him back in, because, "if you would open up," he tells her, "we would find the way out, you saw how it was before, you saw how everything was going so well, just a matter of turning the light on and continuing to search, both of us together" (164).

Every time I read this story, I am struck by Lucho's fateful generalization: "always the same, it's cold, it's cold." Why *always,* one wonders? Has Lucho been thrown out naked and shivering from many apartments? Even more surprising, why is exiting associated with pain and death, and not with liberation, in "No se culpe a nadie" and "Cuello de gatito negro"? Why is darkness deemed desirable, and light menacing? Why is breathing hindered with such insistence? Above all, how does one explain away the protagonists' struggle to return to the threatening environment? Why such determination to go back inside after being hurt?

It could be, of course, that these stories are nothing more than the tale of a poor wretch who falls out of a window, and of his more fortunate counterpart who ends up barely slipping away with the tail between his legs. Such cursory readings pose at least one problem for the critic, however; they fail to explain why the stories "work." What I mean to say is that reading only what is explicit does not make clear why the encroaching space portrayed by Cortázar is so profoundly anguish-producing. One can understand why the bite of a vampire or the threatening approach of an oversized ape would frighten readers, but it is not readily evident why the personal panic button is set off with such vehemence when we read Cortázar's depiction of a man who almost suffocates while putting on a sweater.

The author of *Bestiario* spent his life insisting that his stories were a process of self-analysis channeling a great deal of personal anxiety. But doesn't art mirror the symphony of human concerns regardless of how biographical it purports to be? Can anyone doubt, at this point, that "Cuello de gatito negro" and "No se culpe a nadie" depict "archetypal themes and figures"? Wouldn't this explain why readers react to the latent allusions in these stories? Furthermore, if the material sublimated here were a universal as well as a truly important component of Cortázar's psyche, would it surface in only two of his stories? Would it not be a ubiquitous presence portrayed in many guises throughout his fiction?

Without having to look very far, we find the same narrative underpinnings that are present in "No se culpe a nadie" and "Cuello de gatito negro" in one of Cortázar's most captivating tales. With one difference: This classic goes much further in terms of making available to the reader the latent content that animates all three works of fiction.

Cortázar has beguiled generations of readers with the suggestion that the sacrifice scenario of his cunning "La noche boca arriba" should be taken as "reality," while the more familiar scenario, in which the protagonist "had gone through the strange avenues of an astonishing city . . . on an enormous metal insect that whirred away between his legs" is the actual "marvelous dream" (82). It must have been a perpetual source of merriment for him to watch critics splitting hairs in trying to decide which of the two interwoven tales was "reality" while completely missing the point, being blind to the issues dramatized in this extraordinarily deceptive story.

After all, what does it matter which of the two narrative planes is "real" when we know they are both fiction? Isn't the perversely ambiguous resolution – a playful eenie-meenie about reality and dream – the last hurdle that must be negotiated before one can grasp the sense of the story? Shouldn't our most important concern be to discover what the story means, not whether the Moteca dreams up the man riding the "metal insect" or the motorcyclist dreams up the Moteca? Following such false leads only takes us further from the truth that Cortázar has so artfully screened. Instead, to give some coherence to the mechanism of symbols with which he mines his narrative field, we need to take him at his word (he declared to Prego that "a good many of his stories have grown out of [his] dreams," 182) and analyze "La noche boca arriba" as we would a nightmare.

This double-barreled adventure is rife with references to stifled breathing, tunnels, narrow passageways, "black holes," blood, and a dread of closed spaces. These references appear in the section dealing with the Moteca warrior being readied for sacrifice, but are equally present in the parallel story about the motorcycle rider who is taken to the hospital after an accident.

The action opens with the sentence "In the middle of the long hotel hallway . . ." (72). Soon after, we learn that the sunlight "filtered down amidst the tall downtown buildings" (72). References to long, narrow spaces become more frequent as the story unfolds: When the Moteca warrior is brought from the temple's dungeon to be sacrificed, he slips through a "passage" that "was never going to end," a "corridor with . . . dripping walls" (80). As in "No se culpe a nadie" and "Cuello de gatito negro," the whole scene takes place in total darkness: "coming out of the black pit . . . he was surrounded by an absolute darkness," and, soon after "his fingers closed again on a black emptiness, and the passageway went on endlessly" (until it) "rose, opening like a mouth of shadow" (79, 81). At last, the Moteca prisoner in "La noche boca arriba" "watched the double door open" and "felt grappled by hot hands, hard as bronze; he felt himself lifted, still face up, and jerked along by the four acolytes who carried him down the passageway" (80). Unwilling to open his eyes ("useless to open his eyes and look around in every direction; he was surrounded by an absolute darkness"), he tries to find his amulet, only to discover "that it had been yanked off" his neck (80, 79). Suddenly, he hears "a yell, a hoarse yell that rocked off the walls . . . [followed by] . . . another yell, ending in a moan" (79). As it turns out, "It was he who was screaming in the darkness, he was screaming because he was alive, his whole body with that cry fended off what was coming, the inevitable end" (79). Abruptly, at that point, "he came out in a single jump into the hospital night, to the . . . soft shadow wrapping him round" (81). He let out another scream and "panted, looking for some relief for his lungs" (81).

The ordeal is not over even at this point, however, and the fantasy of reentering the threatening space that we saw in the two earlier stories is reenacted by means of the recurrent dream which keeps putting the victim back in the tunnel when he least expects it: "The passageway went on endlessly . . . with momentary ruddy flares, and face up he choked out a dull moan because the roof was about to end, it rose, was opening like a mouth of shadow" (81). Although earlier in the action "he could barely open his mouth," and it was "useless to open his eyes," as he exits from the long, dark passageway, "shiny with the blood dripping off it . . . his eyes . . . opened and closed in an attempt to cross over to the other side"

(79, 81). He could smell "death in the air, and when he opened his eyes, he saw the blood-soaked figure of the sacrificing priest coming toward him with the stone knife in his hand" (82).

The action of "La noche boca arriba" is emphatic in at least two respects: The motorcyclist's "dream" follows an operation and "death" takes place when you exit from darkness. The dramatic effect of anesthesia on the psyche has been amply documented by medicine since the turn of the century, and psychoanalysis has not lagged behind in its assessment of drugs' effects. Otto Rank observes how, "after an anaesthetic, existing states of anxiety (such as sleeping alone in a dark room, anxiety dreams, nightmares, etc.), occur in greatly intensified form" (56). He goes on to explain this reaction by suggesting that the physical symptoms that follow anesthesia "(for instance, striving for breath), automatically mobilize the birth anxiety and the entire psychical complex connected with it" or, stated otherwise, "that the narcotic sleep goes back again to the primal situation" (56–7).

Might not Rank's remarks shed light on the stifling dread that permeates Cortázar's portrayal of a patient's postoperative trauma in "La noche boca arriba"? Couldn't the narcotic sleep from which the injured motorcyclist's nightmare actually springs be a mere excuse for dramatizing the primal situation?

We know from Freud that birth and the trauma created by "the economic upheaval which birth entails" have to do not only with the pain of a forceful entry remembered by the unconscious but, more particularly, with the violent separation from the reassuring safety of the mother's body (94). Such separation, known in psychoanalysis as "the wound that never heals," would explain the last violent image of the dream described in Cortázar's story (the moment when the victim passes through "to the other side" after being swept along bloody walls). It is also important to point out that the traumatic nature of this expulsion assumes the guise of a repetition compulsion in the story, a perpetually reenacted "sacrifice" (the victim exits or is about to exit several times, but always wakes up and is compelled to relive the traumatic passage over again), in which the experiences of dyspnea, fear, and darkness are ceaselessly described.

Portraying birth trauma as a sacrificial dream is far from gratuitous, because "feeling the loss of the loved (longed for) person" is likened to death in the unconscious (Freud, 75). Although, as Rank points out, "with the thought of death is connected from the beginning a strong sense of pleasure associated with the return to the mother's womb," which is why all three stories culminate with the fulfillment of a death wish: defenestration in "No se culpe a nadie," sacrifice in "La noche boca arriba," and castration in "Cuello de gatito negro" (Rank, 24).[1]

In other words, the patient's recurring nightmare in "La noche boca arriba," Lucho's wish to go back into Dina's room, and Mr. Blue Wool's otherwise inexplicable return into the stifling folds of his sweater, picture not only the pleasurable affect associated with the original condition (i.e., life in utero) but also the separation anxiety allusive of primal trauma. Last but not least, by culminating in death, these three stories enact the wish to return to the womb. The uncanny adventures of a Moteca warrior and a motorcyclist, of a couple who meet in the Paris Metro, and of a man who falls out of a window are simply Cortázar's excuse to detail the experience of being cast out from dark surroundings that are simultaneously threatening and gratifying.

The universal nature of Cortázar's obsession with separation and dislodgement compels us to recognize the validity of a statement he once made to Luis Leal: "It's evident that underneath the symbolic themes," he admitted, "the archetypes that pester me pierce through to the surface" (Leal, 407).[2] These archetypes are not readily evident on the level of the *histoire* in which the adventures of two men living in two separate worlds are described, however. The *histoire* is only an excuse to divert the expression of an instinctual desire from its primitive form. Instead, Cortázar's design is to be found at the level of the *récit*, which takes on its true meaning only when viewed from the perspective of primal trauma. It is from such perspective – and such perspective alone – that the significance of key elements in Cortázar's plots becomes clear.

The amulet around the Moteca's neck, for instance, is a case in point of Cortázar's pivotal use of symbols. Described as "his real heart" and "the life center," the amulet is insistently pictured as the cord that keeps the Moteca warrior alive (80). This is why, once that cord is severed, the warrior "was lost," and "no prayer could save him from the final" (79). As he lies in the belly of the pyramid, bound (a condition difficult not to associate with the pleasurable intrauterine state of immobility) and "surrounded by an absolute darkness," the Moteca waits for the dreadful moment that begins when "he watches the double door open," is grabbed by "hot hands," and feels himself lifted face up "and jerked along . . . down the passageway" (80). As we have seen, the corridor has "dripping walls," and he pants, looking for some relief for his lungs, uttering "another choked cry" because "he could barely open his mouth" (80).

The passageway goes on "endlessly," but when "the roof was about to end" he chokes out another "dull moan" (81). At that point his eyes begin "closing and opening desperately," trying to "pass to the other side" (81). However, the "other side" is not *out*side, as one might think, but within "the bare, protecting ceiling of the ward," which, like the womby maw underneath the pyramid, is wrapped in "tepid shadow" (78).

Shifting back and forth between the hospital and the pyramid, between the "oozing darkness" and the "tepid shadow," the Moteca seems unable to bring about the transition from inside to outside. The story indicates how the preamble to this transition is acted out over and over again without managing to culminate in an ejection. We are immediately reminded that Lucho and the protagonist of "No se culpe a nadie" are equally unwilling to remain outside in the cold air, the former even begging to be allowed to return inside. The protagonists of all three stories are also covered with blood while they attempt to extricate themselves (or are ejected) from engulfing spaces; all three are unable to see; all slide from darkness to light; one is completely smeared with "blue spittle"; two of them travel through what seem like never-ending tunnels; all of them gasp for air; all scream; two feel themselves pulled upward or outward, and experience a pain as if their ears "were being torn off" ("No se culpe a nadie," 287–8).

Can there be any doubt that what Cortázar was staging in these stories was a nostalgic hankering for halcyon days in which characters might have lived out their lives as "rosy little bodies" floating in some aqueous paradise ("Axolotl," 422–3)? Hasn't it become plain by now that he crafted his stories as an attempt to heal a wound that cannot heal, unable to fill "this void, this nothingness, [which] had lasted an eternity"? ("La noche boca arriba," 78). Particularly pertinent to our analysis is that the symbolic descriptions of his personal longing become an actual substitute for the impossible return. In other words, by dramatizing birth trauma in the coded language of phobias, Cortázar was satisfying his most basic unconscious desire. He could act out the impossible in fiction by having his characters meander in darkness through a maze of tunnels suggestive of an actual return that, although more satisfying, was wholly irrational.

What I mean to say is that, when we read all the stories in sequence, it becomes clear that the author of *Bestiario* works the separation from the mother, originally full of dread, into a game of willing concealment in which anxiety and liberating energy are transmuted into writing.[3] The anxiety mechanism is repeated almost unaltered in the cases of phobias

(claustrophobia, fear of tunnels, of animals, of darkness) as the unconscious reproduction of the anxiety at birth. "This first danger is connected
with all subsequent ones," Freud tells us, "they all retain something in
common in that all of them signify in some sense a separation from the
mother, at first only in a biological respect, then in the sense of a direct
object loss, and later of an object loss mediated in indirect ways" (94).

Separation from the mother is abreacted by means of symbolic substitutions, however; instead of depicting the actual separation, Cortázar
substitutes phobias for the anxiety. All of these phobias recall the prena-
tal condition (darkness, tunnels, constricting space) without explicitly
depicting it. Such substitutions have a calming, "therapeutic" effect; they
mimic a reunion with the absent mother, even though such reunion is
purely symbolic. This may seem farfetched, but Otto Rank explains how
"the child . . . works off the separation from the mother . . . in a game
which can easily and often be broken off and repeated at the child's pleasure" (23). In the same manner, Cortázar tailors his separation anxiety
by substituting it for *figuras* allusive to birth and the womb, which
explains why darkness, holes, and tunnels play such a preponderant role
in his fiction, and why the cast of his characters who drown, suffocate, or
have breathing disorders is so revealingly large.

In other words, the bodies that figure in his stories dramatize
Cortázar's own trauma. They are, to cite Peter Brooks, "emblazoned with
meaning within the field of desire, desire that is originally and always, with
whatever sublimations, sexual, but also by extension the desire to know:
the body as an 'epistemophilic project'" (5). Cortázar's stories construct
the desire to know from sexual desire, although by "sexual" we must not
construe "genital" but, rather, as Brooks makes clear, "the complex conscious desires and interdictions that shape humans' conceptions of themselves as desiring creatures" (6). Learning about himself is, for Cortázar,
grasping the sense of his own traumatic experiences, experiences which
contain enough universal elements so that readers, all of us, can identify
with the anxiety they set into motion. The author of *Bestiario* spent his life
dramatizing what his body remembered by means of seemingly unrelated
scenarios. When we look at them closely, however, we see that each and
every one provides a piece of the puzzle. The stifled breathing, the pervasive darkness, the longing to return, the endless tunnels and passageways, are simply the spokes of the wheel which, to paraphrase Brooks, figures Cortázar's conception of himself as a desiring creature.

More than any other author, Cortázar spent his life reenacting in fiction the separation from the maternal body. He dramatized his longing for a lost paradise by having many of his characters die, deaths that must be seen as unconscious expressions of the desire to return to the shuttered environment from which they had been so violently ousted. It is this desire from which all of Cortázar's fictional universe springs. The irrational fears that permeate his writings are simply an open invitation to enter the text through the (author's) body, a body extemporized in a series of *tableaux vivants* in which Cortázar's profound anxiety was vividly depicted. Moreover, this body begs to be stripped of its truth, of the truth that it knows, longs for, and insistently portrays.

With typical insight Barthes once wrote that the novel is an anagram of the body (30). No doubt, by this claim he meant that "the body is the referent of reference itself . . . the ultimate field from which all symbolism derives" (6). Since the beginning of history, all fiction has diverted the expression of instinctual desires from its primitive form, but it seems to me that a handful of modern authors that includes Cortázar are consciously working with the cathartic nature of the process which turns their obsessions into art. More than ever before in the history of literature, works are being designed as anagrams of the body. In other words, what the characters and events featured in these new kinds of stories actually dramatize are the painful pleasures of being – the drives, fears, and attachments of the authors themselves. Readers are usually taken in by one level of the narration – namely, the intricacies of plot and character – but seldom focus on the process that the act of writing implies for the writer. What I hope I have demonstrated is that few have succeeded in coming to grips with this process as skillfully, or achieved higher artistic dividends out of exposing their dirty traumas in public, as Julio Cortázar.

*Notes*

1. Freud explains how castration anxiety "has also separation from a highly valued object as its content" and is another guise for the "'primal anxiety' of birth" (Freud, 76).
2. We know from Jung that "the creative process . . . consists in the unconscious activation of an archetypal image, and in elaborating and shaping this image into the finished work. By giving it shape," Jung explains, "the artist translates it into the language of the present, and so makes it possible for us to find our way back to the deepest springs of life" (Jung, 82).
3. One needs only to recall Lucho's entreaties to Dina to let him back in, and his insistent reminders about "how everything was going so well" when they

were together inside the same dark room, to get some idea of just how dreaded this separation really is ("Cuello de gatito negro," 164).

## References

Barthes, Roland. *Le Plaisir du texte*. Paris: Editions du Seuil, 1973.

Brooks, Peter. *Body Work: Objects of Desire in Modern Narrative*. Cambridge, MA, Harvard University Press, 1993.

Cortázar, Julio. "Cuello de gatito negro." In *Octaedro*, 145–65. Buenos Aires: Editorial Sudamericana, 1974.

*Libro de Manuel*. Buenos Aires: Editorial Sudamericana, 1974.

*Relatos*. Buenos Aires: Editorial Sudamericana, 1970. All references to short stories quoted in this essay are from this edition, with the exception of those from "Cuello de gatito negro."

Filer, Malva. "The Ambivalence of the Hand in Cortázar's Fiction." In *The Final Island, The Fiction of Julio Cortázar*, ed. Jaime Alazraki and Ivar Ivask, 129–33. Norman: University of Oklahoma Press, 1976.

Freud, Sigmund. *The Problem of Anxiety*. Trans. Henry Alden Bunker. New York: The Psychoanalytic Quarterly Press and W. W. Norton & Company, 1936.

Hernández del Castillo, Ana. *Keats, Poe, and the Shaping of Cortázar's Mythopoesis*. Amsterdam: John Benjamin B. V., 1981.

Jung, C. G. "On the Relation of Analytical Psychology to Poetry." In *The Spirit in Man, Art, and Literature*, trans. R. F. C. Hull. Vol. 15 of the *Collected Works* of C. G. Jung, Bollingen Series 20. Princeton, NJ: Princeton University Press, 1971.

Leal, Luis. "Situación de Julio Cortázar." *Revista Iberoamericana* 39 (1973): 399–409.

Picón Garfield, Evelyn. *Cortázar por Cortázar*. Mexico City: La Impresora Azteca, 1978.

Prego, Omar. *La fascinación de las palabras*. Barcelona: Muchnik Editores, 1985.

Rank, Otto. *The Trauma of Birth*. New York: Robert Brunner, 1952.

# PART TWO

## Cortázar Reads Cortázar

# 5

## Betwixt Reading and Repetition
## (apropos of Cortázar's *62: A Model Kit*)

*Lucille Kerr*

When asked about his views of *62: A Model Kit* and its relation to other of his texts, Cortázar once stated the following: "When I finished *Hopscotch,* and above all when *Hopscotch* was published, readers reacted as they normally do when they wait for the author to write something like a second part to the text. . . . [but] that seems to me a completely unacceptable requirement. I have a very good relationship with my readers, but not to the extent of following their instructions" (Cortázar/Sosnowski 1985, 47). Despite his resistance to being instructed, as it were, by his readers, and despite his desire, if not design, to break with the project of the 1963 text and take his next novel in a different direction, Cortázar went on to confess that when he actually wrote *62* he found himself explicitly invoking *Hopscotch* by recalling one of its most important figures' proposals. He explained: "When I felt the desire to write another novel I decided to do something that didn't have anything to do with *Hopscotch*. But, oddly, what is said at the beginning in its title, in *62,* is where I take off from a reflection of Morelli in one of his brief notes in *Hopscotch,* to see if it is possible to write a novel that rejects psychological behavior, the law of causality that determines the different interactions between individuals based on their feelings" (48).[1]

Cortázar's reference to the well-known explanation of the novel's title in what has generally been read as an authorial preface to *62* might be viewed in a number of ways. If one takes his observations as a possible, even necessary, frame for an overall consideration of *62,* one is led not only around that text but also among questions that pertain to how one might read his work overall. Moreover, Cortázar's comments about the

Some material in this essay was first offered at the Twentieth-Century Spanish and Spanish American Literatures International Symposium held at the University of Colorado at Boulder, 18–20 November 1993. My thanks for the opportunity to present some of this work go to the Boulder faculty and especially to Luis González-del-Valle, who organized and hosted the conference.

1968 novel and its relation to *Hopscotch* recall the literary and theoretical questions engaged both by his most famous work and by its successor. Though different stories are told in each of these novels, between the two texts Cortázar addresses pivotal notions about narrative fiction and interrogates conventional critical figures (e.g., author, reader, character) in an idiosyncratic but not insignificant manner.

Cortázar's insistence on authorial prerogative in the face of his readers' actual or potential demands is an odd but apt disclosure. As we recall, *Hopscotch* would have initially involved its readers in a seemingly democratic, if not entirely egalitarian, relation between this same author and his audience.[2] Cortázar's return to the 1963 text's proposals – or rather to the proposals of its resident author-theorist, Morelli – is a telling gesture that both repeats and repositions some of his provocative notions about narrative literature. The author's uncontrollable return to a previous text would, it seems, prescribe the route that any reader of *62* might appear to have to take in order to read the 1968 text properly.

The reading model implicitly proposed by the author, however, would have the reader execute some unsettling maneuvers. The route required for that reading would virtually repeat an authorial operation that is supposedly at the origin of *62*, a text whose originality, and unconventionality, the requisite return to *Hopscotch* also disputes. Furthermore, such a reading would run the risk of belying the redundant, if not tautological, operations that the "required" reading of *62* could entail. However, the readings already produced around this text suggest that it may be difficult, and for some impossible, to resist returning to the previous novel. For many readers it has also been difficult to resist repeating the author's words – more specifically, his critical terminology – that seem to resonate so forcefully around, and also within, *62*. Indeed, Cortázar's novel recalls the uncontrollable repetitions that inform both his authorial activity and the critical corpus generated by this novel.[3]

The author's word around this text (as represented by the quotations above), as well as the authorial words that seem to initiate it (i.e., in the prefatory statement) push one to interrogate the parameters for reading *62* and perhaps even Cortázar's literary project as a whole. One of the questions one might ask after reading, or rereading, *62* is whether it is possible to talk about this text without in some way privileging the author's word about it. By opening with what the reader is urged to take as an authentic authorial statement, and under the guise of guiding the reader to read independently (like *Hopscotch* that precedes it), *62* would underscore the apparent difficulty of reading on one's own. It suggests that one must turn to the author's word not only for instructions about how to read but perhaps also for information about what is being read.[4]

From the outset *62* poses a variety of questions about reading, questions that seem to be anticipated if not answered in the prefatory comments where the author appears to speak directly to the reader about the novel. As we recall, the authorial statement raises expectations about the possibility of breaking with conventional concepts and practices ("Not a few readers will notice various transgressions of literary convention here"; 3).[5] These opening words, which have received much attention, predict readers' reactions to some of the text's unsettling narrative strategies (i.e., it is imagined that some readers "might possibly be startled"; 3). The words guarantee "the reader's option" to read and make meaning independently of the arrangements found in the text prepared and presented by the author (3–4). The statement also locates the text's narrative and theoretical origins in chapter 62 of *Hopscotch,* from which the novel openly derives its title. (The text mentions "the intentions sketched out one day in the final paragraphs of Chapter 62 of *Hopscotch,* which explains the title of this book" and speculates that "perhaps those intentions will be fulfilled in the course of it"; 3.)

That *62* is presented as both a literary experiment and a quasi-theoretical proposition is not insignificant. As both experiment and proposition, it asks questions about narrative categories, and about the formal concepts that may well continue to frame (even if only indirectly) the reading and writing of narrative fiction (i.e., concepts such as verisimilitude and character, author, and reader). As experiment and proposition, it also questions the relation between writing (also reading) and theorizing, and draws connections between these operations. The interrogation staged in this text's narrative – in whatever may be called its story – is explained, however, as the result of a formal inquiry that was begun both abstractly and practically in *Hopscotch,* and in particular in its chapter 62.

The untitled paragraphs of the introductory statement send both a warning and a welcome to the reader. There *62* is characterized as unconventional and transgressive, in both its theory and its practice. The virtual solution to the 1968 text's difficulties, the preface proposes, can be sought and found in the writing and reading of the 1963 novel, which *62* thereby identifies as a "key" for reading.[6] As we recall, the theoretical proposal contained in Morelli's note in *Hopscotch*'s chapter 62 is mainly about the matter of character, a critical concept that has more recently caught the attention of literary theorists and critics unaware of Cortázar's literary practice and proposals. (We recall that Morelli, himself an elusive character in *Hopscotch,* posits the foundation for a future book in which psychological causality would cease to govern characters' actions; in such a book, most of the principles of conventional verisimilitude would also be suspended [*Hopscotch,* 361–3]. What may seem most revolutionary is that Morelli's literary theory is supposedly based on the research of a Swiss neurobiologist who proposes that human behavior is caused by chemical changes in the brain rather than by psychological motivation.)[7]

In reading *62* one may therefore be persuaded to consider, among others, the "question of character" independently, if not also in relation to the "question of verisimilitude," precisely because one seems to be instructed, directly or indirectly, to do so. However, one's attention may be drawn to such topics not so much because the authorial preface suggests them, but rather because the narrative also engages – indeed, problematizes – those concepts' conventionality within its own literary activity. The difficulties of making sense of *62*'s narrative would prod one to consider what terms such as "story" or "character" have been taken to mean, and how they might be adapted to new narrative projects. Moreover, one's attention may be drawn to such concepts, and the overarching questions to which Cortázar seems to connect them in *62,* precisely because it is difficult to sort them out from within the text. One may be compelled, as many have been, to talk not only about character, for example, but also about why one can't talk about the characters of *62* in conventional ways, even though that is precisely the grid against which one is constrained to measure them. "Character" is, for Cortázar's text, as much a controversial concept as it is a conventional category.[8]

Given *62*'s apparent challenge to such conventional terms and concepts, one might be tempted to rely on another vocabulary, one apparently ready-made for reading Cortázar. Indeed, in trying to describe the novel's narrative – that is, in attempting to summarize its story in the wake of the theoretical announcement made in its prefatory page – one might feel compelled to engage the literary material of *62* with a vocabulary that belongs as much, perhaps more, to Cortázar's own lexicon than to that of literary poetics more generally. Such privileged Cortazarian concepts and vocabulary (especially *figura*) precede and yet, the authorial voice of the preface implicitly claims, follow on the writing of *62.* But the reading difficulties announced in the prefatory passages appear not so much as abstract critical matters to be analyzed but rather as practical narrative obstacles to be surmounted.

Indeed, in reading *62,* one must navigate, as it were, through pages in which various figures appear and reappear in episodes and scenes whose temporal and spatial parameters are not always clearly delineated, but which nonetheless, and contrary to what the initial paragraphs suggest, come to make some kind of sense.[9] For example, generally one can say that the novel concerns a group of individuals situated simultaneously in Paris, London, and Vienna, and that it gives glimpses of the relationships and episodes in which they also become involved individually and together. One can name these figures and describe specific scenes or summarize individual events that comprise the novel's narrative material.

However, in speaking further about the text, a good many readers have assumed that one must inevitably move between Cortázar's texts and his theories, for, the implicit argument goes, one cannot make sense of things without framing the narrative elements with the authorial concepts those elements seem to illustrate or explain.[10] Furthermore, it may appear that one needs to consider not only the relationship between chapter 62 of *Hopscotch* and the whole text of *62: A Model Kit,* but perhaps also the novel's affiliation with other of the author's words around it, whether in personal interviews or in texts that would explain the novel's genesis (e.g., "The Broken Doll" and "Glass with Rose").[11] That is, in going further, readers may feel compelled to return to other texts, to read backward and forward around the novel where "key" references appear to be explained and authoritative explanations provided. Thus one may move to *Hopscotch* and Morelli's statements, where, in a sense, the novel has already been plotted out, where the question of convention, explicitly called up in *62*'s opening paragraphs, is thematized as it is theorized in the voice of an authorial figure who attaches himself to critical as well as literary considerations. And one may move to interviews and essays where the author talks about, even seeks to explain, the aims and origins of the novel and, additionally, the meaning of specific narrative elements.

Indeed, *62*'s prefatory remarks authorize a reading beyond its immediate borders. They suggest that meaning is to be found elsewhere, in a previous theory or critical conceptualization which, one might argue, is merely put into practice in this novel. But such a subordination of narrative text to theoretical or conceptual project, which such reading models presuppose, may also be refuted by *62*, whose sense inevitably seeps beyond the borders of any such project. Although the novel appears to respect the aims of a previously articulated, unconventional theory of narrative or narrative character, it critiques blind adherence to prior projects. And even when it seems to serve its primary aims, the unconventional nature of its accomplishments may well be a matter of dispute. I would argue that 62's narrative strategies and anecdotal material also recover conventions and concepts which the previous theory and the present text explicitly challenge.

There are, moreover, a number of ways to situate the novel's prefatory paragraphs. If one takes the preface as an explanation of what the novel will do, one can read the text as the elaboration of a literary project that becomes self-evident in the doing of literature but that nonetheless must also be theorized before the project begins. However, the preface is a retrospective introduction, a statement explaining, after the fact, the aims of the text whose unconventional and potentially controversial effects its readers cannot resist noting and its author, it seems, cannot refrain from explaining. The theory of the novel proposed prior to the narrative is a theory that also follows its own practice; and that practice, in turn, stages what one is supposed to read as its originating theory.

If, as suggested above, one takes the preface at its word, one might be compelled to read 62 as an "application" of theory first proposed in *Hopscotch*.[12] But the 1963 novel can be read as a text that telescopes the distance between theoretical proposal and literary practice, partly because the one form of discourse is mapped onto the other, and partly because the theory *Hopscotch* presents is apparently derived from the discourse assigned to a character in the narrative (i.e., Morelli). Thus, if one finds in *Hopscotch*'s text the supposed origins and aims of 62, one also finds that the 1963 novel's theoretical authority remains unstable. Just when one might think one may visit the one text so as to return with some theoretical certainty to the other, one finds that one's itinerary has changed. For one is forced to wander between texts, or from a theory that can also be read as a practice to a practice that also functions as a theory, and back again. One may imagine that one is traversing a somewhat foreign (even if vaguely familiar) territory, only to discover that one hasn't really gone all that far from home.

One may read 62 as mapping out a familiar and finally conventional reading territory. One may read Cortázar's novel as reaffirming rather than revoking conventional reading practices, the conventions of reading against which, the authorial preface suggests, the novel appears to have been fashioned. One may see this text recuperate perhaps more than resist familiar reading patterns; one may read this novel as an effort to reclaim as much as to reject the reader's and author's conventional activities.

Let us recall the novel's structure and its narrative difficulties so as to plot out the territory for that conventional turn. As is true of any text, there are a number of ways to describe this novel and to summarize its narrative. First, one might describe its textual composition. The novel's text comprises a series of narrative segments comparable to chapters in conventional novels, though neither the prefatory segment, which consists of three paragraphs, nor any of the sixty-nine narrative segments, each of different length, bears a title or number to identify or distinguish it from contiguous segments. Then, one might try to summarize its story as it is presented by the text. The narrative material that follows the authorial statement focuses for the first thirty pages or so (the frontier between spaces and scenes is equivocal) on a personage named Juan, who dines on Christmas Eve in the Polidor restaurant in Paris and whose mental associations and analyses on that evening are elaborated in these pages.[13]

The rest of the narrative moves among three cities, as noted above (Paris, London, and Vienna). It registers the interior monologues and dialogues of, as well as the apparently objective reports about, the characters who form the close-knit group of 62.[14] The interrelations among the group's members are such that one can speak not only about various, and often overlapping, couples (Juan and Hélène in Paris, Juan and Tell in Vienna, Marrast and Nicole in London, Celia and Austin in London, Celia and Hélène in Paris, Frau Marta and the English girl in Vienna) but also about the triangles of desire that bind these figures together (Juan-Tell-Hélène, Hélène-Celia-Austin, Marrast-Nicole-Juan).[15]

Although it is possible to name the characters, describe in the barest of terms who they are (e.g., their occupations or professions), and situate them in one or another city or episode, it is not so easy to describe exactly what the narrative comprises.[16] 62: A Model Kit presents a sequence of interconnected scenes and episodes (one might even argue for describing them as self-contained short narratives) rather than a sustained, coherent linear story.[17] Besides the extended opening scene focusing on Juan in the Polidor, there are other episodes one could describe: for example, that involving members of a group called Neurotics Anonymous who are directed by Marrast to examine a painting in the Courtauld Institute in London; or Juan and Tell's voyeuristic pursuit of Frau Marta's seduction of a young English girl in a hotel in Vienna; or Hélène's seduction of Celia in Paris; or Calac and Polanco's comical shipwreck in the shallow waters of a French pond; or the ceremonious unveiling of a statue sculpted by Marrast for the town of Arcueil – and so on. Readings seem inexorably drawn to describing specific scenes and episodes, and to the reiterating characters' ruminations about themselves and others. Readers seem inevitably pushed to summarize and repeat the themes, myths, and motifs that seem to shape the narrative, or to identify the literary and cultural models, the authors and texts, from which *62* may well derive much of its material (e.g., vampirism, "meaningful coincidences," Michel Butor, psychoanalytic discourse).[18]

Despite the acknowledged difficulties presented by the text's rejection of the narrative conventions of realist "psychological" fiction, the "informed" reader may well have the sense that everything does, in the end, make sense in this novel, but perhaps in unexpected ways. The problem the text seems to pose is how to represent any such sense, perhaps how to translate into intelligible terms the peculiar logic, rather than isolated allusions, themes, or scene, that appears to organize the novel's narrative. In confronting the text's apparent impenetrability, critics have seen that task as a one of decipherment, principally as the need to decode the novel's historical, literary, or cultural references. The goal has also been to disclose the associational logic, the unconventional connections, that link these elements and allow them to make sense.

However, in critics' efforts to delineate the connections among characters and episodes so as to make sense of the novel, *62* seems to have occasioned principally elaborate reiterations of the text's details. Cortázar's novel demonstrates, perhaps, how the desire to interpret critically always runs the risk of collapsing, perhaps unintentionally, into an uncontrolled repetition of and absorption into the text from which critical activity would more properly differentiate and distance itself. In the case of *62*, the repetition of the text's thematic motifs (e.g., the vampire myth), and the circular appropriation of its terminology (e.g., the novel as kaleidoscope, the characters as forming a *figura*) seem unavoidable in reading.[19] The matter of repetition, as informing but also as distinct from reading, is perhaps one of the "key" questions raised as one rereads Cortázar's text.

What seem to get repeated in readings of *62* are not only the thematic or anecdotal details of the narrative or the explicit associations among them, but also, if not principally, the authorial theories and terminology proposed within and around the novel. That such repetitions are inevitable if not required for a reading of *62* is an arguable point. Nonetheless, one might wonder, as suggested above, how one can talk about this text without relating it to *Hopscotch*, without framing one's reading with reference to Morelli's theory that is so explicitly recalled in the authorial preface. Or, how one ought to talk about a text that appears to provide metaphors (e.g., kaleidoscope) if not also critical concepts (e.g., *figura*) apparently so well suited to its own explanation. Or, how, if at all, one can refuse the author's word about the textual relations, theories, terminology, and concepts that seem to figure so weightily in this text and about which Cortázar has so often agreed to elaborate further.

There are, however, different ways to frame such questions. Given the persistence with which the novel's own terms and notions have defined and even subsumed the discourse generated around *62* in critical studies and authorial interviews, one might wonder about the repeated return to such terms, about the dependence on the author's (literary and critical) word. Moreover, one might also wonder whether there might not be something significant in the fact of repetition itself, whether the pattern of tautological reiteration might not unwittingly reveal a significant feature of this novel. On the one hand this feature might demand and, on the other, decry the persistent critical restatement of the text's (or the author's) own words.

Perhaps a return to the much commented upon opening pages of the narrative – those dedicated to Juan at the Polidor restaurant that follow the prefatory paragraphs – will help to suggest another way around Cortázar's writing and around writing about Cortázar. These pages, which have been read as summarizing or already containing all the essential elements of the narrative that follows, are both cryptic and clear. In the broadest terms, they describe the mental rather than physical activity of Juan, who is both subject and object of the narration, which focuses attention on the associative processes that inform his actions and thoughts during his solitary Christmas Eve dinner at the Polidor. Seated facing the dining room's back mirror, he is oddly positioned to see and hear things as they finally need to be seen and heard, for his position allows him access from several positions at once. The process by which he comes to understand how he hears and sees the dinner scene around him seems to acquire significance not only for him, but also, as many readings of the text claim, for the whole novel.[20]

The scene revolves around a sentence, spoken by another diner and heard by Juan in the novel's opening line ("I'd like a bloody castle"; 5). This sentence, which is Juan's automatic, simultaneous translation of "Je voudrais un château [i.e., Chateaubriand] saignant" (5), is the visible – or, rather, audible – result of a process of association of which the reader has no knowledge in the novel's first page but which the text, in the voice both of Juan and of the unidentified narrator, soon explains in subsequent pages of the episode. The pages that follow, and through which additional enigmas and explanations are provided, are notable not only

because they present details whose textual resonances are anticipated in
these initial pages. (One might emphasize the accumulation for example, of, interrelated references to places [e.g., Transylvania] and person-
ages [the countess Báthory] associated with historical and literary vampire stories. The vampire figure resonates from around the bottle of
Sylvaner Juan drinks and the "bloody castle" he "hears" the other diner
order, as well as from the mention of "the countess," Frau Marta, the
basilisk; see note 18.)

It could be argued that the significance of this episode lies in the reading performed by these pages, and in the reading figures this portion of
the text proposes. The novel presents Juan as a character who acts and
thinks, and who both subsequently and simultaneously begins to interpret or decipher his own actions and thoughts. As the acting, thinking
personage, he is a figure somewhat out of control, because initially he is
unable to read properly the text he produces through his actions and
associations. He is a figure of unconscious associations, or rather, a figure
unconscious of the associations he seems automatically to make among
a variety of figures and phrases. As the figure who interprets or translates,
and thus reads, the scene in which he is also situated, however, he is a figure of mastery, for he appears finally to understand not only what but
also how things mean in this scene. Initially he may be presented (or is
presented as presenting himself – the episode is narrated in the first and
third persons, with Juan as the object of both internal and external focal-
ization) as unsure of how to read or as doubting in general that something like understanding can be reached (7). But he eventually seems to
read things (and be read) correctly, if not also completely.

Juan's doubts about comprehending what he has done and/or seen,
and his confrontation with the "useless desire to understand" (7), are
incorporated into the process of interpretation and decipherment as well.
The question repeated in this episode, and that would finally generate his
reading, is "Why did I go into the Polidor restaurant?" (5, 7, 15). (This
question is followed by other related interrogatives, for example, "Why
did I buy a book I probably wouldn't read?" [5]; ". . . why did I buy the
book and open it at random and read . . . ?" [7]; "Why did I ask for a bottle of Sylvaner?" [5].) Given the announced authorial project to refuse
conventional causal logic, the text appears to remain true to its "theory,"
as it refuses to provide definitive answers to these questions about Juan's
so-called motivation. While it refuses one interrogative ("why?") it
nonetheless accepts others ("how?" and "what?" and "where?" and
"when?"), as a reading of nonmotivational connections develops within

Juan's scene. Indeed, in the voices of Juan and the external narrator, the text replies to virtually all the important questions Juan (or the reader) might have about the relations among the apparently unrelated elements of the scene. This reply – the final interpretation – is constructed in the episode's final pages (20–4, 26–7). The virtual appearance of that "decoding" permits the scene's closure and causes, as it were, Juan to leave the Polidor restaurant, the privileged site of reading, seeing, and hearing in and around *62* (see also note 20).

Juan performs as a reading figure whose curiosity, whose interest in "the old human topic – deciphering" (8), leads him (like any good reader perhaps) to attempt what appears to be an exemplary interrogation of and interpretation for *62*. His questions about the connections among his physical actions and about the meanings of his mental associations, as well as his (or the text's) answers to those questions, figure one of the reading projects that Cortázar's reader might feel compelled to complete. Indeed, around the figure of Juan the text also proposes precisely how to read *62;* furthermore, the text privileges a specific type of reading. Juan's reading, along with the text's reading of Juan, in these crucial initial pages would suggest that there are hidden meanings (if not "keys") that can and must be identified in order to make sense of things. That reading suggests that only when one has uncovered such meanings (i.e., allusions, references, associations) can one make sense of this episode and also, some readers would argue, the whole novel.

Juan, a translator by profession, appears as a conspicuous figure of interpretation at the beginning of the text. The professional deformation that would compel him to ruminate reflexively about his interpretive activity and to question the reliability of his reading does not, however, obscure the way in which his overall reading is staged in the text or how it offers a reading model that seems so well suited to *62* (see, e.g., 6). The resistance to reading that the scene's initially impenetrable surface presents to Juan (and to the reader) seems finally to be neutralized by a privileged figure of translation whose task it is to uncover hidden linguistic structures and recuperate original meaning. Juan virtually deciphers what at first seems to present itself as incomprehensible. As he does so, he constructs a route into the text, a way to make sense of what otherwise would appear to have little if any meaning. The reading performed both by and around Juan in this episode virtually finds beneath the scene's and the text's surface the references to which one is led to believe that one must have access if one is to read the novel properly.

Through Juan's reading and the reading of Juan presented by these pages, the novel figures a competent, if not ideal, reader for 62.[21] But the reading figure produced and privileged here calls up a model of reading one can only call authorial. Indeed, the reading performed in this episode succeeds in reading the text only insofar as it seems to repeat, if not reproduce, authorial knowledge and restage authorial activity. For this reading (which, as suggested above, seems to have determined how 62 has often been read) seeks out and apparently succeeds in recovering authorial meaning, the (un)intended meanings presumably required for making sense of 62. The text's reading of Juan, as well as Juan's seeming success in reading, suggests that much if not all that looks opaque can be rendered transparent in Cortázar's novel – that is, if one is willing to repeat the author's steps in reading. Juan's episode at the Polidor thus has as much heuristic as hermeneutical value; it teaches how to read as much as it tells what might be, or actually is, underneath what is being read.

What are the consequences of becoming a reader like Juan? What are the consequences of following the reading models produced by this "master" episode? And, what, perhaps, does Cortázar's text reveal about itself through this reading proposal? It may well be that the "keys" contained in Juan's reading are more varied than those this figure seems to offer in what is arguably the novel's "key" episode. As suggested above, the figures of reading apparently privileged by Cortázar's text finally appear more conventional than they might at first seem, if not counter to what the authorial preface (and all of Morelli's theories in *Hopscotch*) would propose.

A reading such as Juan's (and of course the narrator's reading of how Juan reads or interprets things) would propose that the recovery of meaning (references, allusions) is not only possible but necessary in this text. Such an attempt to recover meaning following Juan's model is at the same time an attempt to return to authorial aims and ideas rather than to produce an independent reading. The reading proposed at the outset of 62 therefore entails an authorial recuperation along with the recuperation of the traditional notion of original (if not final) meaning. Such recovery would necessarily entail repetition, and such repetition, in turn, would serve as evidence of recovery. To read the way the reader seems to be instructed to read at the beginning of 62 is in a sense to try to return (to) the author's words, words that initially appear to underwrite the reader's recuperative repetition. In order to read properly, the initial episode if not the whole novel seems to propose, one must repeat the text, one must reiterate and reauthorize the author's word as it emerges from beneath the novel as well as around it. To read like Juan is, in a sense, to read like Cortázar, and that is the only reading, the "master" episode suggests, which can get one through this text.

Is such a reading of 62 inevitable? What are the possibilities for reading 62 without privileging an authorial reading, without in some way repeating the author's terminology and interpretations? One way is to maintain that 62 aims to resist being read otherwise; that its project, put forth as a transgression of canonical critical concepts and literary practices, finally rests on the most conventional of grounds. Indeed, alongside the figure of the unconventional, transgressive author, which is proposed in the novel's prefatory paragraphs and elaborated in authorial interviews, there surfaces a figure of authorial control and containment. While that figure's word is associated with radical ideas about reading and authoring, his writing still conserves conventional practices and principles.

One can read Cortázar's refusal to comply with his readers' desires, cited at the outset of this discussion, also as a statement of authorial resistance. That statement oddly but aptly compels Cortázar's readers to consider how conventional models of reading are not only figured by the novel's initial, exemplary episode but also are implicitly recuperated by the reading apparently required of its own readers. It may well be that in 62 Cortázar has accorded readers what they feel most comfortable with: a text that tells its readers how difficult it is to read but also ("secretly") plots out a reading strategy that would elicit from them the habits of reading they already know how to repeat.[22] Readers who aim to read otherwise, to read against the grain of repetition and recuperation, would have to reject the reading figured by 62 in order to read in the manner theoretically proposed, either there or elsewhere, by Cortázar.

In the end, if there are any reading lessons to be learned from reading 62 and the ways in which it has been read, they may be lessons that inevitably situate us between reading (or rereading) and repetition. As one attempts to maneuver around the words of Cortázar and the contrary models of reading his writing proposes, one is positioned between texts and terms that Cortázar both reconsiders and recycles in 62. If, while reviewing the readings of 62 and the reading instructions it offers, one considers how this novel works against the "revolutionary" reading practices associated with Cortázar's writing, one might perhaps be able to resist the repetitions inherent in the model of reading it privileges and take one's reading into less conventional territory. However, at the moment one engages the text and moves into its terrain, one is also compelled to respond to, perhaps even by reiterating (but in ways more complex, perhaps, than those who would follow Juan's example), the models of reading that *62* (un)wittingly exposes. It may well be, then, that *62* figures its own reading as a negotiation between alternate practices and principles, which together persist in shaping how one may inevitably wind up reading this text, and possibly others, by Cortázar.

*Notes*

1. With the exception of quotations from Cortázar's texts also published in English, all translations in this essay are mine. See also Cortázar/González Bermejo, 89–90, Cortázar/Garfield, 36, and Prego, 93–6, for related authorial statements regarding *Hopscotch*'s chapter 62 as the foundation for *62: A Model Kit.*
2. See Kerr, *Reclaiming the Author,* 26–45, 178–82, for my previous discussion of the complex figures of the author that circulate around *Hopscotch* and the contradictory roles proposed for the reader in that text.
3. There is hardly a discussion of *62* that does not mention, if not cite directly, its opening paragraphs as a key to interpreting the novel. Moreover, many readings appropriate Cortázar's critical terms in order to explain the concepts he himself has elaborated in other texts and in personal interviews. Many essays return as well to the text of *Hopscotch,* primarily to cite Morelli's proposals in chapter 62 and often to equate the character's words with those of Cortázar. Such readings presume that the author's word is presented directly to the reader in the prefatory paragraphs of *62,* where Cortázar seems to suggest that if one returns to Morelli's notions one will find a transparent explanation of precisely what is attempted, if not accomplished, in the 1968 text. For a sample of such discussions, see, among others, Alazraki 1978 and 1981, Boldy, 97–160, Curutchet, 107–27, Dellepiane, Francescato, and Sicard.
4. Despite questions raised below regarding the privilege *62* and its readers seem to grant to an authorial reading (i.e., a reading that would aim to recuperate original meanings), there is much helpful material in articles that aim to decipher obscure references or narrative elements in *62.* Among the most suggestive are Boldy, 97–160; Hernández; Incledon; and Nouhaud.
5. These words initiate the statement, and are followed by "a few examples" of the text's transgressive nature, which turn out to consist of transgressions from the laws of verisimilitude; therefore the mention below of this concept, along with that of character, as possible foci for critical inquiry.
6. Many readers have focused on the identification and explanation of certain terms and narrative elements and have made explicit reference to the word *key* in the process; see, e.g., Alazraki 1981, Dellepiane, Gyurko, Hernández, and Incledon. Nouhaud, on the other hand, playfully reminds the reader of the instability of "key" meanings while also suggestively proposing the interpretive possibilities for reading some "keys" (220).
7. One might note in addition that this is an idea to which biomedical and pharmacological research, as well as psychiatric practice, has more recently given a good deal more credibility than such ideas received in the 1960s, when they were summarily presented in *Hopscotch.* For overviews of develop-

ments in modern theories of character and characterization, at least until about 1985, see Martin, 116–22, and also Hochman.

8. Borinsky's reading of how specific figures in the novel may "create the kind of currency needed to undo the psychological integrity of the characters" (90) is the most suggestive contribution on this topic, and Ortega's brief ruminations about the space occupied by the novel's characters develop related points (273–7); Yovanovich has also tried to focus directly on "character" in 62 (132–49). Though other readings do not address the concept of character directly, implicitly all assume the difficulties of reading characters in 62 and offer possible ways of answering questions about them. As I have suggested elsewhere (Kerr, 21), one could argue that Cortázar's text offers yet another opportunity to explore how, in its questioning of fundamental literary concepts (in this case, "character"), Spanish American literature has the potential to teach readers a good deal more than the theoretical materials typically consulted about such concepts.

9. Francescato's early reading of the text argues a related point, going so far as to declare that, even if readers are unable finally to resolve all the "enigmas," the novel nonetheless can be comprehended quite well (368); Figueroa Amaral's early discussion also emphasizes the text's "clarity" (377).

10. This argument is made implicitly by all the critical and authorial discussions of concepts such as "*figura*," "constellation," and "coagulation," through which, it is claimed, one may not only understand what 62 is about but also connect the novel to Cortázar's previous works; see, for instance, Dellepiane, Gyurko, Sicard, Yurkievich. The analyses that pay special attention to 62's own peculiar idiom (the concepts "the city," "my paredros," "the zone") and that rely on the novel's explicit definitions of these terms or on Cortázar's statements about his lexicon to explain the novel, include Alazraki 1978 and 1981; Boldy, 97–160; Curutchet, 107–27; Garfield, 115–31; Peavler, 107–10; see also Cortázar/González Bermejo, 93–5; Cortázar/Prego 87–9, 94–6. Cf. Ortega's refusal to read the text in terms of such authorial conceptualizations (232–3).

11. These two short texts are companion pieces, published a year after 62. Whereas "Glass with Rose" clarifies a notion mentioned in "The Broken Doll," the latter constitutes the author's revelations about the varied sources of 62 and his explanations of many "key" references. Critics have both repeated and pursued further these references and have thereby fulfilled, as it were, the reading of 62 already begun by Cortázar. These texts are also mentioned in Boldy, 98, 110, and Incledon, 283, and in Cortázar/González Bermejo, 86–9, 91, 93, and Cortázar/Prego, 89.

12. Alazraki calls 62 the author's "novelistic answer" to Oliveira's search for alternatives or to "Morelli's program" (1978, 14; 1981, 162), and sees it as "the implementation" (15) or "realization" of Morelli's project (1981, 155); Francescato describes it as "the result of the elaboration of the notes by the author Cortázar created in *Hopscotch*" (367); Yurkievich sees the novel as a "sequel" to *Hopscotch* (precisely the notion Cortázar claimed to resist) or as the "putting into practice of Morelli'a narrative proposals," but he also qualifies those descriptions when he claims that 62 is "effective as a novel" but "defective with respect to the program that motivated it" (463); Sicard sees

*62* as an "attempt" to produce the "novel of *figuras*" whose "theoretical bases" are presented in chapter 62 (234).

13. Juan, an Argentine in Paris who works as an interpreter, has been identified as a figure of Cortázar and as a central character, if not protagonist (given their shared biographical details, author and character seem "naturally" identified with each other). This transparent identification is not unlike the Morelli-Cortázar or Oliveira-Cortázar (*Hopscotch*) and Persio-Cortázar (*The Winners*) identifications assumed for, and continued from, Cortázar's two previous novels; see, for instance, Dellepiane, 172, Peavler, 108, Sicard, 233–4, 236–7. However, the most suggestive identification with the author's figure may well be of a different sort, as suggested below.

14. Cortázar's predilection for groups or communities of characters whose interrelations rather than individual actions form the basis of the narrative is discussed in Cortázar/Sosnowski, 49. Cortázar's term for the configurations constructed by such interrelations is *figura* (intimately related to, if not imbricated in, the notions of coagulation and constellation), a term proposed in *The Winners,* discussed and implicitly developed in *Hopscotch,* and, apparently, more directly materialized in 62. Much attention has been paid to this concept's elaboration in 62, and to repeating what Cortázar has said about it; see, among others, Alazraki 1978 and 1981; Boldy, 97–160; Curutchet, 109–27; Dellepiane; and Sicard; also Cortázar/Garfield, 36; Cortázar/González Bermejo, 91–3; and Cortázar/Prego, 687–9. See also note 10.

15. For more detailed summary descriptions of these dyadic and triadic configurations, see Alazraki, 1981, 159–60; Dellepiane, 165, 173; Garfield, 119–22; Peavler, 108–9. Dellepiane also suggests a four-part division of the narrative related to the locations of the different pairs: The first comprises the Polidor episode with Juan in Paris; the second revolves around both the Marrast/Nicole and the Juan/Tell pairs in London and Vienna; the third focuses mainly on Hélène and Celia in Paris as well as on the previously mentioned pairs in the other cities; and the fourth moves principally to Paris where the characters all converge (171). Paz's comments on the novel's spatial, temporal, and erotic orders, as well as his play on the novel's title in Spanish (62 as the transformation of a "modelo para amar" into a "modelo para armar"), suggest still other ways to consider these characters' relations (Paz/Ríos, 37–9).

16. Most of the characters are engaged in artistic, musical, literary, scientific, or educational activities, and are therefore identified with the world of high culture (as, we recall, are most of the principal characters in Cortázar's other novels): Juan is an interpreter, Hélène a physician, Marrast a sculptor, Tell an illustrator, Calac a writer, Celia a university student, Austin a musician. See Jones's observations on the "economic idyll" enacted by the characters in their arguably "pastoral" gathering (29).

17. Dellepiane, 180, and González Lanuza, 75, argue that 62's narrative techniques demonstrate Cortázar's superior abilities as a short-story writer rather than his accomplishments as a novelist.

18. While Hernández reads 62 as a vampire novel, seeing "the central theme of vampirism as a common basis" for the novel's "complex system of cross-

references and allusions" (109), Alazraki argues that it would be a mistake to read the novel exclusively in terms of that code (1981, 156). On the myriad associations with literary and legendary vampire stories and figures, see, besides Hernández's detailed discussion, Boldy, 113–19, 129–35; Curutchet, 108–9; Francescato, 368–9; and Garfield, 125–8. On the Jungian notion of "meaningful coincidences" or "synchronicity," which has been suggested as an explanatory model for the novel's logic and the notion of *figura*, see Boldy, 116, Curutchet, 108, and Dellepiane, 163–4. On the pivotal references to Butor's texts, see Alazraki 1981, 157, Boldy, 115, 141–3, Garfield, 124. On the reference to or reliance on the logic of psychoanalysis and the figure of Freud, see Nouhaud's and Borinsky's readings. On other possible literary, mythological, and cultural derivations and affiliations, see Figueroa Amaral, Jones, Incledon, Boldy passim, and also Cortázar/Prego, 92–3, 96–7, Cortázar/Garfield, 87–8, Cortázar/González Bermejo, 89, 95–6, and of course Cortázar's "The Broken Doll."

19. The kaleidoscope image, which is taken directly from the novel's vocabulary (e.g., 48, 49), is privileged as the "key" critical metaphor by Alazraki, who argues that "the novel is put together like a kaleidoscope" (1981, 158); he is not the first nor the only critic to prefer this authorial term; see, e.g., Francescato, 368 and Garfield, 116. See also note 10.

20. For detailed discussion of this scene, see Boldy, 115–17 (he reads it as a "model of how the text itself produces the *figuras*," 117); Curutchet, 108–10 (he also reads the scene as illustrating the concepts of *figura* and "significant coincidences," 108); Hernández, 109–10 (in her reading, the scene mainly serves the theme of vampirism); Alazraki 1981, 157–8 (he views the scene as "defining an ideogram that the rest of the text desciphers or attempts to decipher," 157). For the present discussion, Nouhaud's is the most suggestive reading (214–18); she engages the figures of the reader and the author through notions both derived and distant from the text (e.g., translation, mutilation, transportation) but which are used to elaborate horizontally, as it were, on the text's associative possibilities rather than vertically on its definitive meanings.

21. That the reader is a very special, if not specialized, figure tied to high culture, a figure with a specific kind of cultural experience and literary knowledge – an experience and knowledge perhaps equal only to that of the novel's author – has been noted by Curutchet, 109, González Lanuza, 72–3, and Nouhaud, 218, 220.

22. If one were tempted to read the author's figure as a figure of secrets and secret maneuvers, one could look to Borinsky's reading and to the perverse figure of M. Ochs for other suggestive reading possibilities.

## References

Alazraki, Jaime. "Introduction: Toward the Last Square of the Hopscotch." In Jaime Alazraki and Ivar Ivask, eds., *The Final Island: The Fiction of Julio Cortázar*, 3–18. Norman: University of Oklahoma Press, 1978.

"*62. Modelo para armar:* Novela calidoscopio." *Revista Iberoamericana* 47 [116–17] (1981): 155–63.

Alazraki, Jaime, and Ivar Ivask, eds. *The Final Island: The Fiction of Julio Cortázar.* Norman: University Oklahoma Press, 1978.

Boldy, Steven. *The Novels of Julio Cortázar.* Cambridge University Press, 1980.

Borinsky, Alicia. "Fear/Silent Toys." *Review of Contemporary Fiction* 3, no. 3 (1983): 89–94.

Cortázar, Julio. "The Broken Doll." In *Around the Day in Eighty Worlds,* trans. Thomas Christensen, 201–10. San Francisco, CA: North Point Press, 1986. Translation of "La muñeca rota," *Ultimo round.* Mexico City: Siglo XXI, 1969. "Primer piso" 104–11.

*Conversaciones con Cortázar.* With Ernesto González Bermejo. Barcelona: EDHASA, 1978.

*Cortázar por Cortázar.* With Evelyn Picon Garfield. Jalapa, Mexico: Centro de Investigaciones Lingüístico-Literarias, Universidad Veracruzana, 1978.

*La fascinación de las palabras; conversaciones con Julio Cortázar.* With Omar Prego. Barcelona: Muchnik, 1985.

"Glass with Rose." In *Around the Day in Eighty Worlds,* trans. Thomas Christensen, 236–7. San Francisco, CA: North Point Press, 1986. Translation of "Cristal con una rosa dentro," *Ultimo round.* Mexico City: Siglo XXI, 1969. "Planta baja" 98–101.

*Hopscotch.* Trans. Gregory Rabassa. New York: Pantheon, 1966. Translation of *Rayuela.* Buenos Aires: Sudamericana, 1963.

"Julio Cortázar: Modelos para desarmar." Interview with Saúl Sosnowski in *Espejo de escritores: Entrevistas con Borges, Cortázar, Fuentes, Goytisolo, Onetti, Puig, Rama, Rulfo, Sánchez, Vargas Llosa,* ed. Reina Roffé, 41–62. Hanover, NH: Ediciones del Norte, 1985.

*62: A Model Kit.* Trans. Gregory Rabassa. New York: Pantheon, 1972. Translation of *62: modelo para armar.* Buenos Aires: Sudamericana, 1968.

Curutchet, Juan Carlos. *Julio Cortázar o la crítica de la razón pragmática.* Madrid: Editora Nacional, 1972.

Dellepiane, Angela, "*62. Modelo para armar:* ¿Agresión, regresión o progresión?" *Nueva Narrativa Hispanoamericana* 1, no. 1. (1971): 49–72. Reprinted in Giacoman, 151–80.

Figueroa Amaral, Esperanza. "Dos libros de Cortázar." *Revista Iberoamericana* 35 [68] (1969): 377–83.

Francescato, Martha Paley. "Julio Cortázar y un modelo para armar ya armado." *Cuadernos Americanos* 3 (1969): 235–41. Reprinted in Giacoman, 365–73.

Garfield, Evelyn Picon. *Julio Cortázar.* New York: Fredrick Ungar, 1975.

Giacoman, Helmy F., comp. *Homenaje a Julio Cortázar.* Madrid/Long Island City: Anaya/Las Americas, 1972.

González Lanuza, Eduardo. "Casualidad y causalidad a propósito de *62. Modelo para armar* de Julio Cortázar." *Sur* 318 (1969): 72–5.

Gyurko, Lanin. "Identity and Fate in Cortázar's *62. Modelo para armar.*" *Symposium* 27 (1974): 214–34.

Hernández, Ana María. "Vampires and Vampiresses: A Reading of *62.*" *Books Abroad* 50, no. 3 (1976): 570–6. Reprinted in Alazraki and Ivask, 109–14.

Hochman, Baruch. *Character in Literature*. Ithaca, NY: Cornell University Press, 1985.

Incledon, John. "Una clave de Cortázar sobre *62. Modelo para armar.*" *Revista Iberoamericana* 41 [91] (1975): 263–65.

Jones, Julie. "*62:* Cortázar's *Novela Pastoril.*" *Inti* 21 (1985): 27–35.

Kerr, Lucille. *Reclaiming the Author: Figures and Fictions from Spanish America.* Durham, NC: Duke University Press, 1992.

Lastra, Pedro, ed. *Julio Cortázar.* Madrid: Taurus, 1981.

Martin, Wallace. *Recent Theories of Narrative.* Ithaca, NY: Cornell University Press, 1986.

Nouhaud, Dorita. "Hay que armar el modelo 'comilfó.'" *Coloquio Internacional: Lo lúdico y lo fantástico en la obra de Cortázar,* 2: 213–21. Madrid: Fundamentos, 1986.

Ortega, Julio. *Figuración de la persona.* Barcelona: EDHASA, 1971.

Paz, Octavio, and Julián Ríos. "Modelos para a(r)mar." *El Urogallo* 3 [15] (1972): 33–40.

Peavler, Terry J. *Julio Cortázar.* Boston: Twayne Publishers 1990.

Sicard, Alain. "Figura y novela en la obra de Julio Cortázar." *Hommage à Amédée Mas,* 199–213. Paris: Presses Universitaires de France, 1972. Reprinted in Lastra, 225–40.

Yovanovich, Gordana. *Julio Cortázar's Character Mosaic: Reading the Longer Fiction.* Toronto: University of Toronto Press, 1991.

Yurkievich, Saúl. "*62: modelo para armar:* Enigmas que desarman." *Cuadernos Hispanoamericanos* 122 [364–6] (1980): 463–73.

# 6

## Cortázar and the Idolatry of Origins

*Gustavo Pellón*

> What though the radiance which was once so bright
> Be now for ever taken from my sight,
>     Though nothing can bring back the hour
> Of splendour in the grass, of glory in the flower
>
> > Wordsworth, "Ode. Intimations of Immortality"

Nostalgia for a lost origin, for a prerational way of perceiving the world, is fundamental to the thematics as well as the aesthetics of Cortázar's writings. Critics of Cortázar's work have emphasized correctly his deep interest in the world of children, in primitive cultures, in the American and English Romantic poets, and in surrealism.[1] As the subject of Cortázar's fascination with the problem of recuperating origins is too vast for the scope of this essay, I intend to survey one of its major tributaries: his changing conception of ancient Greek culture as the origin of Western civilization. In particular I wish to chart the itinerary that led Cortázar from his youthful acceptance of the prestige of classical Greek art and literature (strongly mediated by his assimilation of the views of English Romantic poets) to an attitude of rejection, perhaps best summarized in the words of one of the characters in his short story "The Idol of the Cyclades." Believing that he has managed to recuperate the original insights of Bronze Age Aegean cultures suppressed by classical Greeks, Somoza remarks: "But it was necessary to retrace the wrong paths of five thousand years. It's strange that they themselves, the descendants of the Aegeans, would be guilty of that error" (73).[2] In order to retrace Cortázar's steps as he set out to "unwalk" centuries of rationalist detours, we must first join him beside an empty sarcophagus in Istanbul.

### Epiphany at the Sarcophagus

In the posthumously published collection of poems and prose poems *Salvo el crepúsculo* (1984), Cortázar weaves prose commentaries composed for the publication of the volume together with poems written throughout his life, some of which had previously appeared in *Pameos y meopas* (1971). Among the poems not previously published is one entitled "Gre/ce/cia/ece 59."[3] This remarkable poem and the autobiographical gloss that precedes it seem to mark a watershed moment in Cortázar's relationship with classical Greece. The poem was written in 1959 when Cortázar visited Istanbul and Greece during the trip he described also in "Acerca de la manera de viajar de Atenas a Cabo Sunion," included in *La vuelta al día en ochenta mundos* (1967). "Greece 59" is of particular interest because of the powerful emotional experience to which it refers and because of the insights it provides into Cortázar's changing attitude toward classical Greece and a privileged concept of origin. The poem in turn sheds new light on our readings of "The Idol of the Cyclades" and "The Island at Noon," stories published (and in all probability written) after his trip to Greece.[4]

In the epigraphs from César Vallejo and Clarice Lispector and in his prefatory comments, Cortázar seems very interested in the "distracted" way in which the poem came to be written. This preoccupation with a particular praxis of writing shares space with his description of the epiphanic moment that triggered the poem's composition. Cortázar's gloss enriches our reading of the poem but also guides us to an "authorized" reading of it. In studying both, it is important to remember that commentary and poem are separated by roughly twenty-five years. That distance, as we shall see, makes a difference.

According to the commentary, the experience in Istanbul was one of gnosis, and Cortázar's rhetoric in the commentary harps on "knowing." The first paragraph of the commentary begins with the words "I don't know." The second paragraph begins with the phrase "I also don't know," and continues with the variant "I believe furthermore." It additionally underscores "knowing" in the allusion to Coleridge's Ancient Mariner: "we wake up sadder and more knowing." The commentary ends with the suggestive reflection: "but here I knew I should not suppress or translate like other times. What I will never know is why I knew" (164).

For the site of his epiphany regarding Greece and the genesis of the composition of "Greece 59" Cortázar significantly chose (or was chosen by) the visit to Alexander the Great's sarcophagus in Istanbul.[5] Although he records his half-ironical stance, his emotional distance, by questioning the authenticity of this "alleged" sarcophagus of Alexander, Cortázar describes the epiphanic scene with all its emotional (Augustinian) trappings:

all of a sudden I felt the full blow of adolescence hit me squarely on the chest, the return of the tears that the death of Patroclus in the *Iliad* had torn from me, the fascination of Aeschylus and Hesiod, the unequivocal complacency of the pastoral dialogues of Theocritus, and in the background the greater and more rhetorical shade of Pindar, about whom I wrote an essay that my Greek literature professor had liked so much that he wanted to see it published at the expense of the teachers' college where I studied and whose director, a mathematician and duck hunter, made a corpse-like face and let him know that the funds were not meant to be used for such tomfoolery. *Exeunt* Pindar and great sadness of don Arturo Marasso and the author of the essay, who many years later would burn it together with a six-hundred-page novel (now he regrets it, it was called *Soliloquy* and was perceptibly homosexual, like Alexander whose false sarcophagus was to evoke the whirlwind which has been so badly summarized here). (163)

The association made by Cortázar between the homosexual character of the novel he suppressed and burned and the homosexuality of Patroclus and Alexander helps to underscore the emotional charge of the scene by the sarcophagus. It is not only Alexander's death or the death of Patroclus that wrenches tears from him but the sudden perception of the loss of his former self. Through a rich metonymical connection, he mourns the death of his adolescent world and his vision of Greece in the burning of his novel. The burning of the novel, an act he now regrets, in turn reflects the earlier suppression of his essay by the corpse-faced, duck-killing director of the college. The novel is burned, significantly, together with his essay on Pindar, like the corpse of Patroclus on the funeral pyre. Cortázar's skepticism regarding the true occupant of the sarcophagus of Alexander now acquires further subjective resonance. The tears once intended by the adolescent Cortázar for Patroclus, now withheld by the sadder but wiser Cortázar from Alexander, are actually shed by the author for the death of an earlier self.[6]

What is also at stake here for Cortázar writing circa 1983 is the rejection of what he then (in 1959) saw as an idealized vision of Greece he had held as an adolescent:

I believe furthermore that the trilingualism of the poem – for which I would feel guilty if it were not exceptional – comes from the rejection of the Greece of my adolescent imagination, idealized through Leconte de Lisle, Winckelmann and my teacher Marasso, and substituted now for a vision which I don't know if it is more real but in any case less "classical." And precisely for that, for sharing with the Ancient Mariner that sunset of life in which we wake up sadder and more knowing, my distraction did not exclude irony, the no longer melancholic acceptance of the eternal two sides of the medal, the beauty of the marble lionesses of Delos and the repugnant cough of an old man in the room next door at the hotel. All of that came in three languages, and the distraction did not let me see it until it came time to reread and adjust. It's not the first time that I have happened to write like this, to be alienated up to a modestly babelic point; but here I knew that I should not suppress nor translate like other times. What I will never know is why I knew it. (164)

Cortázar refuses to translate, to repress the trilingualism of the poem, and in his commentary he underscores its importance. He interprets his "babelic" trilingualism as a mark of his rejection of Greek classicism. Certainly the mixture of French, English, and Spanish, with the addition of a couple of phrases in Latin, German, Greek, and Turkish, produces a roughness of texture, a sense of textual fragmentation, and a plurivocality that violate the neoclassical values of smoothness of surface, textual unity, and univocality. Winckelmann's well-known description of the ethos of classical Greece given in *Reflections on the Painting and Sculpture of the Greeks,* "The last and most eminent characteristics of the Greek works is a noble simplicity and sedate grandeur beneath the strife and passions in Greek figures," is thoroughly rejected.[7]

The choice of the three major languages of the poem, however, seems to have also an autobiographical motivation. Because he resides in France, French is the language of Cortázar's daily life and, more problematically, one of the languages of his birthplace, Belgium. Spanish is the language of his childhood and here most importantly of his adolescence. It is also his professional language as a Latin American writer and translator. Besides often being the lingua franca of tourism, English is also a language that is charged with autobiographical significance in this context. It is the language of Coleridge, to whom Cortázar alludes in his commentary; but above all it is the language of Keats, whose works had such a strong formative impact on the young Cortázar.[8] Specifically, Cortázar's "Greece 59" serves as a rebuttal of the famous ode "On a Grecian Urn" about which Cortázar had published the article "La urna griega en la poesía de Keats" in 1946. Keats's last stanza, with its emphasis on the importance of "fair attitude," "silent form," and "eternity," serves now as an antiprogram for Cortázar:

O Attic shape! Fair attitude! with brede
    Of marble men and maidens overwrought,
With forest branches and the trodden weed;

Thou, silent form! dost tease us out of thought
As doth eternity: Cold Pastoral!
When old age shall this generation waste,
   Thou shalt remain, in midst of other woe
Than ours, a friend to man, to whom thou say'st,
"Beauty is truth, truth beauty,"– that is all
   Ye know on earth, and all ye need to know.

The poem "Greece 59" is written over and against this vision of classical
Greece, of beauty, of truth, and of life. Although there is naturally a difference in tone, both the poem and the commentary reject the classical
sublimity of English Romantic models that the young Cortázar had
embraced. This is even evident when he paraphrases Coleridge.
Cortázar's rendering of Coleridge's "A sadder and wiser man," as "sadder
and more knowing" (más tristes y más sapientes) substitutes the sublime
concept of "wisdom" for the more relative concept of "knowing."

I think that, contrary to what Cortázar says in his commentary, there is
a "melancholic" attitude toward the loss of the Greece of his adolescence
in the poem. The acceptance "of the eternal two sides of the medal, the
beauty of the marble lionesses of Delos and the repugnant cough of an
old man in the room next door at the hotel" are more evident in the
commentary than in the poem. "Greece 59" has three parts labeled: I.
Sarcophagus of Alexander the Great, Archeological Museum of Istanbul;
II. Hotel in Athens; III. The Lionesses of Delos. All three parts are trilingual and are characterized by the wordplay and extensive literary and
cultural allusions familiar to readers of Cortázar's subsequent works, particularly *Hopscotch, La vuelta al día en ochenta mundos, Ultimo round,* and *62:
A Model Kit.*

Cortázar begins his poem by literally falling upon a pun: "– Tombe sur
moi, putain, inévitable manigance de l'ennui," with the first word,
"tombe," denoting at once the tomb of Alexander and some sort of
"falling off." The words "putain" (whore) and "manigance" (intrigue)
establish the tone for the entire poem, where Cortázar presents variants
of attractive deceit. The appellation "whore," coming as it does at the
beginning of the poem, functions as a bitter parody of the classical invocation of the muse. This and other appellations in part 1 of the poem (dif-
ferentiated typographically from the musings of the speaker by dashes)
make reference to a prostitute who is engaged in oral sex with the speaker
while he recalls the sightseeing experiences of the day: "fais ton métier
pendant que je médite les Diadoques au lendemain de la Grande Mort
[do your job while I meditate on the Diadochi on the day after the Great

Death]." The "Great Death" refers to the death of Alexander the Great and the melancholy prospect of the Diadochi (Alexander's generals and successors) fighting with each other to carve up the empire. The meditation specifically concerns the death of Alexander's ideal of unity; it may (in a more personal sense) reflect the speaker's feelings about the loss of an idealized image of Greece that cannot withstand the desecration of tourism and modernity. The speaker's mourning, however, is punctuated by a masochistic dwelling on the contrast between his experience of present-day Turkey and Greece and the glamour of antiquity. The fact that Cortázar sets the speaker's meditation in the context of a sexual transaction that is furthermore sordidly described serves as an effective debasement of the ideal. The discourse of the sexual transaction permeates and contaminates the discourse on Alexander. As in the case of the poem's trilingualism, all semblance of unity and purity is exploded. The whole text becomes porous and permeable. Thus, for example, when the third line speaks of "le prestige de ces noms parfumés, musqués" (the prestige of these perfumed, musked names), the figurative meaning of perfume and musk coexists with the literal meaning of the prostitute's perfume. This impression is enhanced when one considers that the figurative meaning of the adjective *musqué* is "studied, unnatural, affected."

The last sentence of the first stanza captures the fear of what is at risk for the speaker in this meditation upon Alexander: "Serait-ce le prestige de ces noms parfumés, musqués, / l'enjeu de cette balade autour du Grand Cercueil, / la longue halte sur les dalles minées par les fourmis?" (Will the stake of this stroll around the Great Coffin, the long stop on the flagstones undermined by ants, be the prestige of these perfumed, musked names?). The prestige, the immortality of the names, is called into question by their association with the superficial, ephemeral nature of perfume and the further suggestion that they may prove no more solid. Indeed, even the apparently solid surface on which the speaker stands is precarious because it is riddled with ant tunnels.

The second stanza presents the problem of "seizing History" and invokes the memory of Pausanias, calling him "fidèle désabusé" (faithful undeceived one), and ironically presenting him as the forebear of modern tourists: "ceux qui ont (presque) complété / leur collection de Guides Bleus, Nagel, Michelin and so forth" (those who have [almost] completed their collections of Blue, Nagel, and Michelin guides, etc.).[9] The third stanza returns abruptly to the (increasingly unsatisfactory) sexual transaction: "– Mais vas-y, ne lâche pas prise, broute toujours, baby" ("Come on, don't let go, keep on grazing, baby"). The speaker then blends his expression of his dissatisfaction with the prostitute's performance with a glamorous description of Alexander: "la nuit était plus leste que toi quand ses étoiles / chatouillaient la peau du jeune lion mieux que le font tes ongles / Apricot Number Two" (the night was sharper/ nimbler than you when its stars tickled / titillated the skin of the young lion better than your Apricot Number Two nails). The skin of the young lion refers metonymically to Alexander, who because of his association with Hercules was often depicted wearing the skin of the Nemean lion. By implication, here it also refers to the speaker's penis. The juxtaposition of the mythological allusion to the Nemean lion and a nail polish color (Apricot Number Two) further contributes to the erosion of the prestige of the classical world before the onslaught of modernity. The nail polish (like the perfume) also contributes to the motif of masking and deception that is central to the whole poem.

The fourth stanza describes the unexpected encounter with the "Alexander sarcophagus." Despite the guidebooks, despite his knowledge, "no se puede saber todo" (you can't know everything), the speaker was totally unprepared for what turns out to be an experience of great transcendence to him. He understands with a suddenness described as "un rayo, un aletazo de águila" (a lightning bolt, a blow of an eagle's wing) that all his tourism has unwittingly, inexorably led him always to this previously unknown goal: "la espiral de tantos viajes Leica en mano / me hundía en este pozo de pasaje, el agujero de la nada" (the spiral of so many trips Leica in hand / was plunging me into this well of passage, the hole of nothingness). *Sarcophagus* literally means "flesh-eating," and the Alexander sarcophagus is the now empty well that serves as a rite of passage for the speaker, this "hole of nothingness" he realizes now has always been his goal. The speaker's epiphany reveals to him the hollowness of his ideal and his ill-placed faith in a source that is dry, an origin that is as spurious as the "Alexander sarcophagus" itself. His eye then catches a skull displayed in a glass case as that of Alexander, and he describes it as the "Omphalos" (navel), the stone that marked the center of the earth at Apollo's temple in Delphi. The speaker realizes that this was "the navel" for him, who had always been magnetized by this coffin without knowing it. The equation of Alexander's skull with the "Omphalos" is crucial to the speaker's pursuit of knowledge. In addition to being the navel of the world, the "Omphalos" was the site of the Delphic oracle, the source of knowledge in antiquity. This gruesome empty "Omphalos," the unwitting goal of his quest, grins at the speaker from the museum display case.

The fifth stanza continues the contemplation of the skull found in the "Alexander sarcophagus." Contemplating the sarcophagus and the skull, the speaker underscores his skepticism, but as his senses become aware of the pistachio odor of the seraglio and the view of the Golden Horn like "a green, amber horn," the irony softens. The mournful phrase "comment ne pas hisser les focs de la douleur" (how can I but hoist sorrow's sails) gives way to an intertextual cascade: "alas, poor Yoricksander, alas, bright boy!, fusillé toi aussi / comme l'ange de l'Oiseleur par les soldats de Dieu! Mais, vrai, j'ai trop pleuré, / Arthur de Macédonie, ne me tiens pas rigueur si devant ce tombeau" (you, too, shot / like the angel of the Bird-catcher by the soldiers of God! But truly, I have wept too much, / Arthur of Macedonia, do not judge me harshly if before this grave). Through the Shakespearean portmanteau word "Yoricksander" the speaker alludes to Hamlet's graveyard scene and then flows into the words that the young French writer Raymond Radiguet used to prophesy his death, according to Jean Cocteau.[10] "Yoricksander" establishes an association between Alexander, Yorick, and more significantly Hamlet, another short-lived prince; but as it is the speaker who is viewing the skull of Alexander, he is placed in turn in the position of Hamlet. "Arthur of Macedonia" draws a parallel between the meteoric career of Arthur Rimbaud and that of Alexander the Great, an image reinforced by the allusion to Raymond Radiguet, whose career was also meteoric. A fact which further suggests a link with Alexander is that nearly all the historical and literary figures to whom allusion is made here were homosexual.

As the stanza ends, we find the speaker returning to his ironical stance with a remark expressing the incongruity of finding the alleged skull of Alexander displayed in the Ingres-like seraglio. This remark is followed by another image of the skull, which grins, "dans l'absence de pensée / et l'impuissance d'agir" (in the absence of thought / and the impotence of action). This comment reaffirms the previous paradoxical association between Alexander and Hamlet. In life Alexander was an extreme example of action. In death he is reduced to Hamlet-like inactivity. The exclamation, "à moi, Héphestion, ombre si chère!" (come to me, Hephaistion, dearest shade!) closes the stanza with a note of pathos. The speaker, mourning Alexander, assumes the voice of Alexander mourning the death of his friend and lover. In Cortázar's game of musical coffins it is often hard to keep track of who is in the coffin and who is out.

The sixth stanza represents another of Cortázar's jolting attempts to demythify and exorcise the classical ambience he has so carefully wrought. We are brought back to the seedy narrative scene where the speaker is still cajoling the prostitute, who seems unable to bring him to a climax. Here Hamlet's political impotence is reflected in the speaker's sexual impotence, which he is quick to blame on the retsina he has consumed: "Tant de vin résiné, on ne tient pas le coup, il faudra s'en sortir" (So much wine with resin, it's hard to take, I'll have to get out of it). The speaker's question to the prostitute, "Your name is Irene, isn't it?" underscores the dehumanized nature of their intercourse, but it may also be another token of the speaker's irony. *Irene* means "peace" in Greek, and the speaker's allusion to her name after he has just complained that she is not aggressive enough may indeed be pointed.

As we saw above, the account Cortázar gives of the autobiographical experience on which "Greece 59" is based reveals powerful affective connections between classical antiquity and Cortázar's youth. In the author's mind, his adolescent weeping over the death of Patroclus in the *Iliad* and the burning of an early novel that Cortázar describes as homosexual are associated in the powerful feelings that overcame him when unexpectedly confronted with the "Alexander sarcophagus." In part 1 of "Greece 59" the mirroring of Achilles and Patroclus in Alexander and Hephaistion (and Hadrian and Antinous, if we consider his poem "Adriano a Antinoo" [Hadrian to Antinous]) seems to show that there is in Cortázar's mind a specific association between classical antiquity, homosexuality, and (less clearly) experiences or feelings from his own adolescence. As we have seen, the theme of homosexual love is also developed through the allusions to modern poets. Thus the constellation of classical homosexual lovers is completed by the references to Cocteau and Radiguet as well as to Rimbaud and (by implication) Verlaine. This affective nexus may help to explain the sexual impotence of the speaker (despite the efforts of the prostitute) better than the speaker's suggestion that it is due to having drunk too much retsina.

The end of the sixth stanza and the beginning of the seventh (and last) stanza of the poem invoke, once again, the memory of Alexander's deeds: "Philip's son, quite a bright boy, a horseman, go ask the Eastern roads," and his death, "(poisoned? Swamp fever?)" Despite his repeated and savage attempts to tarnish the glamour that Alexander's life holds for him, the speaker still declares the greatness of Alexander's historical moment in the first lines of the last stanza. Here he compares Alexander's life achievements to Yggdrasil, the great ash tree that supports the universe in Norse mythology. Alexander was "el fuste de una sed entre Zeus y los hombres" (the shaft of a thirst between Zeus and men).

Part 1 of "Greece 59" ends with a long trilingual sentence. In this apostrophe to Alexander, the speaker restates his wonder at the preordained chance that brought him before the sarcophagus and his climactic experience of anticlimax and disenchantment. This epiphanic reencounter with Alexander (and Greek antiquity) is characterized by the oxymoron: "Alejandro, oh zarpazo de miel" (Alexander, oh honeyed clawing). The skull and the sarcophagus, he declares with some bitterness, have shown him the "exemplary goal of his trips, / the benefits of historical veneration, / the sardonic tableau of a narghile exhibited next to a Macedonian sword." Following the consistent motifs that appear in part 1, the sardonic nature of the tableau would spring from the contrast of the symbol of decadent inaction, the hookah, and the symbol of Alexander's mighty deeds, the sword.

The final words of part 1 describe the speaker's contradictory feelings as "the happy longing of a battered Christian dog / standing exactly between Hellas and Islam, amen." We leave the speaker in the museum standing between the sword (ancient Greece) and the narghile (Turkey), battered and abased by the now adulterated image of classical Greece. Deeply disenchanted with his youthful ideals, the speaker mourns several deaths. He mourns the death of Alexander, the death of the cultural and aesthetic ideal of unity, the death of the Western cultural myth of origin he had passionately embraced in his youth, and the death of a previous self made in the image and likeness of that hollow origin.

Part 2, "Hotel in Athens," takes the reader far from the sarcophagus in Istanbul but not far from death. It is primarily the modality that changes. Whereas the tragic mode predominates in part 1, it is the comic mode (in the sense of Aristophanic comedy) that prevails in part 2. This section of the poem begins with a description of the speaker in his room at the Palladion Hotel in Athens, where he is unable to sleep because a man in the room next door is trying unsuccessfully to clear his throat: "Arrancarse un gargajo no siempre es fácil de mañana, por eso / el señor de la pieza catorce del Palladion Hotel / de siete a nueve lucha contra el ahogo. / ¿Cómo dormir tan cerca del combate entre Gorgo y Tersites?" (Getting out a gob is not always easy in the morning, that is why / the man in room fourteen of the Palladion Hotel / from seven to nine struggles not to choke. / How do you sleep so close to the combat between Gorgo and Thersites?). Phlegm, excrement, and nausea are recurrent motifs of part 2 of "Greece 59." These scatological aspects foreshadow the coprophilia of Horacio Oliveira in *Hopscotch,* but here they do not seem to be connected with any kind of mystical rite of passage. The presence of the excremental in this section is all part of the speaker's prosaic,

demythified vision of tourism in modern Greece. Significantly, although
the hotel's name alludes to classical Greece through its reference to the
"palladion," the wooden statue of Athena whose possession was supposed to assure the protection of Troy, the street by the hotel is called
Venizelos after the patriot and statesman of modern Greece.

The allusion to "the combat between Gorgo and Thersites" is an
obscure one. Thersites, however, seems to offer a key. He appears in book
2 of the *Iliad*, where he is described as "the ugliest man who came beneath
Ilion. He was bandy-legged and went lame of one foot, with shoulders
stooped and drawn together over his chest, and above this his skull went
up to a point with the wool grown sparsely upon it" (82). Known as "Thersites of the endless speech," he is particularly hated by Achilles and
Odysseus, whom he always abuses in council. Through this reference,
Cortázar seems to be alluding to the "endless" gagging of his neighbor.
Furthermore, this antihero, who is a paragon of ugliness, contrasts in
every sense with the beauty of a classical hero like Achilles, by whom he
was eventually killed. In this sense, Thersites (an anti-Achilles and thereby
an anti-Alexander) is the perfect emblem for this section of the poem,
and the perfect counterweight to the image of Alexander presented in
part 1. Here the realm of the heroic is definitely abandoned and the
speaker's major problem is how to pass the day – "the day will be long."
The speaker spares no prosaic details: the food, the cost of the hot shower
"seven drachmae, soap included," the invasion of tourist buses, and soldiers playing cards at the temple of Poseidon. The speaker (as in
Quevedo's famous sonnet) can find no place to rest his eyes that will not
remind him of the death of ancient Greece. Even his description of the
previous night's visit to the Acropolis under a full moon is vitiated by an
inescapable feeling of tourist kitsch: "y en la gran caja de zapatos Partenón
vimos alta a Selene / (anoche, yes, a must, to miss it would be *such* a
shame)" (and in the great shoebox Parthenon we saw Selene high
above / [last night, yes, a must, to miss it would be *such* a shame]). Just as
the speaker's thoughts were punctuated in part 1 by the scene with the
prostitute, here they are constantly interrupted by the gagging of the man
in the neighboring room.

That endlessly gagging man is a harbinger of death. Through this
annoying but hardly extraordinary incident and through several allusions to bodily functions, Cortázar is focusing on human frailties and
mortality. Although the age of the coughing man is not mentioned in the
poem, Cortázar speaks of "an old man" in his commentary, and the
coughing is described as a "râle" (death-rattle) just at the point when it
interrupts one of the few pleasant reveries of this section. After the iron-

ical comments about the moonlit visit to the Parthenon, the speaker relents before the magic of the place: "y es necesario confesar que el cielo me pesaba un poco menos, / que el tres de mayo no era un día con los hombros doblados / por más de cuarenta años que os contemplan; / en el chirriar de un saltamontes ático se asomaba la gracia / de los altos lugares, de las mesetas del corazón: y descansábamos" (and it is necessary to confess that the sky oppressed me a little less, / that the third of May wasn't a day with shoulders stooped / by the more than forty years that look down upon you; / in the chirping of an Attic grasshopper there peeked out the grace / of high places, of the plateaus of the heart: and we rested). It is at this very point that the speaker's reverie is shattered by the coughing of the old man described as a death-rattle. The speaker's middle-aged anxiety, expressed with witty self-deprecation in the parody of Napoleon's famous exhortation to his soldiers before the Battle of the Pyramids, is momentarily dispelled by the "grace" of the Acropolis, but returns with a vengeance when the old man coughs. The speaker considers changing rooms, and this initiates the motif of escape that flavors the rest of the section. He considers and dismisses the idea of escaping to Cape Sunion when faced with the image of ten buses dumping out American students. He then seeks to escape to the Temple of Poseidon, only to find it defiled by soldiers playing cards: "un tres, un seis, ah merde!" ("a three, a six, oh shit!"). It is hard to know if the expletive is uttered by a soldier displeased with his hand or by the exasperated speaker.

His next idea is to flee to the museum to see (significantly) the golden masks found by Schliemann in Mycenae. As he reconstructs the scene of the famous discovery of the "Mask of Agamemnon" his thoughts turn again to death, the horror of Thyestes' cannibal banquet which is the origin of the tragedy of the house of Atreus: "máscaras, rayos verdes y aplastados, / como águilas deshechas contra el flanco de piedra / por las manos del viento, Moiras, Tánatos! / ¡Agamemnon! Ach, Schrecklich!" (masks, crushed green bolts of lightning, / like eagles smashed against the stone flank / by the hands of the wind, Fate, Death! / Agamemnon! Oh, Terrible!). The visit to the museum, meant to be an escape from the memento mori in room 14 of the hotel, results instead in another confrontation with death and an elegy. Although the use of the German word *Schrecklich* follows the previous use of the word *Wunderbar*, attributed in the speaker's reverie to the archaeologist Schliemann, it is clearly and appropriately borrowed from Rilke's first and second *Duino Elegies*, where the phrase "Ein jeder Engel ist Schrecklich" (each single angel is terrible) appears.

What is "terrible" for the speaker beyond the evocation of Agamemnon's grisly fate is that the eyes of his mask seem still to gaze upon the dawn of time: "Con ojos, como sexos de vírgenes, / entremirando un mundo que despierta / y es una pura maldición maravillosa, un bosque de amenazas / a combatir con carros, Ifigenias, caballos, simulacros y aedos" (With eyes like the vulvas of virgins, / squinting at a world that is awakening / and it is a pure, marvellous curse, a forest of menaces / that must be combatted with chariots, Iphigenias, horses, simulacrums, and poets). Cortázar's concern with origins reappears now no longer draped in the clarity of classical Greece but in the Mycenaean darkness and fear portrayed by Aeschylus in the foundational world of the *Oresteia*, a world where Agamemnon can order the sacrifice of his virgin daughter Iphigenia in order to secure a favorable wind for the Argive fleet.

The scene of the next stanza is set back in the hotel, where the motif of escape changes from masks to the blinds of the room. The speaker asks a companion to close the blinds a bit (echoing the motif of Agamemnon's squinting eyes) because he wants to hear better the accordion of a blind man playing in the street. The speaker thus veils his eyes in order to concentrate on the sense of hearing and the sense of smell. The song of the blind accordionist, the sounds of Venizelos Street, and the smell of peanuts and pistachios, both of which rise from the street, remind him of the Pnyx (the hill west of Athens where the assembly of citizens was held in ancient times) and the Areopagus (the supreme court of ancient Athens). In the sounds and smells of the streets, the speaker seems to be able to reconcile momentarily modern and ancient Athens. Breathing a vital earthiness into the classical names Pnyx and Areopagus, the speaker now associates them with the smell of onions and crowds. This reevaluation of the past stands in stark contrast with his previous concept (in part 1) of "the prestige of these perfumed, musked names." This reconciliation or equilibrium is underscored by the observation that the man next door has probably left, as no one is coughing any more. The equilibrium is short-lived as the sound of the accordion (associations with the modern world? with Argentina?) nauseates him slightly and the desire to escape returns: "ganas de irme, / de nadar mar afuera, desnudo de la historia, / marinero de Ulises en el alba del tiempo" (a desire to leave, / to swim out to sea, naked of history, / a sailor of Ulysses in the dawn of time). Thus part 2 of "Greece 59" ends with a clear declaration of the speaker's longing for an origin outside of history. Out at sea, out of sight of land, the speaker would return not only to the dawn of time but to a situation that evokes the dawn of his own life in the womb. This original fantasy, of course, cannot go unpunished, and Cortázar ends part 2 by having the speaker suggest that he and his companion should go have a cocktail: "Et si on prenait l'apéritif, chérie?" ("What about a cocktail, dear?"). The cocktail will be the surrogate for a swim at the dawn of time.

Part 3, "The Lionesses of Delos," is the necessary culmination of Cortázar's settling of accounts with Greek antiquity. Here, in the birthplace of Apollo, Cortázar will exorcise the ghost of Keats. The first two lines correct Keats's vision of beauty, truth, and time: "No sé que es la belleza; esto es hermoso, / la lenta mordedura de la rosa del tiempo" (I don't know what beauty is; this is beautiful, / the slow bite of the rose of time). In his ode "On a Grecian Urn," Keats values and envies the urn for its timeless beauty, which he equates with truth in his famous dictum: "Beauty is truth, truth beauty, – that is all / Ye know on earth, and all ye need to know." Cortázar disposes of both terms in Keats's equation by saying that he doesn't know what beauty is, which (following Keats) implies that he also doesn't know what truth is. Unlike Keats, Cortázar does not feel at ease with absolutes. He feels he can speak of what is "beautiful" but not of "beauty." What Cortázar finds beautiful is also the opposite of what embodies beauty for Keats. The major emphasis of Keats's ode is placed on the fact that the urn and the persons depicted on it are untouched by time: "Thou, silent form! dost tease us out of thought / As doth eternity: Cold Pastoral! / When old age shall this generation waste, / Thou shalt remain, in midst of other woe / Than ours, a friend to man." Cortázar, on the other hand, finds the lionesses of Delos beautiful because of "the slow bite of the rose of time," the marks of erosion on the statues. The urn abolishes the passage of time for Keats, whereas the statues of the lionesses affirm and celebrate it for Cortázar.

Under the sun of Delos, the speaker seems to feel a liberating euphoria akin to that expressed in the fantasy where he imagines himself a sailor of Ulysses swimming "out to sea, naked of history." Here the sun of Delos is associated by the speaker with a type of liberating therapy: "Sol de Delos / con ceñidor de kinesiólogo: a tirarse gritando en lo desnudo, a abrir / cada ventana sobre la carne libre, entre las leonas, / su exasperante guardia de arpías agoreras (Sun of Delos / with a therapist's belt: to hurl oneself shouting into nakedness, to open / each window over the free flesh, between the lionesses, / their exasperating vigilance of oracular harpies). Obscure as these images are, there does seem to be a stress on liberation in them: the reappearance of the motif of nakedness, here used as an index of some form of abyss, and the image of the free fall is followed by the image of opening windows "over the free flesh." But the liberation is not devoid of mitigating aspects; there is darkness even under the Sun of Delos. The euphoric images are qualified by suggestions of danger and fear.

It is the motif of fear that is then developed in the rest of the stanza as the images become increasingly equivocal. Below, the speaker sees the old Roman port, but the baths are oxymoronically "dusty" and "the frogs" violently "are shattering ad nauseam the bottom of the fountain of Meroe."[11] The existential nausea felt by the speaker in the Athens hotel room has returned, albeit in the form of a classical formula, "ad nauseam." The stanza then builds up to a climax that characteristically fizzles into anticlimax. The speaker describes a fearful scene at night amid the ruins, evokes "the Panic horror," and begins to spin a horror story, "They'll have it that some prowling shape / starts looking for a prey at midnight, and" only to break off abruptly and deflate the buildup by turning down the offer of a dark cigarette, as if the "prowling shape" amid the ruins had turned out to be a local stroller. Then, repeating the gesture that closes part 2, he again invites his companion to have a drink: "Let's go back for a drink. Not bad, the local stuff." This second invitation to drink, coming as it does right before the second stanza of Part 2, which describes the speaker's quest for Apollo in Delos, the god's birthplace, seems to be playfully indicating the speaker's choice of a Dionysian corrective to his crumbling but still persistent Apollonian cast of mind.

The second and third stanzas constitute Cortázar's reckoning with Apollo and the Apollonian view of Greek antiquity. Although the second stanza begins with the appropriately rhapsodic invocation: "Te he buscado en la cima, en tu cuna de altura, rubio señor del día" (I have sought you in the summit, in your lofty cradle, blond lord of the day), it becomes clearly parodical when he adds, "sabiendo que no estabas" (knowing you were not there). In addition, the apparently canonical epithet he employs to address Apollo is somewhat vitiated by his alluding to the fact that he smokes "blond cigarettes" when he turns down the Greek cigarette. Abruptly the speaker gives a Geiger counter reading of 40 and describes a reconnaissance flight of three jets over a number of Greek islands. Their report is: "No god, all dead, nothing to point out." The oracular knowledge of Apollo has been supplanted by the technologically gathered data of jets and of a Geiger counter that finds no trace of the god's "radiance." After this rupture, the stanza nevertheless reassumes the rhapsodic tone to evoke the primal scene of Leto giving birth to Apollo: "Así, de Leto abriéndose en la cima con su dolor radiante entre los muslos" (Thus, of Leto splitting in the summit with her radiant pain between her thighs). The speaker looks in vain for traces of this origin in the red earth, "in the silence where a cricket scrapes," "in the burnished sea at noon." Instead he finds what he calls "the dialectic of Delos: Flee, stay," and concludes sadly, "there are no gods, it is all sad pottery / and a mediocre beach, the resin in the wine, a dog / howling in the veranda (the postcards, two drachmas, in the hall)." The next three lines frame a question: "what is this rhythm of broken clouds, the black sea trembling in the columns, the perfect procession of the void?" That void is the nauseating hollowness the speaker has felt throughout. The last stanza takes up once more the motifs of the mask, the emptiness, and the quest: "Máscara de isla, hueco tambor quemándose: no te vayas, viajero / reconóceme, encuéntrame, I was a God, a radiant King, golden Apollo!" (Mask island, hollow burning drum: don't leave traveler / recognize me, find me, I was a God, a radiant King, golden Apollo!).[12]

The speaker of "Greece 59" has journeyed to the source and found it empty and dry like the Roman baths at Delos. I believe that the paradigm of ancient Greek culture operating in "Greece 59" is Nietzschean. Contrary to what Cortázar declares in the commentary written years after the poem, I do not see in the poem itself any kind of resolution. Much less do I see "the no longer melancholic acceptance of the eternal two sides of the medal, the beauty of the marble lionesses of Delos and the repugnant cough of an old man in the room next door at the hotel" (164). The acceptance of the "eternal two sides of the medal" will come to the mature Cortázar, but this poem is full of melancholy. The irony and iconoclastic gestures that punctuate the poem recur even in part 3, as if to acknowledge that the previous applications have failed to inoculate the speaker against the glamour of the past. Instead of acceptance, what we find in "Greece 59" is revelation and mourning. What we also have in the end is a clear rejection of the Apollonian view of Greek antiquity in favor of a Dionysian one. Tellingly, anticlimactic moments in the poem are followed by invitations to drink or seek oblivion in erotic release.

### The Lessons of the Greek Islands

The short stories "The Idol of the Cyclades" and "The Island at Noon" can be read as Cortázar's further exorcisms of the persistent nostalgia for origins. "The Island at Noon" seems to be an elaboration of the fantasy described toward the end of part 2 of "Greece 59" where the speaker yearns to swim in the Aegean Sea "naked of history" like one of Ulysses' sailors. In "The Island" an airline steward, Marini, becomes fascinated by a Greek island that his airplane routinely passes at noon, and he too day-dreams about swimming naked in the coves in the northern part of the island (99). Marini's desire becomes so great that it comes to dominate his whole life. His coworkers are surprised when he rejects a transfer to the more desirous New York flight and eventually loses his girlfriend, Carla, because of his obsession. The dénouement of the story is well known and owes much technically to Ambrose Bierce's "An Occurrence at Owl Creek Bridge." To simplify grossly, what we as readers have taken to be the fulfillment of Marini's fantasy turns out to be a daydream. Marini only makes it to the island as a corpse after his plane crashes nearby. The Greek fishermen who pick up his body wonder how he had the strength to swim all the way to shore.

Just as Goethe is said to have exorcised his failed love affair by writing *The Sorrows of Young Werther* and killing off that aspect of himself in the character of Werther, so Cortázar washes away his "original sin" in poor Marini's blood. Given his disappointing experiences as a tourist in Greece, perhaps Cortázar could justify this as a "mercy killing."

"The Idol of the Cyclades" is a far more complicated story. Its basic thematic structure, nevertheless, is straightforward enough. A Parisian married couple, the Morands, and their South American friend Somoza find a Cycladic idol during their vacation on a Greek island. Shortly after the idol is discovered, the vacation and their relationship go sour as the Morands begin to suspect that Somoza has fallen in love with Thérèse Morand. When they return to Paris, Somoza is allowed to keep posses-sion of the idol but not allowed to see Thérèse. Besides the sexual rivalry (real or imagined), there is an epistemological rivalry between Morand and Somoza. The ironical and refined Parisian is an archaeologist and believes the idol must be understood through science. The earnest and impulsive South American, whose profession is not revealed, believes that he can reach the idol through other than rational means. What we have, therefore, in "The Idol of the Cyclades" is a dramatic reenactment of the conflict between rationalism and irrationalism. Irrationalism, of course, wins. As the story ends, Morand, having killed Somoza, crouches naked behind a door licking a bloody stone ax as he waits to ambush his wife.

By choosing a Cycladic idol as the focus of the story, Cortázar has dealt a further blow to the idea of the birth of Western culture in the ethos of classical Greece. Cycladic idols have traditionally held the position of "origin" for classical Hellenic art. Having sought "origin" in a primitive non-Western culture in a story like "The Night Face Up," Cortázar now seeks to undermine the very origins of Western culture in "The Idol of the Cyclades." The choice of Cycladic culture as the background for his story allows him to posit an irrationalist foundation for the culture that is taken to be the origin of rationalism.

Cortázar's earlier works, of course, frequently demonstrate an interest in the irrational, as did his fascination with the life and works of Edgar Allan Poe. What is taking shape in "Greece 59," "The Idol of the Cyclades," and "The Island at Noon," however, is the wholesale attack on rationalism that will serve as the principal philosophical stance in *Hopscotch*. Irrationalism, too, informed Cortázar's aesthetics as he expanded his writing practice from the crafting of classically perfect short stories (which he never abandoned) to the examination of open forms: *Hopscotch* and the collage books, *La vuelta al día en ochenta mundos* and *Ultimo round*. The concept, presented several times in "Greece 59," of the unknown goal toward which one has always been unwittingly striving becomes one of the major preoccupations of Oliveira in *Hopscotch*, as he sees that the more he searches the less he finds, while la Maga, who does not search, constantly finds. Likewise, Cortázar's emphasis on the "distracted" writing of "Greece 59" would seem to create retrospectively a genealogy for all the purposely "pointless" and "goal-less" games in *Hopscotch*. Horacio's and la Maga's attempts to run into each other in Paris without agreeing on a time and place is a correlative of "distracted writing." Thus, although Cortázar's speaker in "Greece 59" abandons the pathetically pleading voice of Apollo in Delos, Cortázar's unresolved preoccupation with reason and light will organize *Hospcotch*, albeit negatively; but in Oliveira's distracted ramblings Apollo will appear under a new avatar: Descartes.[13]

## Notes

1. For a study of Cortázar's interest in the "pre-Adamic" primitivism of the Cuban author Lezama, see my *José Lezama Lima's Joyful Vision* (1989), chap. 6.

2. Unless otherwise noted translations are mine.

3. The title actually appears as:

CE

GRECIA 59

ECE

4. "El ídolo de las cícladas" (The Idol of the Cyclades) is not included in the first (1956) edition of *Final del juego (End of the game)* but appears in the second edition (1964). "La isla a mediodía" (The island at noon) was first published in *Todos los fuegos el fuego (All fires the fire)*, (1966). The stories reflect

Cortázar's travel experiences in the Greek islands both in their vividly described settings and in their attitude toward the nostalgia for origins felt by the characters Somoza ("The Idol") and Marini ("The Island").

5. Cortázar's skepticism regarding the authenticity of the "Alexander" sarcophagus exhibited in the museum of antiquities at Istanbul is fully justified by the consensus among art historians.

6. For the parallel commonly drawn in antiquity between the lovers Achilles and Patroclus and Alexander and Hephaistion, see Fox, 56. The motif of homosexual lovers in classical antiquity is of some interest to Cortázar. In classical antiquity an association was made between the love of Achilles and Patroclus and that of Alexander and Hephaistion. In later antiquity, a parallel was drawn by Arrian between Achilles and Patroclus and the emperor Hadrian and his lover Antinous. Cortázar, who translated Yourcenar's *Memoirs of Hadrian* from the French into Spanish (probably in 1954) wrote a sonnet entitled "Adriano a Antinoo" (Hadrian to Antinous). That sonnet is included in *Salvo el crepúsculo* but was first published in *Pameos y meopas,* where it appears in a section labeled Buenos Aires, Paris, 1944–57. My guess is that the sonnet was inspired by Yourcenar's book and written around the time Cortázar was translating it. This is not the only instance of the influence of *Hadrian's Memoirs* on Cortázar. The title of his collection of short stories *Un tal Lucas* (A certain Lucas, 1979) is curiously taken from the last sentence of the note in which Yourcenar gives her sources and explains her methodology: "Let us add finally that a phrase of the description of Antinoopolis, attributed here to the emperor, was taken from the account of the trip of a certain Lucas, who visited the region at the beginning of the eighteenth century" (273).

7. Quoted in *Dictionary of the History of Ideas* (3:367).

8. See Hernández del Castillo, 4.

9. Pausanias was a Greek traveler and geographer of the second century whose *Description of Greece* is the source for most of what we know about the ruins of ancient Greece.

10. I am grateful to my colleague Roland Simon, of the French department at the University of Virginia, for helping me to identify the reference to Radiguet's prophecy of his own death. Jean Cocteau, whose veracity has been questioned (see McNab) is the source for this prophecy. Cocteau's anecdote, related in his preface to Radiguet's *Count d'Orgel* (*Oeuvres complètes,* 2:10), is as follows: "Listen, he told me on the ninth day of December, listen to a terrible thing. In three days I shall be shot by the soldiers of God" (quoted in McNab, 35). Cocteau employed the second sentence in his poem "L'Ange Heurtebise," part II (1925). "L'Oiseleur" refers to Cocteau; see, e.g., his book *Le Mystère de Jean l'oiseleur. Monologues* (1925). Cortázar's "l'ange de l'Oiseleur" is therefore Radiguet.

11. The frogs in the fountain may be an allusion to a tradition associated with Leto. When she was fleeing the jealous Hera with the infants Apollo and Artemis in her arms, she asked to drink from a pond only to be refused and insulted by the locals. She prayed that they would be punished and they were turned into frogs. See Bulfinch, 67.

12. The similarity of these verses to Milton's "On the Morning of Christ's Nativity" is striking: "The oracles are dumb, / No voice or hideous hum / Runs through the arched roof in words deceiving. / Apollo from his shrine / Can no more divine, / With hollow shriek the steep of Delphos leaving."

13. See, e.g., *Hopscotch,* chapter 18, where Oliveira exclaims: "¡eh Cartesius viejo jodido!" (eh Cartesius, you fucked-up old man!).

## References

Aldington, Richard, ed. *The Viking Book of Poetry of the English-Speaking World.* 2 vols. New York: Viking, 1958.

Bulfinch, Thomas. *Bulfinch's Mythology.* Comp. Bryan Holme, intro. Joseph Campbell. New York: Viking, 1979.

Cortázar, Julio. *Final del juego.* Buenos Aires: Sudamericana, 1983.

*Salvo el crepúsculo.* Buenos Aires: Editorial Nueva Imagen, 1984.

*Todos los fuegos el fuego.* Barcelona: Edhasa, 1982.

*Rayuela.* Buenos Aires: Sudamericana, 1968.

Fox, Robin Lane. *Alexander the Great.* New York: Dial Press, 1974.

Hernández del Castillo, Ana. *Keats, Poe, and the Shaping of Cortázar's Mythopoesis.* Amsterdam: John Benjamins B.V., 1981.

Homer. *The Iliad.* Trans. and intro. Richmond Lattimore. Chicago: University of Chicago Press, 1967.

McNab, James P. *Raymond Radiguet.* Boston: G. K. Hall, 1984.

Pellón, Gustavo. *José Lezama Lima's Joyful Vision.* Austin: University of Texas Press, 1989.

Rilke, Rainer Maria. *Duino Elegies.* Trans. J. B. Leishman and Stephen Spender. New York: Norton, 1967.

# 7

## Supposing Morelli Had Meant to
## Go to Jaipur

*Andrew Bush*

### *Julio Takes a Camera*

In or near Saignon, I suppose, and simultaneously on the upper story of a two-floor book (Cortázar, *Ultimo,* 22), a breach opens between the remains of a medieval structure – likewise two-tiered, arch surmounting arch – and, across a narrow passage, a stone house (Fig. 1). A clerestory and a nave(?), the arches are lodged in the past, shorn of their original function. But the house is inhabited in the present. Under a lintel that shows signs of repair, a door is closed, still dividing inside from out according to its primordial purpose, while farther down the wall, and more tellingly, a window is open. The eye scans the static image, progresses from part to part, and so introduces a "novelizable quantity" (Lezama, *Oppiano,* 132), rebuilding the house from the missing stones of the ruined arches and adjacent wall, mapping the interval between past and present as a simultaneous coexistence abutting an interstitial space. But whether the same stones were literally carried across (*trans-latus*) from the church, if it was a church, to the house or houses, or if instead to read that continuity, is arbitrarily to turn back the loose ends upon themselves in a narrative knot, to "*rizar el rizo,* as they adeptly translate English texts on aviation in Barcelona" (*Ultimo,* 28), the historical novel that might be inferred is founded upon the photo that is. And in the photographic composition sight lines converge from the framing buildings of the foreground to the interstitial space, the breach, where the eye is caught by the dark side of the *contraventana* that opens the house to the light. A translator, let us call him Julio or Paul Blackburn (*Ultimo,* 17, upper story) or Juan (*62*), moving between a certain *francoesperanto, anglohispano* and *francoinglés* (*Ultimo* 18, upper story), as in *una de tantas conversaciones de Saignon,* may discover a paradox: a *persienne* ajar? No, no slats. A *contrevent* or *contraventana,* a shutter, an open shutter. A projection of the lens. A photo created in the camera's own image.

Kurosawa's Derzu Uzala transforms a surveyor's tripod – it is also used for still photography – into the makeshift ribbed vaulting of a house of marsh grasses, a shelter *against* an ominous *wind*.

Figure 1

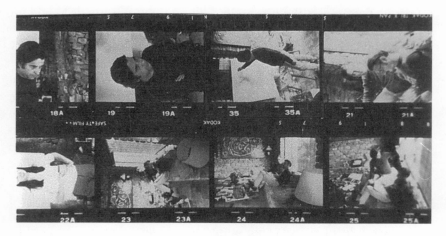

Figure 2

Cortázar also takes photographs of his house guest, Julio Silva. This Julio is a painter whose culinary science reminds Cortázar of a Persian sultan

"You will say they are Persian, but let them be changed," says Lear (III. 6). Jai Singh attached himself to no particular school but studied Hindu, Muslim and European methods impartially. He collected astronomical books and had certain of them translated; he organised and certainly used some of the Arabic or Persian text-books on the astrolabes, of which there were a great many available. (Kaye, 3–4)

and of José Lezama Lima (*Ultimo*, 18, upper story). First, a full-length view of Julio before his canvas in progress, the photo numbered frame 35 (*Ultimo*, 17, upper story; Fig. 2); it is out of sequence, intercalated into the roll of frames from 18 to 25 (substituted for frame 20, posing frame 20 beneath a screen image). Cortázar returns to the image in two more close-ups, blowups as it were. He moves in for a half-length shot (*Ultimo* 18, upper story; Fig. 3) and then again, closer still, he isolates the painting hand at work (*Ultimo* 19 , upper story; Fig. 4). Ruined arches, stone house, open shutter: The photo of the buildings in or near Saignon forms the next frame, a dispensable chapter in that self-reflexive series. Another form of continuity: beyond psychological coherence, beyond causal relations. Not so much as a metaphor of one another, but rather a resemblance mediated, translated by a metaphor – unseen, unspoken – of a camera.

The open shutter does not arrest the image as it flees into the breach along traditional orthogonal lines. (The arch on the ground floor offers a parallel escape for the perspectival illusion. But this is a dead end for the eye. A labyrinth must also have its false leads.) Distant, paler than the sky, a building stands, almost illegible, in the background. Flat black spaces of doorway and window are separated by a line of an open gallery, or is it a blind arcade; and beyond, or is it attached (and if so, at what oblique angle?), is a tower or belfry at a vanishing point in the very center of the photograph. The specificity and variety of the foreground – sacred versus secular, public versus private, then versus now – are narrowed down to that *mirador* from which an unseen eye may return the gaze of the photographer, itself overlapping an eye, my eye, that scans the photograph.

Elsewhere, pen in hand, in *62/modelo para armar,* Cortázar identifies the architectural imago that fills the breach in time as well as in the psychogeography of everyday life simply as *la ciudad,* the city. But here he

Figure 3

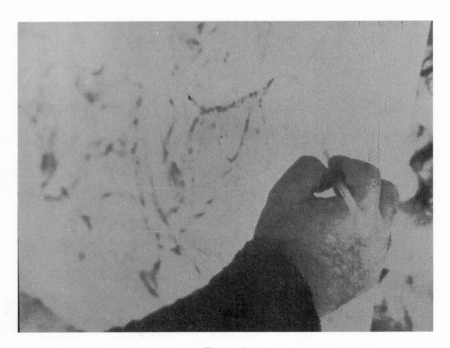

Figure 4

takes a camera and records an evanescent archtype; may I say, to give it a name, an observatory.

## Take Two

1968: *62* goes into print; Cortázar goes to India. He takes his camera with him to the sultan Jai Singh's observatory in Jaipur.

The Jesuit missionary Joseph Tieffenthaler remarked of his visit to the observatory complex in the eighteenth century, not long after Jai Singh's death, that "what attracts most attention is a gnomon (*axis mundi*), remarkable for its height of 70 Paris feet, and for its thickness. . . . On the summit of this gnomon is a belvedere, which overlooks the town and is so high that it makes one giddy" (quoted in Kaye, 54). Oliveira was giddy, too, perched in his belvedere above the *axis mundi* of *Rayuela*. Now it is Cortázar's turn, camera in hand; photographs of the *mirador* of the observatory (front cover and 8; Fig. 5) form the first impressions of *Prosa del observatorio*.

Yet one need not enter through the front door. The back-alley photographer finds a breach in the fantasmal architecture of superseded aspirations – science having long since marched relentlessly on (*Prosa* 65; Fig. 6). From an angle, a walkway is reduced to a narrow passage, framed obliquely by two buildings in the foreground. The vanishing point is occluded by the building to the right, while on the left, a wall with impenetrably black windows extends to the midpoint, dividing the photo at the center. In the very midst, though half-hidden in the breach, is another of Jai Singh's great astronomical instruments. Entering here, turning back somewhere between pages 51 and 55 (the pagination of *Prosa* is disturbed there), the breach opens – indeed, the breach in time and space that is Cortázar's recurrent concern is named *lo abierto*, the open, the opening, in *Prosal del observatorio* (e.g., *Prosa*, 63–5, which frames the photo of the half-hidden instrument between two pages of prose). There, the same instrument is fully revealed, spreading its symmetry broadly over facing pages, the luminosity of its concentric rings made brighter still by the work of the darkroom that blackened out the foreground and the sky (Fig. 7). An image of the camera once again.

And of the eye behind the lens. The instruments of the observatory realize a passion for the stars: "Eroticism of Jai Singh at the end point of a race and a history, ramps of the observatories where the vast curves of breasts and thighs yield their paths of pleasure to a gaze that possesses by transgression and challenge and that leaps to the unnameable from the

Figure 5

catapults of its trembling, mineral silence" (*Prosa*, 45). The eye of Actaeon fleeing Diana, fleeing Hélène (*62*); but Actaeon in India turns at Jaipur: "Actaeon will survive and return to the hunt until the day in which he finds Diana and possesses her beneath the leaves, snatching away her virginity that no clamoring defends any longer" (*Prosa*, 67). Allegorize, allegorize ("Diana the history of man [*sic*] . . . the enemy history with its dogs of tradition and commandment" [*Prosa*, 67]), but Cortázar insists upon a mythology of rape. It is condensed in the prose and photography at Jaipur. The defiling eye of this astronomical machine is, simultaneously, a marble Mount of Venus (compare the photos of "/que sepa abrir la puerta para ir a jugar," especially *Ultimo*, 142 and 152, upper story) at once subject and object of the violence of the gaze.

In the upward curve of the flanking structures there is a reminiscence of horns. The whole instrument becomes a great taurine mask, just as it

Figure 6

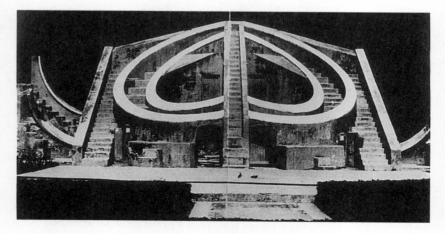

Figure 7

is also and at the same time a labyrinth of stairs and passageways. Tropo-logically, it is both container and contained, which is to say, topologically, a great Klein bottle: a self-reflexive opening (*lo abierto*) that denies the primordial division of inside and out. Hence, an "antiliterary language," as Cortázar says (Harss and Dohman, 236), a post-Romantic challenge, that is, to "the language of the door" (Lezama, *Oppiano*, 9) which consti-tutes Romanticism's master inside–outside trope.

The hint of a minotaur stages self-reflexivity's primal scene (González Echevarría) – were it but primal; but before Los reyes, "La casa de Aster-ión," a house whose doors "are open day and night" (Borges, *El Aleph*, 67). And before Cortázar's reflections on the nature of reading and writ-ing posed as a mutual annihilation that is in fact self-slaughter, Borges's final interview between Lönnrot and Scharlach: "'In your labyrinth there are three lines too many,' said [Lönnrot] at last. 'I know of a Greek labyrinth that is a single, straight line. So many philosophers have gotten lost on that line that a mere detective could well get lost too'" (Borges, *Ficciones*, 158). But Cortázar transposes the Eleatic conundrum by cor-recting Lönnrot's argument *more geometrico* (Borges, *Ficciones*, 151). The one-line labyrinth becomes, with a non-Euclidean twist, "simply a Moe-bius strip" (*Prosa*, 11).

The Moebius strip might be conceived, for narrative, as an infinite loop that wards off the double death of the subject and the story, a *cuento de nunca acabar* analogous to Borges's race of Achilles and the tortoise – or so it is for John Barth (1–2; see also 37). But for Cortázar it is rather the *hilo conductor* that leads him out of the strictures of Borges's labyrinth by displacing all sense of an ending, that is to say, by abandoning sequen-tiality and its correlative logic. The Moebius strip of stars above or of eels below (*Prosa*, 71), and more so the ring that joins the eels to the stars, obverse and reverse on a single side, is the mathematical model for the alternative logic of the breach, simultaneously a figure of continuity and of discontinuity. And it may even be that through the logic of the Moe-bius strip, all of Cortázar's writing is a *prosa del observatorio:* Perspective is the crucial but unstable element, which, in its shifts, makes a single story line appear two-sided, only to reveal an unsuspected unity.[1]

Even the primal scene is a scene of instruction (Bloom), a confronta-tion with what is more primal still. Cortázar met Borges in such a scene and translated Yu Tsun's Garden of Forking Paths to the Jardin des Plantes of his "Axolotl," and the bifurcating lines of a temporal labyrinth into the geometrical problem of a Moebius strip (though not, or at least not only, as Bertín Ortega imagined it) in which one and the other side of the glass in the aquarium turn out to be the same side. And it is to this scene that he obsessively returns, as he does, for instance, in *Rayuela,* where Talita is arrested on her plank bridge, a victim of Zeno, unable to cross until Oliveira eliminates the distinction between this and that side (Talita and la Maga) in the transfigurative experience of a purloined kiss in the morgue.

Even and ever more primal, Cortázar's myth of rape, the motor of metamorphosis, as it was for Ovid and the Greeks, assimilates the geometry of the Moebius strip, most explicitly in the rape of Janet under the title of "Anillo de Moebius" in the late story collection, *Queremos tanto a Glenda.* But if Freud was wrong and Abraham and Torok right, then the primal scene is not a true eyewitness account, but rather a lie intended to guard the secret of a source of shame. The Wolfman's recollection through analysis of coitus between his father and mother, may have been a cover-up (Abraham and Torok, 1976). The omniscient narrator in Cortázar's "Anillo de Moebius" might then be ranged alongside Freud: He allows the eyewitness to be distracted too easily from the real trauma. There and elsewhere, the secret trauma, figured as rape for Cortázar, is a vicious allegory for the subjection of the reader to the "tradition and commandment" of the text. If he designates such a reader as *hembra* in *Rayuela,* the term pertains far more to Oliveira than to la Maga, and most of all to the early erudition of Cortázar himself.

From victim to victimizer, another reflexive arc: an eye for an eye, a rape for a rape. The would-be *lector macho* will avenge his emasculation in the fantasy of a resurrected Actaeon. Indeed, he has already done so at Jaipur in Jai Singh's "maniacal and cadenced retaliation of an Endymion who turns the tables and hurls a net of marble spasms against Selene" (*Prosa,* 45). The writer, analogously, would throw off his passivity, his sleep beneath a panoply of captivating allusions, and free his page of its explicit references. Such, at least, was Cortázar's promise to himself as he worked on *62* (see *Ultimo,* 105, upper story): "it is possible that [the reader of *62*] may not have noticed that its writing does away with all immediate adherence, that the references to others' points of view, the quotations of authors or deeds sympathetically linked to the central plot, had been eliminated for the purposes of a narrative as linear and direct as possible" (*Ultimo* 104, upper story). But the flight from the characteristic excesses of *Rayuela* as an encyclopedic catalogue of high and low culture threatens to trap Cortázar in Lönnrot's rectilinear labyrinth. The active repression of the pleasures of allusion leads inevitably, it might appear, to a return of the repressed primal scene of instruction. Thus, *62* gives the lie to the claim in "La muñeca rota" that "It is rare that the characters allude to

other literary elements or texts that their situation momentarily para-
phrases: the whole is reduced to some references to Debussy, a book by
Michel Butor, a bibliographic item concerning the countess Erszebet
Bathori, vampire" (*Ultimo* 104, upper story). The explicit reference to
Butor in the opening pages introduces an uncanny coincidence ("coinci-
dencias inquietantes," *Ultimo* 105, upper story) between an allusion in
Butor's text and a random snatch of dialogue overheard in a café. But
below the surface of explicit reference, the situation translates the opening lines of Borges's "Tlön, Uqbar, Orbis Tertius": Juan, too, owes the discovery of "another order" (*62*, 10) – the order of coincidence itself, of the
"*clot*" ("coágulo," *62*, 8; Boldy's emphasis), the order of Moebius – to the
conjunction of a mirror and a book (see Borges, *Ficciones*, 13).

Yet if Cortázar must always separate himself anew from Borges, the
Moebius strip has a flip side in the period of gestation of *62*, of the assembly of *Ultimo round* and *La vuelta al día en ochenta mundos,* and the trip to
India. This is also the period of his work on the edition of *Paradiso* and
his essay "Para llegar a Lezama" (originally published in *Unión* [Havana]
in 1967). In this light the same opening passage of *62* reads as an implicit
reference to Lezama, who is present in the *comensal gordo* himself, whose
large appetite and equivocal French ground the linguistic duplicity that
confounds, momentarily, even a practiced interpreter like Juan, like Julio
– "'*Quisiera un castillo sangriento* [I would like a bloody castle],' the fat fellow diner had said" (*62*, 7); "*Je voudrais un château saignant,* the fat fellow
diner had said" (*62*, 8). The logic of the Moebius strip seamlessly joins
the opening line of "Tlön" to the closing line of *Paradiso*, where the voice
of Oppiano Licario, a *mémoire d'outre-tombe*, presides over a ghostly scene
of instruction and announces, "we can begin" (Lezama, *Paradiso*, 490).
And so he does. He begins *62*, a tale of discovery, in which an apparently
fictitious world, *la ciudad*, invades, reforms, and disintegrates quotidian
reality (see Borges, *Ficciones*, 18); and in the wreck of causality and familiar forms of coherence: "Everywhere the reminiscence of an uncondi-
tional [*un incondicionado*] that we do not know, engendered by a causality in the visible, that we regret like the lost city that we recognize anew"
(Lezama, *Obras*, 2:1215).

### Double Reflex

*. . . I only find that approximate word: ingenuousness. An American ingenu-
ousness, insular in the plain and simple sense, an American innocence.*

(*La vuelta*, 2:54)

Play it, che.

*. . . inexhaustible juvenile paideuma*

(Lezama Obras, 2:1187)

Aligning his reading with the paradigm of the *Club de la Serpiente* of *Rayuela* and the quirky, close-knit collection of friends and lovers of *62* then in the offing, Cortázar focuses on Lezama through the lens of an imaginary "club *very exclusive*" (*La vuelta,* 2:42) of potential readers, a defense of *Paradiso* against a broader and disingenuous readership that enfolds *Rayuela* as well (ibid. 2:57). Therein lies a clue: The creation of a mythic "Lezama Adam before the fall" (ibid. 2:54) constitutes a rewriting of *Rayuela* by imagining a super-Traveler – implicitly as a foil to Cortázar's own role as a redeemed Oliveira – an American who achieves spiritual enlightenment without the apprenticeship of European *Wanderjahre.*

Lezama repays the compliment, translating the epithet "ingenuousness" into the denomination of Cortázar as pupil, *paideuma:* "'a learner rather,' says Dedalus" (Joyce, 35). The variation on Cortázar's critical theme is not unambiguous. Lezama writes as a reader of *Rayuela* and of "Para llegar a Lezama," but not yet of *62,* so he needs to foretell, rather than simply describe, the beginning of "the other novel" that is to come. For Lezama, the pupil is still an Icarus, and "The verbal icarus ended in the perplexities of wax" (*Obras,* 2:1187). Lezama applauds the exuberance of *Rayuela,* but in defining it as a labyrinth, the principal trope of his essay, he also condemns it to a waxy translucence, never a true transparency, "a grotesque and irreparable breach between what is said and what one wished to say, between the breath inspired into the word and its configuration in the visible" (ibid.).

A gloss of Lezama is perhaps always in order. All the more so in that the structuring principle of his prose is the gloss: expanding restatements of a nucleus which, however, in Lezama's work is often omitted and always evasive. It is the structuring principle of *62* as well: a long narrative gloss on its first, oracular line – as is, say, Blanchot's *Le pas-au-delà.* The gloss I choose here is Lezama's own, as he traces the distinction between the sacred spirit (or even the divine inspiration) of the Word and written texts through the two registers of Cortázar's polyphony:

That labyrinth [*Rayuela*] allows itself to be penetrated by an ancestral language, where one finds the stammering of the chief of the tribe, and by an esperanto, a universal language of clues and roots that is reduced from the former by an analytical decantation. There is an interposition in the ancestral language, the accumulation of unmediated speech, behind the words of communication hide or half-open others that weigh as much as their other external manifestation. Sequestered beats, contractions, creakings that breathe secretly behind an extended and visible verbal mass. The other language, an esperanto of the late Joyce, that places an infinite scenography behind the unmediated speech, a dilated concentricity that proceeds through dilated irradiations. (*Obras,* 2:1193)

Lezama then attempts to situate Cortázar's characteristic voice as it is framed between the polar opposition of those languages, while recalling, fleetingly, the dialogue in progress between his own essay and "Para llegar a Lezama" (recalling that his own essay glosses not only itself but also Cortázar's). "Between both languages," writes Lezama, "stretches a labyrinth where the emphasis and belly laughs, the oaths and the blows are interwoven in nucleii and in the infinity of *sandy* folds" ("pliegues arenosos," *Obras,* 2:1193; my emphasis). This last image, that is, picks up Cortázar's thread: "Para llegar a Lezama" is a title derived from Lezama's poem "Para llegar a Montego Bay," whose verses provide an epigraph for Cortázar:

Después que en las arenas, sedosas pausas intermedias,
entre lo irreal sumergido y el denso, irrechazable aparecido,
se hizo el acuario métrico . . .

Afterwards in the sands, silken intermediate pauses
between the submerged unreality and the dense, irrefutable
   appearance,
the metric aquarium was formed. . . .

Ultimately, Lezama's essay is a gloss of his own poetry via a dialogue with Cortázar: the "irreparable breach" a severe version of the "silken pauses," "the submerged unreality" and the "irrefutable appearance" marking the division of language into "unmediated speech" ("the inspired word") and "its other external manifestation" ("the visible"); "pliegues arenosos" (cf. *pliegos sueltos*), a reminder that the sands are pages, at once manifest and invisible – a text, yes, but constantly slipping away like the grains of the hourglass that poetry measures but cannot arrest.

The more immediate subject, however, is *Rayuela,* and Lezama fixes his attention there to close the passage: "With a demoniacal pulse, extraordinarily rich, Cortázar administers those derived conversations with the two languages, between the chief of the tribe and the shipwrecked admiral. One language traces its labyrinth over the other, that of the ancestral hauling and that of the analytical separation, seeming to cite the phrase of Malcolm Lowry that Cortázar liked so much: 'How will the murder victim persuade the murderer not to appear to him?'" (*Obras*, 2:1193; note that the question attributed to Lowry could just as well be Lönnrot's). Though he admires the dexterity, Lezama detects a hierarchical ordering in this superimposition in which Cortázar's game is always lost – the reductive, analytical gloss of Cortázar's modernist irony covering over the sacred language of the primordial tribe, much as even that language in its human expression glosses over a divine intention.

Lezama discerns that Cortázar's very conception of language is predicated upon a breach, a premise that he shares and upon which he himself expounds with frequency, usually through the metaphor of insularity. But Lezama believes firmly in the possibility of the sea voyage that can cross the *pausas intermedias*, that can reach Montego Bay – he calls the crossing poetry – bringing the spirit to rest safely on the sands of the farther shore. If, as he maintains, that same opening is articulated as a labyrinth in *Rayuela*, then Lezama raises a doubt, shared by Oliveira, that the breach can ever be mended and the ancestral language of the tribal elder, whether the hieratic Oppiano Licario or his analogue come down in the world, Morelli, can ever be communicated to and through Cortázar as *paideuma*.

Paradiso *could well not be a novel . . . for the lack of a plot that might give narrative cohesion to the vertiginous multiplicity of a content. . . . Nevertheless, it is not these disorders in the narrative montage that most eliminate the novelistic character from the book:* Paradiso *is removed from the usual concept of the novel in that its events are not situated in a viable (i.e., liveable) spatio-temporal nor psychological flow; in some fashion each and every one of the characters is seen in essence much more than in presence; they are archetypes rather than types. . . . they seem to move in an absolute continuum, outside of all historicity, understanding one another beyond the reader and the immediate circumstances of the story, in a language that is always the same language, and that all reference to cultural and psychological verisimilitude makes immediately inconceivable.* (*La vuelta*, 2:60)

Elementary, my dear Julio, *Choral unity and total dispersion of the individual.* (Lezama, *Obras*, 2:1198)

In contrast to Lezama's suspicion of the irremediable breach in the language of *Rayuela* that buries the sacred under a rich overlay of irony, Cortázar recognizes a wholly other novel, *la otra novela*, in *Paradiso* precisely for its univocity, a stylistic manifestation of what Lezama calls "extasis of participation in the homogenous" (*Obras*, 2:1215; Lezama's emphasis), a dissenting opinion *avant la lettre* to contemporary critical values schooled in the writings of Bakhtin. The analysis is perspicacious. The response is simple: a choral unity. Eschew the high modernist (or late Romantic) faith in style as the fingerprint of literary identity that commits the text to spiritual alienation and formal fragmentation. Sacrifice the individual to a vision of overarching cohesiveness (let Oppiano Licario die and in his place arise the triumvirate of Cemí, Fronesis, and Foción).

But Cortázar did not come to Lezama as a pupil only. He, too, used the occasion of this dialogue to gloss his own concept of "figures":

The problem is not only to replace a whole set of images of the world but, as Morelli says, to go beyond imagery itself, to discover a new stellar geometry that will open new mental galaxies. Here is where the "figures" come in. . . . The concept of "figures" will be of use to me instrumentally, because it provides me with a focus very different from the usual one in a novel or narrative that tends to individualize characters and equip them with personal traits and psychologies. I'd like to write in such a way that my writing would be full of life in the deepest sense, full of action and meaning, but a life, action, meaning that would no longer rely exclusively on the interaction of individuals, but rather on a sort of superaction involving the "figures" formed by a constellation of characters. I realize that it isn't at all easy to explain this. . . . (Harss and Dohman, 236)

The source of his theoretical formulation is not in Lezama's work, close as the affinity might be, but rather was already present in the words attributed to Morelli in chapter 62 of *Rayuela:* "'If I were to write that book, standard behaviors (including the most unusual, the deluxe category) would be inexplicable by the normal psychological instruments . . .'" (417). Yet a full explanation remains difficult for Cortázar at that moment, because his Oliveira, however suggestive, may always be brought back to the plane of a personal psychology, his most exceptional moments still comprehensible within a scheme stretched only far enough to include the deluxe model of hallucination. The figures, were Cortázar able to execute them, would carry him beyond *Rayuela,* dispersing the individual into a constellation of characters whose unity of action exceeded the bounds of their self-consciousness. Instructions for a model kit.

*I am not a critic: some day, which I suspect will be distant, this prodigious summa will find its Maurice Blanchot, because it is from that race that the man will need to be who might penetrate this fabulous larvario* (*La vuelta,* 2:45). [Translator's note: Lezama's "larvario," recalling the interests of Oppiano

Licario, may be an experimental chamber or laboratory of morphological change, such as larvae undergo; but Latin "larva" is also a ghost, specter, or hobgoblin, and has so remained as a secondary meaning in Spanish, hence "larvario" may also be a collection of ghosts, an enchanted dwelling, a *casa tomada.*]

Lezama had not, has not, found his Blanchot. Nor Cortázar. The Blanchot who, for instance, was also no critic, but rather raised the question of what criticism might be from the perspective of the breach: "poetry has a form, the novel has a form [*Blanchot's note:* Or, better yet, poetry, the novel is form, a word which now, far from clarifying anything, bears the full weight of the interrogation]; research, that in which the movement of all research is at stake, seems to ignore that it has none, or, what is worse, refuses to question itself concerning that which it borrows from tradition" (*L'Entretien,* 1) – a question that Blanchot poses thus: "How to speak in such a way that speech is essentially plural?" (ibid., 9).[2]

*Larvario, eh? Tú tampoco has encontrado a esa Mme. Bauchot, grandote porteño.*

### Putting His Camera Aside, Julio Has a Vision

Julio takes his camera to Jaipur, takes his photos of the observatory, and takes them home to Paris, to Saignon. And he begins to wait (*l'attente,* one of Blanchot's names for the breach). The pictures of the observatory are not yet ready to be the *Prosa del observatorio.* Jai Singh's cosmic erotomania is a story worth telling. But the apprenticeship of *Rayuela,* the assembly of *Ultimo Round,* the photos themselves, had shown that to escape the labyrinth of Western rationality required a breach, first, across which the two opposite sides could yet be one – "a sort of apex of the theme of the double, to the extent that they would tend to illustrate connections, concatenations existing between different elements that, from a logical standpoint, would seem to be entirely unrelated," Cortázar says (Harss and Dohman, 239) – a Moebius strip. A stage is missing as yet in the metamorphosis. The photos, in all their ghostly splendor, are yet an incomplete or intermediary form. The unseen stars require a double. The years pass. He reads, by chance I suppose, "an article by Claude Lamotte published in *Le Monde,* París, April 14, 1971" (*Prosa,* 5):

Know, Apollo has become the God of newspapermen. And his servant is whoever tells him the facts truly (Hölderlin, "Die beschreibende Poesie," 1:229). A tenacious fact in the madness of Hölderlin: Sr. Scardinelli stuck his tongue at him from a mirror. To intuit as a central continuum of the novel the absorbing serpent known as *lampalagua*, that swallows an air like a magnet and attracts the distant and monstrous to the instantaneity of its transmutative dream. (Lezama, *Obras*, 2:1207)

. . . Hölderlin has read Marx and doesn't forget it. (*Prosa*, 79)

where he learns about *anguilas* – their procreation in the Caribbean, their long ocean crossing in the form of "minute and oily *larvae*" (*Prosa*, 17; my emphasis) to the rivers of Europe, their final transmutation into the *anguilas* who return to the Caribbean to spawn – through the research of scientists. Of these, he addresses one:

> dear señora Bauchot,
> tonight I have seen the river of eels
> I have been in Jaipur and in Delhi
> I have seen the eels in the rue du Dragon in Paris . . .
> (*Prosa*, 57)

"They will have landed," thinks Lily Brisco. (Woolf, 309).

Julio has had his vision and the book is completed before the year is out.

### Dispensable Chapter: Julio Makes a Camera

In a few brief pages in *Ultimo Round,* which is to say between the trip to India and the publication of *Prosa del observatorio,* Julio, or perhaps *mi paredro,* calls upon Polanco to be his witness, the world of science requiring such proof of the "reproducibility of research findings." But the inference of continuity with *62* – name: Polanco; temperament: irascible – is undermined, literally, by a text placed beneath much though not all of "Los testigos," recounting there on the ground floor of the two-story book the critical mischances of Julián Garavito (Julio Garabatos? Jules the Scribbler?), who startles Cortázar by informing him that the Luis Funes of "Sobremesa" must be the same character as the Luis Funes of "Bestiario." "I find it dizzying when they come to me and tell me you used the same character in two stories in order to demonstrate the constant," writes Cortázar (*Ultimo*, 30, ground floor); and yet, "half perplexed and half hopeful; it may just be true" (ibid. 31, ground floor). It may just be that this Polanco is *the* Polanco and that "Los testigos" is a chapter *de otros lados* (*Rayuela*, 405) of *62*. Even so, Polanco declines his "moral obligation" (*Ultimo*, 33, upper story), so I will attend to the experiment in progress myself.

Julio, I'll call him that, has his reading of *Oliver Twist* interrupted by a fly gone belly-up ("one of those flies" – there were three – "was flying

upside down" [*Ultimo*, 28, upper story]) and a radical departure from the
novel ensues – not the other novel, but *the* novel, Dickens, no less.

"And what I read first were . . . Dickens, T. S. Eliot," Rosario Ferré said to me.
(Bush, 75)

Experiments in narrative do not always require ever more *scriptible* texts
(Barthes, *S/Z*) like *62,* but rather, as Borges already anticipated in
"Pierre Menard," revised strategies of reading may suffice. And the new
reader may be no more than *desocupado,* in search of distraction from the
realities of Paris, Vienna, London, or Saignon, and may continue to find
distraction even with book in hand. No text, no discourse impervious to
the breach.

And so one courses through the forest clearings analogously to the way one
discourses through classrooms, from classroom to classroom, with vivid
attention that drops off at times – surely – and even collapses, thus opening
a clearing in the continuity of the thought to which one is listening: the missing word that never will return, the meaning of a thought that departed.
(Zambrano, 17)

------------------------------------------------

----------------------------------------

The text to which the text refers is missing in the original manuscript [Ed.]
(Lezama, *Oppiano,* 185)

The temporal and spatial coordinates of Dickens's London, the London
of Nancy and Sykes, are overlaid by a new plot.[3]

The relation between Dickens and the fly appears entirely fortuitous,
but Polanco reveals the overarching *figure* in a surreptitious translation in
his peroration:

"Look, it isn't normal or decent for a fly to fly on its back. It's not even logical, to tell the truth."

"I'm telling you that's how it's flying," I shouted, shocking some local
bystanders.

"Of course it's flying that way. But in reality that fly keeps flying like any
fly, only it turned out to be the exception. That it gave a half twist [*media
vuelta*] is all there is to it." (*Ultimo,* 33, upper story)

The *media vuelta* or half-*twist* of the fly translates Dickens title – a coincidence, like the sudden appearance of the dog Rilke just at the moment
when Cortázar had heard the echo of "a Rilkean voice" while reading the
poetry of Graciela de Sola on a morning in Saignon (*Ultimo,* 16, upper
story), or like the intersection of a stray allusion to Chateaubriand in a
book by Butor and the voice of the fat fellow diner ordering his *château*

*saignant?* The breach disrupts one logic to implant another, the logic of the constellated figures, the logic of the Moebius strip, whose geometry is realized in practice by giving a surface a half-twist. *La constante*, then, is not so much Polanco as the fly, or more precisely its violation of the rules of flight, "the canonical posture disdained" (*Prosa*, 44), as Cortázar says of Jai Singh's rape of the stars.

(A psychoanalysis of the text might suspect the bravado and recon-struct a primal scene in which the *lector macho* is forced to succumb to a *noche boca arriba:* "Hélène's rape of Celia, that is not *of* a woman but *by* a woman – the agent" [*Final del juego*, 170] – may be the rule rather than the exception for Cortázar. Hence, Polanco's repugnance in the face of the inverted posture of the fly, and Julio's anxiety: "my diminutive although *alarming* discovery" [*Ultimo*, 29, upper story; my emphasis].) The discovery of a missing word, or rather, since the primal scene may be expected to obscure more than it reveals, the maddening buzz of an allo-some (Abraham and Torok) and its variants in the lexicon of the text, the haunting of an incubus ("íncubo," *La vuelta*, 2:54).

Julio acts to realize his twin goals, "to investigate and to communicate to the world of science" (*Ultimo*, 29, upper story). He recognizes that the rapid to and fro of the fly will inhibit his designs. So he determines to employ special research methods: "I decided that the only solution was to go on reducing the dimensions of my room until the fly and I remained enclosed in a minimum of space, an essential scientific condi-tion on the basis of which any observations would be of an indisputable precision (I would keep a diary, take photos, etc.) and would permit me to prepare the corresponding communication" (*Ultimo*, 31, upper story). The laboratory setup is a slapstick comedy. Julio gradually empties his room of human furnishings as he installs a series of cardboard parti-tions that diminish the flight path of the upside-down fly: "the last set of screens that reduced the observation space to such a point that it was no longer possible for me to remain standing and I had to construct for myself an angle of observation on the floor" (*Ultimo*, 32, upper story). Looking up, presumably, like Jai Singh at his stars.

The method appears to replicate Lönnrot's trap in three dimensions. On the one hand, successive reductions of space will never bring Julio quite close enough; whereas, on the other, his attempts to do so succeed in building a labyrinth ("At this point in my efforts the problem was to get in and out" [*Ultimo*, 33, upper story]). The procedure is that of Cortázar's own "Casa tomada," only seen from the other side of the door, were it still licit to speak of this side and the other side. But I suppose it is not. Instead, in this parody of the observatory, Julio and the fly inhabit the camera obscura, again like Jai Singh within the astronomical machines at Jaipur. The hybrid monster, an insouciant but still a pathetic thing, is made up of the copresence of man and beast in the maze.

### An Inconclusive Unscientific Supposition

Chapter 62 of *Rayuela* gave rise to two experiments, two transgressions ("the prefix is added to several others that turn upon the root *gressio:* aggression, regression, and progression are also inherent in the intentions sketched one day in the final paragraphs of chapter 62 of *Rayuela*" [62, 5]). There is *62/modelo para armar,* of course. And there is *Prosa del observatorio.*

First, the formal resemblance. A coincidence identifies a breach, "the congealing outside of time, the privileged horror, exasperating and delicious, of the constellation, the opening to a leap that had to be taken and that [Juan] would not take because it was not a leap to anything definite nor even a leap" (62, 21). No, not so much as a leap. Merely a step, perhaps a faux pas. "Why did I enter the Polidor Restaurant?" (62, 7), *¿por qué di ese paso?* the question that marks the return from the breach in the "Kantian categories," as Cortázar says (Harss and Dohman, 236), to the analytical frame of mind: Juan's defense against epiphany. While in *Prosa del observatorio,* as the camera shows, one may but need not enter through the front door, the first page. The formal analogue appears rather late, just before the apostrophe to Mme. Bauchot. There it is not a matter of coincidence precisely, for space and time are simply left out of account, but perhaps *rapport:* "Entrons dans ce rapport" (Blanchot, *Le pas,* 7).

Lamotte's newspaper article (or Butor's book) entering into relation with "to step on an eel in rue du Dragon" (PO, 55) – *gradus* (whence "gressio"), both "a step, pace" and "that on which one steps" (Lewis and Short). *Prosa del observatorio* being the more radical departure, Cortázar does not withdraw into the analytical mode, does not raise a question, "Supposing that he who tells a tale does so in his own way, that is, that much has already tacitly been told" (62, 18). But I shall. Why did he step on the *anguila,* do you suppose, why set it underfoot? Saint Julio – le *pauvre* – with no more than an eel to slay on the rue du Dragon. "Things ridiculous or terrible" (*Prosa,* 55): Without this step the observatory of Jaipur remains on the other side, the night sky, that "dragon with so many eyes" (*Prosa,* 75), merely above; with this step Cortázar translates himself from the one side to the other, and from below to above and back again. He loops the loop. He discovers his Moebius strip: "an eel that is a star that is an eel that is a star that is an eel" (*Prosa,* 13).

Then a formal distinction. *62* may in fact be "the other *novel*" that
Lezama glimpses through *Rayuela. Prosa del observatorio* is not. Its genre is
without clear designation. "Discourse" suggests itself, as the term is thematized in the text in the "discurso, decurso" of "the Atlantic eels and the
eel words" (*Prosa*, 11) and, moreover, it is the same to and fro movement
(*discursus*, a running to and fro; Lewis and Short) that characterizes the
frenetic flight of the fly:

... his discourse [referring to Pascal] ... is manifest as a dis-cursus, a
course disunited and interrupted that, for the first time, imposes the idea of
the fragment as coherence. (Blanchot, *L'Entretien*, 2–3)

But the term has entered contemporary critical vocabulary on a different
tangent. So instead I will designate the genre of *Prosa del observatorio* an
inconclusive unscientific supposition. In this light it may be seen more
clearly as a return to the form of chapter 62 of *Rayuela*, remarking that
Lamotte's article from *Le Monde* cited in *Prosa del observatorio* takes the
place of the note on neurobiology attributed to *L'Express* by Morelli (*Rayuela*, 415–16 n. 1). *Supponere*, I recall, is "to put in the place of another,"
but also "to substitute falsely or fraudulently," takes all but the place, as
it is not set below, at the foot of the page in a counterfeit of academic
style, but rather suffuses the whole and animates the text.

The history of scientific observation is the logical link that brings Jai
Singh together with Mme. Bauchot, a categorical similarity in the foreground that frames the breach. But *Prosa del observatorio* is written on the
Moebius strip and so pursues a different mode of concatenation. The
*anguilas* are an undercurrent beneath the passion of Jai Singh, a hilari-
ous and a horrifying dispersal of the individual in the multiple (Serres).
Far more than Juan and Hélène and their constellation of intimates in
*62*, more even than the stars in the Indian sky, the *anguilas* embody the
"chemical theory of thinking" of Morelli's Swede: "Such are things, an
agreeable extrapolation suffices to *postulate* a human group that believes
it reacts psychoanalytically in the classical sense of that old, old word, but
that represents no more than an instance of that flow of animate matter"
(*Rayuela*, 47, my emphasis).

To postulate: *62/ modelo para armar;* to suppose, no more: *Prosa del
observatorio.*

### Notes

1. " ... in science we must give unambiguous communication the highest priority, since reproducibility of research findings is an indispensable require-

ment for valid science. Still, I would argue that clear communication must
be valued also in literary analysis, and that, even if scientific terms such as
nonlinearity and stochasticity are permitted broader connotations, it is
important for the practitioners of postmodernism to be aware of their original scientific meanings, lest they be led to false conclusions through quasi-
scientific arguments," writes John W. Clark from the McDonnell Center for
Space Sciences (236) in reply to John R. Rosenberg's discussion of Espron-
ceda. So, too, I suppose, for mathematical terms.

An unusual dialogue, and an argument from an unexpected quarter in
favor of the etymologizing, a poor man's philology, that has been the lot of
literary criticism for the past generation. But who are these practitioners?
Shall we disqualify the use of Mandelbrot's term *fractals* to Brazilian poet
Horacio Costa, who appropriates it as the title of his excellent collection of
verse, the archly (that is, self-consciously and at times self-parodying) postmodern *O livro dos fracta*? Or is it only off-limits to Rosenberg? Should
Cortázar hunt down his old geometry textbooks – that is, if he may be considered postmodern (by no means an open-and-shut case but, in an anticipation of the term, "postmodernism" may have been what he meant when
he referred to "the Atomic Age" ("the voice of the announcers on Radio
Luxemburg mixing with Buddhist litanies at dusk, *mantras + flashes:* WE ARE IN
THE ATOMIC AGE, BABY" [*Ultimo* 15, upper story; the emphasis is Cortázar's and
the italicized words are in English in the original]). Should I?

The polemic of *Prosa del observatorio* focuses directly upon "the very practice of science," which, Clark states, "presupposes the existence of an objective reality possessing quantifiable spatial and temporal regularities – otherwise science would not make any sense at all" (245). Supposition is
Cortázar's stock-in-trade, but not presupposition, especially not those presuppositions, above all, the last about making sense. He might well have
found Clark's very next remark more heartening, however: "And, as I have
stressed, we cannot leave Mother Nature out of the loop" (245), though
Cortázar's fiddling with geometry suggests that he would have rather stressed
the loop. Clark, too, may have mislaid the stress, which, if my ear is rightly
tuned, falls on the *we*, we scientists.

Well, if it must be us and them, *we* cannot leave out the text, whereas Clark
begins his discussion – compelling and above all lucid throughout, though
also, as he confesses, "brusque" (246) – by doing just so (227). Were we,
whoever we are, to return to *El diablo mundo*, a different question would arise
than that which concerns Professor Clark, namely, does the vocabulary of
chaos theory, as Rosenberg presents it, illuminate the fragmentary character
of the poem? Does it allow an approach to the text that remains closed to the
vocabulary of the Romantics themselves, or is his critical apparatus more
obtrusive than instructive?

And those other practitioners? Cortázar determines to write, is determined
to write a book that is two-in-one – "In its way, this book is many books, but
above all it is two books" (*Rayuela*, ix) – a hybrid. Shall he make metaphors of
the minotaur? It's been done. He did it himself. Move on. Open a physical
breach by cutting the book and refer to the continuously paginated section

above as the "upper story" (*Ultimo* 219, upper story) and that below as "ground floor" (*Ultimo* 220, ground floor). An architectural imago. A house divided. The layout allows for the multiplicity of *Rayuela* without the counterrevolutionary *Tablero de dirección*. But the crucial issue remains how to conceptualize the relation that is merely materialized by the breach. This is not quite the same as looping the loop in the lab with Mother Nature, as Professor Clark rightly acknowledges ("Literary theorists as well as creators of literature are continuously involved with manipulations of virtual reality and of meaning. In their world, they are free to construct, deconstruct, fragment, even to deny reality. In science we do not have those luxuries" [245] – though not, I reiterate, to deny the reality of the text.)

Working with a static version of the same format in his discussion of Blanchot and Shelley, Derrida theorized the breach in terms of translation and comparative literature. And I have drawn from that source. Cortázar is under no obligation to be so explicit. He is revealing, however, in the centerpiece of *Ultimo Round:* "La muñeca rota" on the upper story and "Cosas de Polanco" on the ground floor, in the middle of their respective series of pages (see also the photo of the doll in the middle of the front cover; but symmetry is not everything: "Mensajes recurrentes," which details more *cosas de Polanco,* begins on the left column of the cover). The upper and ground floors reattach here with a twist. The framing device around the photos of the doll suggest a negative, but a positive image is reproduced. Positive, negative – the remembering of texts above, the dismembering of the doll below – metaphors for the obverse and reverse: the invitation to view one and see the other, two sides becoming one. A Moebius strip.

Cortázar takes a narrow view of science when he declares that "The poet must devote himself to hunting for the exceptions and leave the laws to the scientists and the serious writers," though his explanation is telling: "Exceptions . . . offer what I call an opening or a fracture, and also, in a sense, a hope" (Harss and Dohman, 243). It gives some sense of the evolution of the relation between literature and science to find that his argument is a precise inversion of Arnold's apology for literature against a scientific method, which, for him, consisted of the "unsatisfactory and tiresome" effort of "for ever learning lists of exceptions" (336). But Cortázar is chastened to a different view by his reading of Lezama Lima, "Because Lezama is concerned with the total mystery of human beings, *the existence of a universal that governs series as well as exceptions*" (*La vuelta,* 2:63, quoting *Paradiso*). From here it requires no more than a half-twist to rejoin to Clark: "The *phenomenon* of chaos certainly demolishes naive, stereotyped 'totalizing, globalizing' Newtonian ideas about how dynamical systems move through time or organize themselves in space. . . . But chaos *theory* seeks new totalizing, globalizing descriptions in terms of which we may come to a rational understanding of these putatively radical or 'deviant' forms of behavior. To the scientist, the excitement of chaos science (beyond the sense of liberation inspired by the beauty and richness of nonlinear systems) is that chaos theory is revealing the *order* underlying the overt disorder of chaos" (242). The half-twist would eliminate the word *rational* and translate the dialectic of order and chaos into the confrontation of sense and senselessness. (Certainly, for Lezama sense, meaning, wins out; Cortázar remains skeptical.)

The Moebius strip is by no means chaotic, and yet it still challenges the rational order of an Aristotelian either/or. It also eliminates the breach; at least in theory. A virtual reality. But the textual reality, for Cortázar the practitioner, depends upon the breach that marks the supposition that meaning is possible only in an irreducible plurality of senses.

2. One answer that Blanchot gives to the question comes in the form of a reference to a mathematical model: "so, it is to this hiatus – the strangeness, the infinity between us – that responds, in language itself, the interruption that the waiting introduces. Only let us understand clearly that the arrest here is not necessarily nor simply marked by silence, a blank or void (how vulgar that would be), but by a change in the form or the structure of language (since to speak is first of all to write) – a change comparable metaphorically to that which made of the geometry of Euclid that of Riemann. (Valéry confided to a mathematician that he intended to write – to speak – on a 'Riemann surface')" (*L'Entretien,* 109). Blanchot appends a note to that remark by Valéry in which he recounts the exchange from the point of view of the mathematician M. Montel, citing a passage from Judith Robinson, *L'Analyse de l'esprit dans les Cahiers de Valéry.* I quote his quotation at length, my note on his note: "Mathematicians use a tool called the Riemann surface: it is an ideal notebook containing as many leaves as is necessary, of which the total thickness is always zero, and which are attached one to another according to certain rules. On that multileaved surface, they inscribe numbers of which several occupy the same place on different leaves. In the course of a conversation, Valéry said to me: 'Don't you find that conversations take place on a Riemann surface? I make a statement to you, it is inscribed on the first leaf; but at the same time, I prepare on the second leaf what I will say to you next; and also, on a third leaf, what will come afterwards. On your side, you respond to me on the first leaf, while holding in reserve on other leaves what you count on telling me later.'" Blanchot then comments: "Of course, the image remains very unsatisfactory, since the discourse here, instead of implying a true dehiscence of language, only makes appeal to what one could call the principle of delayed speech" (*L'Entretien,* 109–10 n. 1).

It would be less unsatisfying, however, if, given the infinitely thin girth of the leaves, the various pages were read simultaneously. This would not only give a virtual model, akin to Freud's Mystic Writing Pad, for language as an open semiotic system, but also would illustrate one of the instrumental functions of Cortázar's figures. For it would be possible for a conversation to take place between two such Riemann surfaces in which the notebooks were opened arbitrarily to noncorresponding pages. Any immediate coherence might well be lost (or an unplanned coherence might be discovered), yet were the whole notebook, the whole surface kept in view, the overarching relationship would be clear. Here we have an alternative mathematical model to the Moebius strip for the format of *Ultimo Round.* Moreover, the text of "La muñeca rota" reconfigures *62* as a Riemann surface by recollecting some of the allusions and coincidental associations that are written on

the lower stories of the novel (to recall the architectural metaphor), the supposed pages of the *surface feuilletée,* but rendered invisible there by a willful
act of suppression by the author, or, following this model, by the more than
ideal opacity of the text. Were one to abandon "the school composition or
dissertation" as the model for research (Blanchot, *L'Entretien infini,* 1), I suppose it might be possible to render visible once again the surfaces set under
the discursive exposition. Would the intermittent interposition of quotations, set off in small print and forming an interrupted column of their own,
accomplish that goal?

3. The plot of reading. These words are framed by two conversations. On the
one hand, an interview with Rosario Ferré and Antonio Skármeta, talking
about Cortázar (Bush) as part of a broader dialogue on "La herencia de
Cortázar" in the *Revista de Estudios Hispánicos,* which included, for example,
Carlos Alonso's "Julio Cortázar: The Death of the Author." That conversation continues. And, on the other, not so much a closing frame as an opening door. When I was discussing the formal character of these pages with
Argentine poet Mercedes Roffé, she suggested that I read Charles Bernstein
on Charles Reznikoff – a new, oblique light on Cortázar's "numerical
labyrinth" (Lezama, *Obras,* vol. 2), and more directly on the possibilities of
the essay as a self-questioning form. A new page, too, in the *surface feuilletée.*
A new twist in the plot of reading.

*References*

Abraham, Nicolas, and Maria Torok. *Cryptonymie, Le Verbier de l'Homme aux Loups.*
  Paris: Aubier-Flammarion, 1976.
Alonso, Carlos J. "Julio Cortázar: The Death of the Author." *Revista de Estudios
  Hispánicos* 21, no. 2 (1987): 61–71.
Arnold, Matthew. "Literature and Science." In *Selected Poetry and Prose,* ed. Fred-
  erick L. Mulhauser, 326–46. New York: Holt, Rinehart & Winston, 1960.
Barth, John. *Lost in the Funhouse: Fiction for Print, Tape, Live Voice* (1968). New York:
  Bantam, 1969.
Barthes, Roland. *S/Z.* Paris: Seuil, 1970.
Blanchot, Maurice. *L'Entretien infini.* Paris: Gallimard, 1969.
  *Le Pas au-delà.* Paris: Gallimard, 1973.
Bloom, Harold. *The Anxiety of Influence: A Theory of Poetry.* Oxford: Oxford Uni-
  versity Press, 1973.
Boldy, Steven. *The Novels of Julio Cortázar.* Cambridge University Press, 1980.
Borges, Jorge Luis. *El Aleph.* Buenos Aires: Emecé, 1957.
  *Ficciones.* Buenos Aires: Emecé, 1956.
Bush, Andrew. "'Señalar las discrepancias': Rosario Ferré y Antonio Skármeta
  hablan de Cortázar (Entrevista)." *Revista de Estudios Hispánicos* 21, no. 2
  (1987): 73–87.
Clark, John W. "Views for the Ivory Tower's Basement: A Commentary on 'The
  Clock and the Cloud: Chaos and Order in *El diablo mundo.*'" *Revista de Estu-
  dios Hispánicos* 26, no. 2 (1992): 227–50.
Cortázar, Julio. *Final del juego.* Buenos Aires: Sudamericana, 1964.

*Prosa del observatorio.* Photographs by Cortázar with the collaboration of Antonio Gálvez. Barcelona: Lumen, 1972.

*Queremos tanto a Glenda.* Mexico City: Nueva Imagen, 1980.

*Rayuela.* Buenos Aires: Sudamericana, 1963.

*62/modelo para armar* (1968). Barcelona: Bruguera-Libro Amigo, 1981.

*Ultimo Round.* Mexico City: Siglo XXI, 1969.

*La vuelta al día en ochenta mundos* (1967). Madrid: Siglo XXI de España, 1980.

Costa, Horácio. *O livro dos fracta.* São Paulo: Iluminuras, 1990.

González Echevarría, Roberto. "Los reyes: Cortázar's Mythology of Writing." In *The Voice of the Masters: Writing and Authority in Modern Latin American Literature.* Austin: University of Texas Press, 1985.

Harss, Luis, and Barbara Dohman. *Into the Mainstream: Conversations with Latin American Writers.* New York: Harper & Row/Harper Colophon, 1967.

Joyce, James. *Ulysses.* New York: Random House/Vintage, 1961.

Kaye, G. R. *The Astronomical Observatories of Jai Singh.* Archaeological Survey of India, New Imperial Series, 40. Calcutta: Superintendent Government Printing, India, 1918.

Lezama Lima, José. *Obras completas.* 2 vols. Mexico City: Aguilar, 1977.

*Oppiano Licario.* Mexico City: Era, 1977.

*Paradiso.* Mexico City: Era, 1968.

Ortega, Bertín. "Cortázar: 'Axolotl' y la cinta de Moebius." *Nuevo Texto Crítico* 3 (1989): 135–40.

Rosenberg, John R. "The Clock and the Cloud: Chaos and Order in *El diablo mundo.*" *Revista de Estudios Hispánicos.* 26, no. 2 (1992): 203–25.

Serres, Michel. *Genèse.* Paris: Bernard Grasset, 1982.

Woolf, Virginia. *To the Lighthouse* (1927). New York: Harcourt, Brace & World/Harvest, 1955.

Zambrano, María. *Claros del bosque* (1977). Barcelona: Seix Barral/Biblioteca de Bolsillo, 1988.

# PART THREE
## Reading Politics

# 8

## "Apocalypse at Solentiname" as Heterological Production

*Alberto Moreiras*

### *Political Violence and the Rupture of Mimesis*

If certain segments of Julio Cortázar's text seem to have aged rather dramatically in the last ten years or so, the 1976 short story entitled "Apocalipsis de Solentiname" has not met with the same fate. "Apocalipsis" is a great political text, probably one of the most succinct and economical instances of the testimonial literature of solidarity that arose as a response to the horrifying brutality of the Central American counterinsurgency regimes of the 1970s and 1980s. Yet one grows impatient with critical accounts that cannot manage to justify the effectiveness of Cortázar's text except by recourse to its political intentionality and commitment.[1] Cortázar's short story can move the reader emotionally and politically, just as *Me llamo Rigoberta Menchú, Harvest of Violence, The Massacre at El Mozote* or *Unfinished Conquest* can also move one.[2] But literary effects are not to be automatically identified with the efficacy achieved by a testimonial, social-scientific, journalistic, or historical text. By routinely accepting that the overwhelming human truth embodied in Cortázar's text – that is, the reality of brutal and indiscriminate repression in Central America – is also the overwhelming fact that can account for the story's sustained literary interest, we engage in a dangerous form of political cant. Demanding the truth of political violence in literature is in fact, and taken by itself, not necessarily far from endorsing forms of writing that surreptitiously cater to the kind of postmodern enjoyment that George Yúdice has identified as "the aesthetic fix" provided by the productive representation of abjection (25): Texts such as Omar Rivabella's *Requiem for a Woman's Soul* come to mind; or even a book that has the dubious merit of being among the most repulsive and at the same time the most fascinating of Latin American political/testimonial novels I know, Miguel Bonasso's *Recuerdo de la muerte*.

One must wonder if in fact Cortázar's short story, over and beyond its good intentions, is itself immaculate and totally brutality-free in its rhetorical mechanisms. And one must then confront the disquieting thought that perhaps the enjoyment it provides cannot be totally severed from a certain reenactment within the text, at a certain nonsuperficial level of textual constitution, of the very same violence it so blatantly and efficaciously denounces. Perhaps the political trip that "Apocalipsis de Solentiname" really offers can only be found in that self-confrontation – perhaps it could even be said that, for Cortázar himself, there was nothing in the writing of his short story except for said self-confrontation, a nontrivial descent into a personal heart of darkness that does not disqualify the more obvious call for solidarity in the text, but that, on the contrary, sets the call for solidarity onto firmly political, and not merely pious, ground.

"Apocalipsis de Solentiname" manages to break away from a weary but surprisingly persistent ideologeme: the notion that high literature is structurally conditioned to serve the interests of the hegemonic social formation, as it can only at most engage in a vertical representation of the oppressed from an always already privileged perspective. Granted, the text itself is centrally and symptomatically concerned with the issue: but it effectively enacts it so as to better demolish the conventional responses to it. "Apocalipsis" does not reject, but rather embraces the structural fact of its privileged form of representation, and it does so on the basis of its unavoidable structurality; it does not abdicate from high literature procedures, but on the contrary intensifies them so as to put them at the service of a complex form of solidarity with the oppressed; it renounces the possibility of unmediated commitment by showing that commitment can only be mediated; it returns, finally, to a rigorous, almost uncanny, theoretical self-interrogation through which, and only through which, the very possibility of a literary praxis opens up. In so doing, Cortázar gives literature back to us; that is, he puts it back in business, after retrieving it from the ash heap of history to which a certain pervasive contemporary desperation had consigned it.

But there is something else. "Apocalipsis de Solentiname" might not be primarily concerned with the expression of a solidarity whose necessity Cortázar could in fact have taken for granted, given his long involvement in Latin American struggles for social and political liberation. I think that we have not really started to read the 1976 text, in the sense that we have not begun to consider the extent of the epistemological and aesthetic propositions Cortázar was able to develop and offer to us. "Apocalipsis de Solentiname" is not just another brilliant Cortázar short story but, as I hope to show, a cardinal and emblematic instance of the sort of work that needs to be developed if Latin American literature is to remain a significant site of cultural production over and beyond aesthetic considerations.

Anticipating developments, let me suggest that Cortázar, in "Apocalipsis," was moving toward the full literary expression of something that was already glimpsed in earlier texts, notably *Rayuela*, "Las babas del diablo," even *Prosa del observatorio*, to name just a few: a notion that literature can only properly effect an anaclitic investment in its object of expression that will reveal said object as fully opaque, always resistant to appropriation.[3] "Apocalipsis de Solentiname" moves from a primary investment in an object perceived as originary to a secondary investment in the same object through which the impossibility of recuperation of the object of anaclisis as such is symbolically enacted. "Apocalipsis" will in that sense show itself to be a text pervaded by a thwarted ontological infatuation. What thwarts the ontological drive is the heterological materiality of the real. The greatness of "Apocalipsis" resides in its capacity to affirm a certain constitutive impossibility for the work of art to engage in ontological constructions while at the same time also affirming that the work of art depends, in its very constitution, on such constitutive impossibility. This has serious consequences regarding the possible effects of literature on political thinking and the social articulation of cultural work. For Cortázar, as I will try to show, solidarity cannot depend on mimesis; community cannot depend on ontology. It is rather the rupture of mimesis, and the disaster of ontology, that can make us accept, out of a radical destitution, the common bind on which thinking, literature, and emancipatory politics sometimes blindly thrive.

### *Lying the Truth*

"The jackal howls, but the bus passes" is an intriguing sentence at the beginning of the narration (120; 18).[4] The Spanish reads: "el ómnibus pasa," that word, *ómnibus*, meaning the vehicle that carries all things and all, like a metaphor. To listen to the howl of the jackal when the totality of things moves by, when metaphor slips by and at one with it, implies a certain capacity to empathize with things, to feel pain at a distance, as in sacrifice. Cortázar, both author and narrator, remarks that the small plane that takes him to the primary scene of the text, a Piper Aztec, takes him "straight to the sacrificial pyramid" (120; 19). Pain at a distance finds an apotheosis there, as we shall see. Every sacrificial moment is necessarily, after all, a telepathic moment.

Cortázar will tell us about his visit to "a life surrounded by fear and death" (122; 20), a visit, however, emphatically and apparently not into a heart of darkness, but rather into a "first vision of the world" (121; 20), whose consequence nevertheless will imply "[to cross] a limit" (126; 24; translation modified) and to fully enter the "idiocy" (127; 24; translation modified) of hallucination and delirium (24): that is, the idiocy of the phantom. The jackal in Cortázar's text foretells an extraordinary act of ectoplasmic translation. A jackal is the Central American animal whose howling culturally translates the howling of the wolf in other latitudes: ominous, portentous. There is a dark, hermetic mention of the wolf in "Apocalipsis de Solentiname," but it is so cryptic that one would think it is nothing but language's own joke.

At the beginning of the story Cortázar sees himself dead, at the gates of the otherworld, and imagines that either Saint Peter or his devilish counterpart ask him the customary questions, among them the following: "Don't you think that down there you used to write too hermetically for the people?" (120; 18; translation modified). "The people" is *Volk* in German, and it is true that Cortázar is just about to engage in an experience which is to a certain extent folkloric, because he talks of himself as a visitor or tourist who goes to the Christian community of Solentiname to see and admire the folk painting produced there by Nicaraguan peasants. But *Volk* means "wolf" in Russian. Beyond the fact that a short story partially written in Havana in full contemplation and anticipation of Sandinista insurgency might be quite open to some Soviet influence, one would think that Cortázar has nothing to do with that Russian word. Why, then, the delirious outburst concerning Saint Peter's questions, provided they were Saint Peter's, on hermeticism and the people? There is room to wonder whether in fact something is hidden in the people, whether "the people" conceal(s) something. In any case, I would like to raise the possibility that in Cortázar's cryptic writing about the people, about the folklorist peasant-painters of Solentiname, a hidden wolf might lurk, something like a translated jackal howling at the real. "Apocalipsis de Solentiname" reveals a radical experience of lycanthropy which is likely to stimulate our cathartic, telepathic pain.[5]

"Understand by nihilism a certain kind of critical awareness which will not allow you to make certain affirmative statements when those affirmative statements go against the way things are," says Paul De Man commenting on Walter Benjamin's "The Task of the Translator" (De Man, 104). In translation – translation understood as an "event" – De Man finds a certain active, antimessianic, antiutopian nihilism of which he says that it is "possibly preparatory to a historical act" (103). For De Man, interpreting Benjamin, translation is an antimessianic, antisacred political intervention whose fundamental act is the decanonization of the original. In decanonization "all that is idiomatical, all that is customary, all that is quotidian, all that is nonsacred, all that is *prosaic* in the original" is brought out (97). This revelation, the particular form of apocalypse that Benjamin would place in the realm of "pure language" (*reine Sprache*), is in my opinion the general reference of "Apocalipsis de Solentiname." In the story we can find an instance of resistance literature whose fundamental tactic is not utopian projection but a thinking of mourning, a usage of memory and of mnemonic repetition designed to corroborate a loss and to attempt to survive it in opposition to its sinister attraction.

Two years after writing his story, in 1978, Cortázar commented, at the Stockholm Pen Club:

["Apocalipsis de Solentiname"] narrated a clandestine visit that I paid in 1976 to the Solentiname community, in Nicaragua's great central lake . . . that narration was . . . sadly prophetic, for a year after I wrote it the troops of Dictator Somoza razed and destroyed the small, wonderful Christian community led by one of the great Latin American poets, Ernesto Cardenal. (*Argentina*, 85)

The story ended up being prophetic. If it had not been prophetic, if Somocista troops had not attacked Solentiname, Cortázar's narration would still be available as a written text, but it would have markedly different reading effects. If the story had not been prophetic in the most terrible and elementary way, the question about the intentional genesis of "Apocalipsis de Solentiname" could conceivably be raised with a different force, and might have a larger resonance. The question nevertheless needs to be raised of why, in fact, Cortázar should write a story whose presupposition is the imaginary destruction of the theological community of Solentiname. Obviously enough, Cortázar did not want to be prophetic when he wrote the story. "Apocalipsis de Solentiname" should therefore not be retrospectively interpreted, in view of its lamentably and counterintentionally prophetic content as a sociorealist narration in the traditional sense.

From the perspective of a hypothetical 1976 reader, the sentences pronounced by Cortázar in Stockholm in 1978, sentences that retrospectively interpret the story as a prophetic story, are sentences that lie – sentences that lie the truth, if you wish – and that by doing so rebuild and strengthen a mechanism of concealment that was already present in subdued form in the 1976 text: In 1976, Cortázar represents himself as a foreigner who witnesses and gives testimony of an atrocious happening. But that testimony, that is, the truth of what Cortázar sees, can only be given, in 1976, as a phantom, hallucinatory projection upon the libidinal screen that Cortázar keeps in his Paris house. Cortázar's testimony, far from being a realist testimony, is, in "Apocalipsis de Solentiname," primarily a libidinal projection. When, in 1978, that libidinal projection is understood to be prophetic, and therefore true, Cortázar commits fraud: He presents his symbolic production as in a strong sense engaging the order of the real. In his 1978 intervention Cortázar encrypts himself, so to speak, in the real. The alleged realism of "Apocalipsis" becomes an important mechanism of concealment superimposed to the text: a caesura, a rift, an interruption at the most essential level of meaning constitution.

But isn't this break in mimesis, this caesura in mimetic procedure, really consubstantial to all literature?[6] Fraud may in fact be structurally necessary to realist literature if, as Nicolas Abraham and Maria Torok say, "the metapsychological concept of reality refers to the place, in the psychic apparatus, where the secret is buried" ("Topography," 62). Abraham and Torok allude to the well-known analytic fact that "the notion of reality is one we do encounter . . . albeit in a disguised, even unrecognizable form. For us, as analysts, it is this very masking and denial which attests, more than anything, to the presence of that which has the status of reality for our patients" (62). I do not want to psychoanalyze the text: only to say that the text itself is following a psychoanalytic notion of reality such as the one just defined.

Which would then be the secret of the Cortazarian text? From the perspective of the secret, from the hermetic key announced in the delirious sentences concerning Saint Peter or the devil, "Apocalipsis de Solentiname" would be a way of talking impossibly about the secret, of talking silently. In that specific kind of lying-the-truth I would locate the pulsional aim of Cortázar's narration. Accordingly, Cortázar's narration, following Abraham's and Torok's vocabulary, must be considered "cryptophoric." And "for the cryptophore, a desire, already directly fulfilled, lies buried, equally incapable of rising or disintegrating. Nothing can undo its having been consummated or efface its memory. This past is thus present in the subject as a *block of reality;* it is referred to as such in denials and disavowals" (65). Let us, then, try to unbury the destructive revelation "Apocalipsis" hides, but not completely. I am of course arguing that a key to the secret is at least formally given in the translation apparatus present in the text – an apparatus geared for a decanonization of the original understood as the site of a secret, that is, of a repressed desire; a textual symptom, then.

### Two Writings, and the Semiotic Ghost

In the story Cortázar, at the same time narrator and character, goes to the theological community of Solentiname for a visit and there he sees the naïf paintings made by the peasants: little houses, midget cows, cane fields, green-eyed horses, Arcadia. In those paintings Cortázar recognizes or identifies the possibility of a "first vision of the world" (121; 20). He takes some pictures, and when he projects them onto his slide screen back home in Paris, it so happens that the images in which he finds himself engulfed have apparently nothing to do with what he thought he had photographed: They are images of torture, death, destruction (*somocistas* against *campesinos*). I will understand in this scenario a reference to two different possibilities of writing: on the one hand, a foundational writing, orphic, world-giving, an ontological and poetic writing, which is the one offered in the peasant paintings; a writing engaged in the equivalence or unity between representation and being; on the other hand, a kind of writing that I will call sacrificial, following Georges Bataille's notion: a writing of expenditure and horror, nihilist, essentially destructive, which is the sort of writing that is carried out in the act of translation that Cortázar's camera operates on the pictographic text.[7] The relationship between the two forms of writing defines the cryptophoric dimension of the text.

Those two kinds of writing are not in a balanced relationship within the text. They are not homological, but heterological with respect to each other. Translation between them, from one into the other, which is ostensibly the fundamental theme of the story, only manages to establish their reciprocal discord and heterology. Through his own autographic investment in the second form, through his use of the photographic metaphor for it, a metaphor of metaphor, properly speaking, that he had already used for similar goals in "Las babas del diablo," Cortázar seems to privilege the second kind of writing, a writing of expenditure and destruction, which is a kind of writing refractory to any appropriation by the good conscience, hostile to any domesticating reinscription. In *Hopscotch* (1963) Cortázar had also attempted to enframe at the same time poetry and the disavowal of poetry, looking not for a writing of addition – poetic accumulation, construction of a world – but for "an implacable *subtraction.*"[8] What are the political consequences of a theory, and a practice, of untamable writing – a writing affirming loss, dissolution, and death? How can we understand it as a writing of resistance, with an emancipatory potential?[9]

Cortázar's second writing, a writing of translation and subtraction, is a writing upon the first kind of writing, poetic writing. The second writing is then not just a resistance against the formation of a world, but also an active belligerence against it. We are dealing with a conception of writing where what receives privilege is apparently the nihilist moment – an antipoetic, antisymbolic writing. The fact that Cortázar's way of representing his notion of a second writing passes through the phantasmalization of murder and torture must be read as follows: In the struggle between foundational writing and destructive writing, the former is apparently subordinate, and it prepares its reprisal as such. The second writing is always a translation of the first: translation happens out of a lack in the original, but translation, always a supplement, cannot in itself reach sufficiency. The second writing essentially depends upon the first: foundational, naïve, first writing preinscribes all that is depraved and abject, and what is depraved and abject is so in virtue of its opposite possibility. Emancipation is the theologico-pastoral possibility of the first writing, but the struggle for its manifestation necessarily involves a heterological dimension: the ontology that underlies any emancipatory project is thus subject to heterological critique.

Two semiotic systems are at play: one geared toward an original epiphany; the second one, translating it. In their ceaseless confrontation a mimetic moment comes into play that uncannily doubles them, and releases undecidability. This doubt is, finally, the certain heterological projection of Cortázar's narrative: a doubt that belongs in the text itself, that constitutes the text as a text caught up in the impossibility of accepting an ontology or a dialectics and the necessity of affirming such an impossibility as paradoxically constitutive. The text is cryptophoric precisely because in it the secret, the buried ontological desire, "is equally incapable of rising or of disintegrating" (Abraham and Torok, "Tropology," 65); it is there, but always in the form of a block of reality (a possibility granted by ontological writing) present in the denials and disavowals orchestrated by the second writing.

Let me propose the term *semiotic ghost* to refer to what is produced in the heterological relation between those two forms of writing.[10] The semiotic ghost is a translation effect. It occurs at the intersection between original text and the task of translation – an intersection between two sign systems. It happens when the symbolic fracture in the original, the originary crypt, stretches over into its cosymbolic supplement, translation; when the translator, in the process of fulfilling his task, touches the crypt, and experiences it, we could say, telepathically.

At the beginning of the story Cortázar lands in San José de Costa Rica, the one-before-the-last stage where he will board a Piper Aztec plane for Nicaragua. Cortázar cannot help thinking that the plane takes him "straight into the sacrificial pyramid" (120; 19). During the press conference in San José someone asks, "Why was *Blow Up* so different from your short story?" (119; 18). *Blow Up* is a film made by Michelangelo Antonioni about or from "Las babas del diablo." Between *Blow Up* and "Las babas del diablo" there is something other than a simple process of photographic or cinematographic translation. The short story as well as the movie thematizes photographic translation in general, and they are both therefore essays on metaphotography. "Apocalipsis" is thus from its beginning enframed by references to multiple semiotic systems. The sentence in "Apocalipsis" about *Blow Up* and "Las babas del diablo" refers to a polysemiosis, to an exemplary complication of the relationship between different sign systems. It announces or forewarns the apparition of the semiotic ghost. The semiotic ghost is an out-of-control, heterological appearance within the text: that which language excretes out of the tension obtaining between the text's signifying elements, a tension which is part and parcel of an ongoing translation process that certainly transcends the translating subject, but that implies him and requests the payment of a debt. We are about to witness a heterological production.

### Heterological Mimesis and the Optical Unconscious

Heterology has to do with the relationship between what Bataille considers the two most basic human impulses: excretion and appropriation. Production in general would be for Bataille the excretory phase of a process of appropriation. Appropriation is subordinate to excretory processes even in borderline cases where appropriation would seem to prevail. As an instance, Bataille refers to the elementary case of sacrificial consumption, the orgy, where "the incorporation in the person of irreducibly heterogeneous elements" such as sperm, menstrual blood, urine, or fecal matter serves the purpose of increasing the strength which is necessary for a more intense expulsion ("Notion," 95). Let me carry this model over to translation, considered as a game of appropriation and excretion.

Translation is not merely excretion of what has previously been appropriated, but production of a specific remnant which remains heterogeneous regarding the appropriated and every act of appropriation. From
this perspective, translation, as heterological production, is a production
of the different out of the identical: it is the waste of the identical, a
mimetic feast where absence and lack play a primordial role. Translation
always significantly translates what is not there. Photography, which is
always a practice of capturing what is not there, is in this respect synonymous with translation. Translation reads "what was never written": Benjamin uses this last phrase to refer to the mimetic faculty, an ancient
human faculty that would structure the perception of what Benjamin in
his own way defines as "nonsensuous similarities": " 'To read what was
never written.' Such reading is the most ancient: reading before all languages, from the entrails, the stars, or dances" (336).

Benjamin's notion of mimesis is radically conditioned by an operating
assumption concerning the absolute irreducibility of the mimetic relationship to a sensuous relationship. As mimesis is the practice of nonsensuous similarity, Benjaminian mimesis does not organize the homoge-
nization of the world, but its very opposite: its heterological proliferation,
in the rifts of the homogenizing element, which is the semiotic element.
Mimesis comes in sudden flashes of perception, in the blink of an eye,
which is also the eye's entry into its own failure and negation:

The mimetic element in language can, like a flame, manifest itself only
through a kind of bearer. This bearer is the semiotic element. Thus the
coherence of words or sentences is the bearer through which, like a flash,
similarity appears. For its production by man – like its perception by him – is
in many cases, and particularly the most important, limited to flashes. It flits
past. (335)

In my interpretation, "Apocalipsis de Solentiname" entirely under-
writes the Benjaminian concept of mimesis. In the intersemiosis of
translation from one into another sign system, from paintings into photographs, for instance, the rupture of semiosis is unavoidable or consubstantial: It therefore facilitates, or even causes, the apparition of the
phantom. The semiotic element, as naked bearer, always incorporates
the possibility of a phantom, which will then manifest itself in a blink: the
Benjaminian flash. For Benjamin this production of a ghost is the properly epistemological moment of artistic practice. The possibility of aesthetic knowledge therefore itself depends upon, and is affirmed in, the
recuperation or retrieval of an antiaesthetic, antisensuous moment, a

ghostlike moment where, paradoxically enough, similarity in the world, and thus the world's translatability, is ascertained.

Rosalind E. Krauss, in *The Optical Unconscious,* has attacked what she presents as the ideology of opticality underwriting high modernism's powerful notion of the autonomy of art: "The mapping of the retinal field onto the modernist pictorial plane, with the positivist expectation that the laws of the one would legislate and underwrite the autonomy of the operations of the other, is typical of the form in which high modernism established and then fetishized an autonomous realm of the visual" (126). According to Krauss, an antioptical or antivisual stream developed within the historical avant-garde, but remained hidden in the face of opticality's hegemony as the most obvious ideology able to ground or legitimize autonomous aesthetic practice. The fetishization of the visible was nevertheless countered in the work of those, such as Marcel Duchamp or Max Ernst, who understood that opticality is not an objective datum, but a product of the intervention of the body in phenomenal perception. These artists moved "to arrive at the threshold of desire-in-vision, which is to say to construct vision itself within the opacity of the organs and the invisibility of the unconscious" (125); "there now arises the density and opacity of the viewing subject as the very precondition of his access to sight" (125).

Krauss adapts Benjamin's 1931 notion of the "optical unconscious" to make it mean "an externalized [projection] within the visual field . . . of the way that human vision can be thought to be less than a master of all it surveys, in conflict as it is with what is internal to the organism that houses it" (179–80). The semiotic ghost, the production of the mimetic moment as a flash, as a diaphragmatic blink, is likewise not an opening of the visual field, but a retinal rupture toward the opacity of unconscious desire: which is why a photograph always necessarily photographs what was not there, and couldn't be – because it was always elsewhere. "Apocalipsis" reenacts Krauss's antioptical option.

### *Visual Disturbances and the Task of the Translator*

As Cortázar arrives at Las Brisas, José Coronel Urtecho's ranch and the last stage before boarding the boat that will take him to the island, somebody brings out a Polaroid camera that frightens him, making him wonder about the phantom, the "disturbing ectoplasm" (121; 19): "what would happen if sometime after a family snapshot the sky-blue paper started to fill up with Napoleon on horseback?" (121; 19); "I was filled with amazement as I saw . . . faces . . . coming out of nothing, of the little sky-blue square of nothingness" (121; 19; translation modified, as Rabassa leaves out the highly significant "sky-blue square of nothingness." It also needs to be noted that "sky-blue" translates the Spanish "celeste," in which a reference to heaven is very much inscribed). "The sky-blue square of nothingness" is of course a field of writing, here presented by Cortázar as a membrane of pure and uncertain possibility, if normally constituting the hymen for the semiotic encounter of model and translation, of original and copy. But why "nothingness"? The possible appearance of the semiotic ghost – the phantom of mimesis within semiosis – does not contradict the function of the field of writing as a field of similarity: on the contrary, the production of the ghost is an excretion of nonsensuous similarity; just as for Bataille nothingness, as well as its analogues absolute and infinitude, are excretions of philosophical thinking: the wasteful remainders that thought cannot endow with positive content, a scandalous difference that even dialectics can hardly control ("Notion," 96).

In mimetic or photographic translation the field of nothingness is the place for sacrifice, for sacrificial incorporation and loss. Cortázar is frightened, and the text announces its heterology in the ominous, portentous nothingness of the blank paper. The concern with nothingness, with avoiding the site of nothingness, recurs in another crucial moment in the text. While looking at the peasant paintings, where Cortázar imagines himself to be contemplating the expression of "a first vision of the world," he decides to photograph them "carefully, one by one, centering them so that each painting filled the viewer completely. Chance is like that: I had just the number of exposures as there were paintings, not one was left out" (123; 21). Nothing is then left out: What was important was to ascertain a total coincidence between the different semiotic systems, painting and photography, so that translation could be exact enough, with no loss, no holes for phantoms to hide in. The "sacrificial pyramid" of the story's introduction is now topologically revealed as the pyramid of vision, whose summit would be the optical, and theological, center of the photographic pupil. Cortázar's Solentiname anxiety over the photographs is curiously and fascinatingly confirmed in a testimonial account of the visit by the Nicaraguan writer Sergio Ramírez:

Somewhere, perhaps by the lateral door of the little church, I hold the primitive paintings so that Julio can photograph them in the first morning light. I think: even great writers resemble gringo tourists. [Why does he photograph these paintings? Julio,] don't forget the apocalypse, and stop fucking with folklore, little cows, little huts, and stars in an all-too-blue sky, perhaps because there was nothing but the paintings [*sic*]. What matters is the apocalypse. (47)

Expelled from the margins, deprived of a dwelling frame, those irritable phantoms will make their appearance in the only place left to them, the very center, and they will completely take over the projection screen, the pyramidal basis, which is in principle nothing but a faithful screen for the reproduction of what was perceived in the originary moment of vision, at the time of photography. This return of the excluded can be nothing but an interference of the optical unconscious, of the opacity of bodily drives, in the presumed optical transparency so "carefully" sought by Cortázar the photographer.

There was nothing in that, really, at least nothing ultimately surprising for a Cortázar who does define his carefully staged transposition into photography as a theft or a kidnapping in view of later liberation. But a liberation into what? In fact, the translator was doing his job: "It is the task of the translator to release in his own language that pure language which is under the spell of another, to liberate the language imprisoned in a work in his recreation of that work" (Benjamin, "Task," 80). Thus the narrator says: "When Ernesto came to tell us that the outboard was ready, I told him what I'd done and he laughed, art thief, image smuggler. Yes, I told him, I'm taking all of them, I'll show them on my screen back there and they'll be bigger and brighter than these, screw yourself" (123; 21). The screen projection is, then, nothing but a legitimate continuation of the projection of desire that took Cortázar into the theft of the image. The erotic character of the translating relationship accounts for its thwarted fulfillment: Desire cannot be satisfied. The lack in the original, the law of the original instituting the need for the supplement of translation by another, organizes the debt of the translator. But the debt, once incurred, has to be paid.[11]

Sigmund Freud's text on "Psychogenic Visual Disturbance According to Psychoanalytic Conceptions" (1910), which Krauss also quotes, can be used to indicate the libidinal, desiring character of the semiotic ghost. For Freud, the eye can perceive an erotic attraction in objects; it does not limit its function to the perception of modifications in reality that could threaten the preservation of life. When ego instincts, which seek preservation, and sexual instincts enter into conflict, then the ego sets up the repression of the eye. If ocular lust "has drawn upon itself defensive action by the ego-instinct in consequence of its excessive demands, so that the ideas in which its desires are expressed succumb to repression and are prevented from becoming conscious; in that case there will be a general disturbance of the relation of the eye and of the act of seeing to the ego and the consciousness" (*Standard Edition*, 11:216; modified translation in Krauss, 139). Anti-opticality, in the sense defined by Krauss, is nothing but the acceptance of the submission of the eye to processes of libidinal investment.

Cortázar's screen projection is a monumental act of excretion for which the previous appropriative act has been preparatory. The act of projection is the purely or properly sacrificial or mimetic moment, and what is produced by it is the loss of semiotic coincidence between model and copy. If the loss of coincidence is the apocalyptic revelation of "Apocalipsis," then the semiotic ghost, understood as that which was concealed but that revelation unveils, is its heterological similarity. In that sense, the epistemological moment must here be understood as a repression of desire, the site of a secret. I would propose the term *preservative repression,* following Abraham's and Torok's designation ("Tropology," 65), to indicate the specifically literary procedure through which, in the struggle of the two forms of writing, in the noncoincidence between sign systems, the ghost comes into mimetic existence.

We have to understand on the one hand that the reactive formation caused by repression, that is, the semiotic ghost, is in a mimetic relationship with the repressed. On the other hand, we have to explain what in the Solentiname peasant paintings attracted the lust of Cortázar's eye, and, more fundamentally, the retaliatory measure of its repression. If Freud is right, a conflict between ego instincts and sexual instincts must be brought to light.

The ego instincts would have moved against the pleasure of seeing that makes Cortázar want to capture the images conveying a "first vision of the world." The ego reacts against the Arcadian investment, looking for its own preservation. But then the repressed instincts will look for revenge:

The repressed instinct takes its revenge for being held back from further psychical expansion by becoming able to extend its dominance over the organ that is in its service. The loss of conscious dominance over the organ is the detrimental substitute for the repression which had miscarried and was only made possible at that price. (*Standard Edition*, 11:216)

The substitute formation will cause a visual disturbance in the sense that the repressed instinct will gain power over the eye.

### A Failed Fetish

Toward the end of his paper Freud wonders whether this psychic mechanism can be entirely explained in recourse to the functioning of the ego instincts or whether the existence of certain "constitutional constellations" could be posited that would intensify the tendency of the visual organs to play an erogenous role and thus to provoke instinctual repression. For Freud, such constellations would belong in the organic not the psychic constitution of the body. They would organize a "somatic compliance" of the eye (218). I will not appeal to the organic reduction of the psychic, since it will be easier to assign the power of somatic compliance to the work of writing itself. After all, if the semiotic ghost appears within writing as a sign, its epistemological import will be differentially related to the signs it displaces or reacts against. Writing makes the subject of writing produce and release a reactive formation when what is threatened is the survival of writing itself in the face of its encounter with the properly monstrous, the first world, the world of origins.

What is there in the Solentiname paintings that can have attracted not just the lust of the writing eye but the retaliatory measure of its repression? Cortázar's eye will be disturbed by the work of a substitute formation that begins to produce itself at the moment in which the pleasure of seeing the peasant paintings requests their appropriation in photographic reproducibility. Translation will then not be merely reproductive. The peasant paintings, as they transform themselves into images of horror, must be understood as the failed site for the construction of a fetish: namely, the fetish of full poetic, ontotheologic writing, world-giving. Cortázar reformulates from this perspective Roland Barthes's notion of the *punctum* in the photographic image (*Chambre,* 48–9ff.). *Punctum* is here the failed site or the fissure in the construction site of the fetish of ontotheological writing. This *punctum,* which in "Apocalipsis" manifests itself with a violence that is the result of repressed libidinal investment, makes of "Apocalipsis de Solentiname" the scene of a writing profoundly marked by mourning, open to phantasmatic relapse.

In *Hopscotch,* Horacio Oliveira engages in his own drunken delirium:

He wasn't so drunk that he didn't have the feeling that his house was a shambles, that inside nothing was in place but at the same time – to be sure, marvelously sure – on the floor or on the ceiling, under the bed or floating in a washbasin there were stars and chunks of eternity, poems like suns and enormous faces of women and cats where the fury of their species was fired up, in the mixture of garbage and jade plaques in their own language where words were woven night and day into furious battles between ants and centipedes, blasphemy existed with the pure mention of essences, the perfect image with the basest slang. . . . All disorder had meaning if it seemed to come out of itself, perhaps through madness one could arrive at that reason which is not the reason whose weakness is madness. "To go from disorder to order," thought Oliveira. "Yes, but what kind of order can there be which does not mimic the basest, most debased, and most unhealthy of disorders? The order of the gods is called cyclone or leukemia, the poet's order is called antimatter, firm space, flowers of trembling lips." (18:74–5; 18:209–10)[12]

Also in "Apocalipsis" blasphemy, in the form of torture and murder of the innocent, will coexist with the pure mention of essences, the first vision of the world; ants will also fight centipedes. The black suns of antimatter refer to the contradictory drives of the desiring, lustful eye, and the foci of disorder give out the anti-optical, antitheological strength that will resist, from the opacity of the unconscious, the constitution of poetic, founding, Orphic writing, displacing it toward the site of a madness where the insane order of the poet aspires to settle.

In *Histoire de l'oeil,* Bataille staged the focus of desire on the drive toward a rupture of the eye – a literal, violent breakage, not far from a sadistic will for destruction: "The eye, she said, had the shape of an egg. She asked me to promise her that, when we could go outside, I would throw eggs up into the sunny air and I would break them with shots from my gun" (46). But that is precisely what happens in Cortázar's story, where the rupture of the eye is staged on an antioptical, phantasmatic vision. Within this delirious logic, there is a similar moment in *Prosa del observatorio,* at the moment in which Cortázar describes Jai Singh, the sultan, builder of the seventeenth-century Jaipur observatory. Jai Singh, in Cortázar's unsettling description, is engaged in a struggle to the end against the eye that looks at him. First the combat is translated:

against the spindles of height distilling their threads for a complicitous intelligence, spiderweb of spiderwebs, a sultan wounded with indifference raises his enamoured will, challenges a heaven that once again proposes transmissible letters, initiates a slow, interminable copulation with a heaven that requires obedience and order, a heaven that he will rape night after night in every bed of stone. (43)

The anti-optical option is then revealed as an intensification of opticality into the space of desire: "Jai Singh's eroticism at the end of a race and a history, observatory ramps where the vast curves of breasts and thighs yield their courses of delight to a gaze that possesses through transgression and challenge and that leaps onto the unnamable from catapults of trembling mineral silence" (44). But what is truly unnamable, that which Cortázar frequently calls, following Rainer Maria Rilke, "the Open," is here the place of entry into "the true revolution" (67), the utopian site, then, where poetic writing is posited, the region of an "image where everything is waiting" (77). Also in *Prosa del observatorio* the accomplishment of such an ecstatic image is thwarted beforehand through the sadistic drive that posits it, through a rape that takes place "night after night in every bed of stone" (43). The fundamental irresolution that organizes not only the structure of *Prosa* but also its dramatic texture, the quality of its prose, which is also, in its full resonance, the antivisual prose of the place of the eye, is an irresolution between poetic writing and a writing of destruction.

The "primitive" paintings of the Solentiname peasants, the paintings that granted a "first vision of the world," the pastoralism of cows, sugar huts, and poppy fields, turn on Cortázar's Parisian giant screen into desolating images of death, sadism, and destruction. The photographic transposition reveals what was not there but nevertheless was there through its very absence: the boy shot in the forehead by the Somocista officer, the scene of cadavers turned face-up, the image of the young woman with a cattle prod between her legs, the pieces of bodies, and girls running in terror. How can this production of bloody ghosts come out of the initial pastoral? What demonic translation has taken place? I think writing as somatic solicitation has acted, and the result is a reactive formation which nevertheless has the character of a substitute formation; a mimetic, nonsensuous similarity acting in the cracks of the semiotic systems, taking advantage of the fact that only in the vulnerability of translation can the demon of displacement, of transposition, of play, intervene. The erogenous is always already the very debt inscribed in the original, anaclitically paying.

### Scopic Wolves

Cortázar is not the only boom writer affected by a similar constitutional constellation. We can also see it, for instance, in Guillermo Cabrera Infante's best work, *Tres tristes tigres*, in the figure of Bustrofedon, the producer of language and the encrypted image of its author. Bustrofedon operates out of a brain lesion acquired in childhood, a lesion that claims its due progressively, dissociating writing and thought, opening thought to the work of a reactive formation. As Roberto González Echevarría puts it:

Bustrofedon's brain lesion is special because it is the source of language, that is, of a new language whose naming skills depend upon a foundational negativity, whose hyposthasis is the lesion itself, the cut, or death. . . . In this language game the logos, as ontology, is the gap of disfunction, the language game announcing disfunction in its proclivity for malformation and error. Malformation and error are the gaps between the I and the world, and between the I and its intentional representation in language. (141)[13]

In those gaps the semiotic ghost dwells. As a sign or a set of signs, it tropologically inscribes itself in the signifying chains surrounding it and proceeds to create nonsensuous similarities where the epistemological power of writing settles. In "Apocalipsis" the semiotic ghosts produce images of expenditure and destruction. What is excreted in the translation process is in Cortázar's story the doubling at the level of the signified of the excretion itself, which takes place at the level of the signifier: The concrete content of the images that appear on Cortázar's projection screen is symbolic of the processes of semiotic transposition the story describes, including the translation act. In "The Notion of Expenditure," Bataille says that literature, insofar as it provokes dread and horror in the symbolic representation of degradation and death, "can be considered synonymous of expenditure; it in fact signifies, in the most precise way, creation by means of loss. Its meaning is therefore close to that of *sacrifice*" (120). Cortázar's reading or mimetic translation extracts out of the Solentiname paintings a hidden sacrificial meaning. What does it consist of?

Cortázar is not just writing about Somocista repression, and that is the most disturbing aspect of his story. He is also writing about the repression of the eye in the task of the translator. Some analogies between Cortázar's text and the psychoanalytic text need to be drawn. In brief, in Solentiname, Cortázar as narrator makes a strong object investment that we have to understand as a regression toward narcissism. Cortázar travels, in other words, toward "the lake with little boats like shoes and in the background an enormous fish laughing with turquoise teeth" (122; 20). That fish gaping in the bottom of the peasant paintings is the image – an image that was already explicit in "Axolotl" – of an ego in a state of primary narcissism.[14] Cortázar's attempt to appropriate the paintings through photography refers to what Freud would call the psychic stage of sadistic-anal organization. The aggressive treasuring is specified in words already quoted: "when Ernesto came to tell us that the outboard was ready, I told him what I'd done and he laughed, art thief, image smuggler. Yes, I told him, I'm taking all of them, I'll show them on my screen back there and they'll be bigger and brighter than these, screw yourself" (123; 21).

In "Instincts and Their Vicissitudes" (1915) Freud mentions that in the sadistic-anal libidinal position the ego instincts "dominate the sexual function" and "impart the qualities of hate to the instinctual aim as well" (*Standard Edition*, 14:139). This explains the sadistic destruction in the Paris hallucinatory activity. When Cortázar wants to project what had previously been introjected, what occurs is the hallucinated vision of a split ego in a state of ambivalence. Cortázar in Paris suffers a symptom caused by a narcissistic object investment. The semiotic ghost pierces consciousness in radical anxiety. Cortázar's text brings us close to schizophrenia understood as a narcissistic psychoneurosis.

I would say that Cortázar's text reaches its full political relevance precisely in this bringing together of the mimetic function and the sadistic function. That it was possible to do so has a lot to do with the fact that Solentiname was a theological community, a community of peasants led by Ernesto Cardenal, who instructed them in the word of God. Textual ambivalence also implicates the apparent concord and peace obtaining within the community. Paradise, we seem to be told, is always a paradise dominated by affective drives involving the father. But a father can always become a wolf, can always open those gates of hell that Cortázar mentions at the very opening of the narration (120; 18). The scopic regime in Cortázar's text, where we go from the pleasure of seeing and being seen to the anxious horror of the same, is a paterno-theological regime.

If translation is possible, if Cortázar can photograph the Solentiname peasant paintings, that happens because the original "wasn't there without a fault, complete, full, total, identical to itself," as Jacques Derrida says commenting on the Benjaminian text on translation ("Des Tours," 232). Cortázar's task is the task of the translator – that is, "to release in his own language that pure language which is under the spell of another, to liberate the language imprisoned in a work in his recreation of that work." The semiotic ghost of heterological production hands over, in a flash, pure language, which is not poetic language or sacrificial language, but is the language that *says* the deep coimplication of those two poles of writing.

In "The Use Value of D. A. F. de Sade," Bataille writes a sentence that at first sight seems as enigmatic as repulsive: "without a sadistic understanding of an incontestably thundering and torrential nature, there could be no revolutionaries, there could only be a revolting utopian sentimentality" (101). Bataille's sadistic understanding is what enables

Cortázar in the first place to introject the "first vision of the world," that is, enables him to realize a violent libidinal investment in it. But then, does it remain possible later to conjure the destructive drive, to escape the thanatological will?

"Apocalipsis de Solentiname" opens itself to the struggle between writings and becomes the site for its expression, but not for its outcome, unless the outcome can be thought to be irresolution itself. Cortázar's complex writing, in "Apocalipsis," upon nonresolutively coimplicating orphic and sacrificial writing produces itself as a heterology the effects of which must, but cannot, be controlled.

"Apocalipsis de Solentiname" is a writing of resistance insofar as it is a writing of mourning for poetic, ontological writing. It is a disutopian writing that not only states the loss of the Orphic function of writing, but that is openly traumatized by it. As such, it is a writing of pain at a distance, a telepathic writing – a writing of solidarity because the very possibility of solidarity is first put into question, and then only accepted as an expression of thwarted, mimetic desire. It is not really the Solentiname paintings that constitute a "first vision of the world": They only allegorize it, as they become the encrypture for a reality whose possibility remains only in its ceaseless concealment. And of that possibility, in negation, Cortázar gives testimony: a utopian writing, then, *because* it is prosaic, unholy, translated into destruction.[15]

Sergio Ramírez, commenting in the book previously quoted on Cortázar's personal option in favor of Sandinista Nicaragua and for Central American liberation struggles, fails to note the fact that for Cortázar the option itself was also to be taken into an exploration of the very motivations of writing, what writing could and what it could not do, what writing therefore was obliged to do if such an option, for Cortázar as a writer, was to go beyond declarations of intent and purely political work.[16] As a practitioner of literature whose work had struggled to engage the world from a cosmopolitan, universalist location, it was not up to Cortázar to step out of his professional skin and simply assert a solidarity with the Nicaraguan people that would have run the risk of being more deeply felt than adequately expressed. Didn't he always write "too hermetically for the people" anyway? What would the political implications be of a sudden clarity, of a drastic reduction in the complex way in which Cortázar's literary production had attempted to follow the call of thinking?

"Apocalipsis de Solentiname" is a poignant document in which solidarity is put to the test of the unconscious: Cortázar disavows the possibility of a sympathetic vision, of a merely affective commitment to the plight of the Nicaraguan dispossessed, which would have smacked of

Latinamericanist desire, of "a neocolonial reworking of primitivism," to apply words Michael Taussig used in a similar context.[17] Instead, Cortázar writes a text where an anaclitic perspective on the impossibility of desire fulfillment, on the impossibility of merely subscribing to any and all "first visions of the world," comes hand in hand with a rigorous self-critique concerning destructive tendencies in his own relationship with representation. What in Central America seemed an expression of hope became in Paris the occasion for the manifestation of sacrificial dread and horror. But sacrificial dread and horror do not for that reason become the ultimate horizon for symbolic expression; on the contrary, sacrificial dread and horror are then shown for what they are – namely, reactive formations caused by the conflictual relation between erogenous, originary object investments, and the self-involved ego instincts of a cosmopolitan writer who long ago had had to give up nostalgic delusions for the sake of artistic/narcissistic self-preservation.

In "Apocalipsis de Solentiname" Cortázar shows, with a perfect economy of means, how solidarity with the destitute needs to be expressed first through a thorough self-renunciation, which in the case of a First World–located intellectual such as Cortázar can only mean a thorough critique of the strategies of representation on which the power of First World cultural production is established. For a First World intellectual, the pain of solidarity can only be pain at a distance: But telepathy is precisely not that easy an apparatus of affect. First, one's own pain needs to be tapped into, so that a common destitution is at the very least rehearsed.

Pain is what mnemonic repetition strives to understand. The alternation between memory/first vision of the world and destruction/sadistic-anal hallucination is in the last instance the matrix of the Cortázarian story. It operates a powerful matricial tropology because, far from giving the story a form, it destroys its form and its structure: a dismorphic form, a crypt. Cortázar's anaclitic representation in "Apocalipsis de Solentiname" satisfies a need for solidarity, but not the desire for it. There is no retrievable object of solidarity: only a lost object, encrypted, hermetically sealed, which excreted us and which we should not try to appropriate. The "first vision of the world" refers to the site of a secret, that is, to a denial and disavowal of reality, to a permanently entombed desire equally incapable of rising or of disintegrating. The semiotic ghost attests to the pain of the eye in contemplating it.

One of the dreams of the wolf-man, the Russian citizen Sergei Pankeiev, whose case is rendered by Freud in *History of an Infantile Neurosis,* is: "My mother and I are together in a room. In one corner the entire wall is covered with holy pictures. My mother takes the pictures down and throws them on the floor. The pictures fall and break into pieces. I am astonished that my pious mother should do such a thing" (Abraham & Torok, *Wolf Man*, 66). For Abraham and Torok this dream makes clear "the economic function of keeping alive at all costs the traumatic scene of witnessing" (67).[18] Cortázar's sadistic production is an attempt to incorporate that first vision of the world, the primal scene, the "holy pictures" in Pankeiev's dream; it is equally and by the same token an attempt desperately to resist the destructive effects the primal scene can have upon the narcissistic ego.

"The traumatic scene of witnessing" is for Cortázar the site of an aberrant self-mourning. The fact that trauma comes to appear in the place of the failed constitution of a fetish, indeed the fact that a fetish cannot be constituted at all, indicates the presence of an open crypt in Cortázar's textual unconscious. But the innocence we feel the desire to postulate in any "first vision of the world" depends upon leaving the crypt alone, of not ever touching it. For Pankeiev, touching it meant to open the window and see a tree full of wolves. Pankeiev's vision is not far from Cortázar's poisonous gift against false innocence, against exculpatory, Orphic writing.

### Notes

1. "Apocalipsis" is more frequently informally discussed than written about. For political readings, see Barbara Harlow, 75–80. See also Muñoz, 546–51, and Tittler. See Alazraki for a summary analysis of Cortázar's thematization of the political, and also Cortázar's interview with Omar Prego, "Juego y compromiso político" (Prego, 127–45; but not all of it is relevant). Finally, see Cortázar's own *Nicaragua* and *Argentina*.

2. Authored or edited respectively by Elizabeth Burgos-Debray, Robert M. Carmack, Mark Danner, and Víctor Perera.

3. "Anaclisis" is a neological term used by translators of Sigmund Freud to render nominal notions related to the German verb *Anlehnen*, meaning "to find support." Jean Laplanche, while proposing an alternative translation for French, *étayage* (which Jeffrey Mehlman translates as "propping"), has given it the importance of a "fundamental term in Freud's conceptual apparatus" (*Life*, 15). The sexual drive would originally be propped upon a nonsexual, vital function. For instance, the infant sucks its mother's breast for self-preservative reasons, but cannot avoid deriving erotogenic satisfaction from it. "Thus the 'propping' consists initially in that support which emergent sexuality finds in a function linked to the preservation of life" (Laplanche, 17). What interests us, however, is the fact that, "in an immediately subsequent phase, we witness a separation of the two, since sexuality, at first entirely grounded in the function, is simultaneously entirely *in the movement which disassociates it* from the vital function" (18). Subsequently, needs will find satis-

faction; but desire, in virtue of its originary disassociation from the object of satisfaction, will not. My point is that the literary is similarly propped on a lost object, the literary thing itself, language understood as a bodily need; but literature is simultaneously entirely in the movement which disassociates it from language understood as a vital function. This essay is ultimately an attempt to study the reflections of this structural situation in "Apocalipsis de Solentiname." On anaclisis, see also Rosalind E. Krauss, 140.

4. The first page number corresponds to the English translation, the second to the Spanish original. I follow Gregory Rabassa's translation unless otherwise indicated.

5. "Lycanthropy" is mentioned, but not elaborated upon, in the already mentioned essay by Muñoz, which deals partially with "Apocalipsis," 543.

6. On mimesis and caesura, see Philippe Lacoue-Labarthe, "La Césure du spe-culatif."

7. On the two kinds of writing, see Gerald Bruns, *Modern Poetry and the Idea of Language* (New Haven, CT: Yale University Press, 1974), for an alternative presentation. I entirely subscribe to Bruns's notion of Orphic writing but prefer to talk about another writing, for which I borrow certain notions from Bataille, that Bruns does not contemplate in his elaboration on hermetic expressiveness.

8. Toward the end of *Hopscotch,* with a certain finality: "If the volume or the tone of the work can lead one to believe that the author is attempting a sum, hasten to point out to him that he is face to face with the opposite attempt, that of an implacable *subtraction*" (chap. 137, p. 526). However, it needs to be said that *Hopscotch* incorporated to a maximum degree the search for a "first vision of the world," and that in fact the problematic – not necessarily of the two writings, but certainly of two opposite attempts at dealing with the world, one constructive, the other destructive – finds in *Hopscotch* a classic expression. Cf., among other important passages, chaps. 71, 90, 99.

9. If Solentiname aesthetics can exemplify the first kind of writing as I define it, it is not because the peasant paintings necessarily express a "first vision of the world," but only because that would be their presumed intentionality. I think it would be as fair to assume that the Solentiname paintings were for Cortázar, at least in "Apocalipsis de Solentiname," the site of an allegory: a symbolic production that could be posited to be "governed by a mythical or ideal unity of word and being" (Bruns, 1); in other words, a symbolic production whose very literality would result in an ontology. But the "primitive" style – or Cortázar's loaded version of it – should not deceive us. Betty La Duke learned, in the course of her own visit to a rebuilt Solentiname community in 1981, that there was nothing primitive about Solentiname primitivism: "My main objective was to learn about the 'primitive' painting, but as I spoke with the Guevara family and other artists and community members, I soon realized that Solentiname 'primitive' painting was a profound expression of personal evolution connected with a broadened religious and political perspective" (97). See the rest of the essay for an interesting account of Solentiname painters in their personal life and political and aesthetic positions.

10. I adapt the term from a short story by William Gibson called "The Gernsback Continuum" (29). The photographer-narrator in this story must carry out a quasi-sublime task: to rescue ruins, to trace a remainder. He needs to photograph whatever is left of 1930s and 1940s U.S. futuristic architecture, what the text calls "American Streamlined Moderne" or "raygun Gothic" (24). In the process of investigating what could have been and was not, the photographer, to use Cortázar's appropriation of Horacio Quiroga's favorite sentence, "crosses the line": "And one day, in the outskirts of Bolinas, when I was setting up to shoot a particularly lavish example of Ming's martial architecture, I penetrated a fine membrane, a membrane of probability. . . . Ever so gently, I went over the Edge" (27). "The Gernsback Continuum" is a curious North American translation of the Latin American experience at the same time partially and excessively (but accurately) registered in "Apocalipsis de Solentiname."

11. The anaclitic "propping" of sexuality on "bodily functions essential to life" also opens the need for the repayment of a debt.

12. The first page number corresponds to Rabassa's translation; the second to the original Spanish in Andrés Amorós's edition.

13. See also, for instance, the work of Humberto Peñaloza/Mudito in José Donoso's *El obsceno pájaro de la noche*, or of Oppiano Licario in José Lezama Lima's *Oppiano Licario*, among other illustrious examples.

14. On "Axolotl," see Brett Levinson's unpublished essay "Cortázar as Latinamericanist: The Periphery as the Un(A)Voidable." My analysis of "Apocalipsis de Solentiname" parallels in many important respects Levinson's own interests in his reading of "Axolotl," but nowhere does Levinson say that there is something like primary narcissism attached to Cortázar's involvement with *axolotls*. His reading is in fact opposite: "The axolotls of Cortázar's tale play (almost to the law of the letter) the role of the Lacanian analyst. Creatures that stare silently at the man without ever closing their eyes, the axolotls are the embodiment of the terrifying witness, of the omniscient reader, of the subject-supposed-to-know. The protagonist's conversion into an axolotl is thus his coming to see first-hand the particular nature of axolotl knowledge – and there is none" (12).

15. On Cortázar's difficulties with writing solidarity, see Levinson, 12–19.

16. See Ramírez, 86–92, 99–103, and 120–4.

17. Taussig's context relates to a definition of "magical realism" and to the political uses of it: "The mythic and magical space fixed by the image of the New World Indian is one studded with political irony" (*Shamanism*, 171). The passage quoted in the text is on page 172. Cortázar could not just use Solentiname paintings in order to claim them as the ground of his redemptive effect.

18. The scene of witnessing is, in this case, the scene of a *coitus a tergo* between Sergei's parents, which Freud already knew. But Abraham and Torok's particular interpretation of this particular "dream of the icons" includes many presuppositions that can hardly be given here in succinct form; see *Wolf Man*, 66–7, but really also the totality of their analysis. What is important for us is the conclusion that "the words of the [dream] scene allow him to pre-

serve another word, endowed with another function and precious above others. This is the precious and magic word *tieret* [*coitus a tergo*]" (67). In "Apocalipsis" the scene of witnessing is also the reversed scene of the first vision of the world: its economical function is, generally speaking, to preserve the possibility of writing.

## References

Abraham, Nicolas, and Maria Torok. "The Topography of Reality: Sketching a Metapsychology of Secrets." *Oxford Literary Review* 12, nos. 1–2 (1990): 63–8.
*The Wolf Man's Magic Word.* Trans. Nicholas Rand. Minneapolis: University of Minnesota Press, 1986.
Alazraki, Jaime. "Imaginación e historia en Julio Cortázar." In *Los ochenta mundos de Cortázar: Ensayos,* ed. Fernando Burgos, 1–20. Madrid: Edi-6, 1987.
Barthes, Roland. *La Chambre claire. Note sur la photographie.* Paris: L'Etoile/Gallimard/Seuil, 1980.
Bataille, Georges. *Histoire de l'oeil.* Paris: Pauvert, 1967.
    "The Notion of Expenditure." In *Visions of Excess: Selected Writings, 1927–39,* ed. and trans. Allan Stoekl, 116–29. Minneapolis: University of Minnesota Press, 1985.
    "The Use Value of D. A. F. de Sade." In *Visions of Excess: Selected Writings, 1927–39,* ed. and trans. Allan Stoekl, 91–102. Minneapolis: University of Minnesota Press, 1985.
Benjamin, Walter. "On the Mimetic Faculty." In *Reflections: Essays, Aphorisms, Autobiographical Writings,* trans. Edmund Jephcott, 333–6. New York: Harcourt Brace Jovanovich, 1978.
    "The Task of the Translator." In *Illuminations,* trans. Harry Zohn, 69–82. New York: Schocken, 1969.
Bonasso, Miguel. *Recuerdo de la muerte.* Buenos Aires: Bruguera, 1984.
Burgos-Debray, Elizabeth, ed. *Me llamo Rigoberta Menchú y así me nació la conciencia.* Mexico: Siglo XXI, 1981.
Carmack, Robert M., ed. *Harvest of Violence: The Maya Indians and the Guatemalan Crisis.* Norman: University of Oklahoma Press, 1988.
Cortázar, Julio. "Apocalipsis de Solentiname." In *Nicaragua tan violentamente dulce,* 18–24. Buenos Aires: Muchnik, 1984.
    "Apocalypse at Solentiname." In *A Change of Light and Other Stories,* trans. Gregory Rabassa, 119–27. New York: Knopf, 1980.
    *Argentina, años de alambradas culturales.* Buenos Aires: Muchnik, 1984.
    *Hopscotch.* Trans. Gregory Rabassa. New York: Pantheon, 1966.
    *Rayuela* [1963]. Ed. Andrés Amorós. Madrid: Cátedra, 1984.
Danner, Mark. *The Massacre at El Mozote.* New York: Vintage, 1994.
Derrida, Jacques. "Des Tours de Babel." In *Difference in Translation,* ed. Joseph Graham, 209–48. Ithaca, NY: Cornell University Press, 1985.
Donoso, José. *El obsceno pájaro de la noche.* Barcelona: Seix Barral, 1970.
La Duke, Betty. "The Painter-Peasants of Solentiname, Nicaragua." *Chicago Review* 34, no. 3 (1984): 94–124.

Freud, Sigmund. "The Instincts and Their Vicissitudes" [1915]. *The Standard Edition of the Complete Psychological Works,* James Strachey, General Editor. Vol. 14 [1914–16], 109–40. London: Hogarth, 1957.
   "Psychogenic Visual Disturbances According to Psychoanalytic Conceptions" [1910]. *Standard Edition.* Vol. 11 [1910], 209–18.

Gibson, William. "The Gernsback Continuum." In *Burning Chrome,* 23–35. New York: Ace, 1987.

González Echevarría, Roberto. *The Voice of the Masters. Writing and Authority in Modern Latin American Writing.* Austin: University of Texas Press, 1985.

Harlow, Barbara. *Resistance Literature.* New York: Methuen, 1987.

Krauss, Rosalind E. *The Optical Unconscious.* Cambridge, MA: MIT Press, 1993.

Lacoue-Labarthe, Philippe. "La Césure du spéculatif." In *L'Imitation des Modernes,* 39–68. Paris: Galilée, 1986.

Lezama Lima, José. *Oppiano Licario,* ed. César López. Madrid: Cátedra, 1989.

Levison, Brett. "Cortázar as Latinamericanist: The Periphery and the Un(a)voidable." Unpublished manuscript.

De Man, Paul. "Conclusions: Walter Benjamin's 'The Task of the Translator.'" In *The Resistance to Theory,* foreword by Wlad Godzich, 73–105. Minneapolis: University of Minnesota Press, 1986.

Muñoz, Willy. "Julio Cortázar: Vértices de una figura comprometida." *Revista Iberoamericana* 15 (1990): 541–51.

Perera, Víctor. *Unfinished Conquest: The Guatemalan Tragedy.* Berkeley: University of California Press, 1993.

Prego, Omar. *La fascinación de las palabras. Conversaciones con Julio Cortázar.* Buenos Aires: Muchnik, 1985.

Ramírez, Sergio. *Julio, estás en Nicaragua.* Buenos Aires: Nueva América, 1986.

Rivabella, Omar. *Requiem for a Woman's Soul.* New York: Random House, 1986.

Taussig, Michael. *Shamanism, Colonialism, and the Wild Man: A Study in Terror and Healing.* Chicago: University of Chicago Press, 1987.

Tittler, Jonathan. "Los dos Solentinames de Julio Cortázar." In *Los ochenta mundos de Cortázar: Ensayos,* ed. Fernando Burgos, 85–92. Madrid: Edi-6, 1987.

Yúdice, George. "Testimonio and Postmodernism." *Latin American Perspectives* 18, no. 3 (1991): 15–31.

# 9

## The Man in the Car/in the Trees/behind the Fence:

### From Cortázar's "Blow-Up" to Oliver Stone's *JFK*

*Frederick Luciani*

In a 1973 interview, Julio Cortázar offered the following opinion regarding the influence of his work on cinema: "Yo no creo que mi obra haya tenido ninguna influencia en el cine, absolutamente ninguna. A lo sumo una influencia muy, muy indirecta" ("I don't think that my work has had any influence on cinema, absolutely none. At most, a very, very indirect influence").[1] Coming just a few years after Antonioni's celebrated film adaptation of his "Blow-Up" ("Las babas del diablo"),[2] Cortazar's denial of influence is difficult to assess. Is it attributable to modesty? To his fatigue with a question that, in one form or another, he had encountered in countless interviews? Or to a sincere conviction that – Antonioni notwithstanding – film art of the late 1960s and early 1970s remained largely unaffected by a body of work that had had such a decisive impact in literary circles?[3]

Although Cortázar's estimation of the issue seems to have been directed toward European filmmaking (he went on to mention Godard's *Weekend* as an example of a film that is indirectly based on his work), it applies equally to an American context. Specifically, it captures the apparent relationship between his work ("Blow-Up," in particular) and a line of film stretching from Antonioni's seminal film through a generation of prominent American directors of the sixties, seventies, eighties, and nineties. Despite the acknowledged debt of these directors to Antonioni's *Blow-Up,* Cortázar's story and his work in general seem either absent from, or indirectly (sometimes misdirectedly) present in their films. Given the apparent aspiration of the directors in question – Brian De Palma, Francis Coppola, Oliver Stone – to "high art" as well as commercially viable filmmaking, the remove at which their films stand from Cortázar – their literary grounding – is noteworthy. It can be explained, perhaps, in larger contexts, such as the gulf between American popular culture and Cortázar's own "high art" sensibilities, and the linguistic, commercial, and ideological disjunctions between Latin American, European, and North American culture in general.

The intent of this essay is to examine this line of American film and filmmakers – Cortázar's wayward and unrecognized Hollywood progeny – with the goal of exploring the absence and ambiguous presence of Cortázar's "Blow-Up" in them. The essay will focus on thematic and discursive connections and disconnections, and on the philosophical, existential, or political concerns that underlie them. Those connections and disconnections will be traced chronologically; the effect will be to create a kind of artificial genealogy, not to be construed as a history of "influences." The chronological scheme will also facilitate a discussion of the relationship between these works and a set of issues that are historically embedded, such as the divergent political sensibilities of Cortázar, De Palma, Coppola, and Stone, and an evolving public consciousness in the United States of certain social and civic issues – a public consciousness that, in the consumer-driven world of Hollywood film production, is inseparable from the film art of the directors in question.

Cortázar returned explicitly to the "Blow-Up" theme in a politically charged short story of the 1970s, "Apocalypse at Solentiname."[4] Both stories will be placed within the "genealogy" that this essay will trace, with the distance between them serving as a yardstick of Cortázar's political and literary evolution. Because the connection between the "Blow-Ups" of Cortázar and Antonioni has long constituted a critical cliché, I shall discuss Antonioni's film mostly in terms of its function as a bridge between Cortázar and the directors who are the essay's primary concern: De Palma (*Greetings, Blow Out*), Coppola (*The Conversation*), and Stone (*JFK*). Alfred Hitchcock's *Rear Window,* which predates Cortázar's story by several years, will serve as a starting point for the genealogy to be traced, as the coincidences between Hitchcock and Cortázar are noteworthy, and because *Rear Window* can serve as an example of the conventional Hollywood "genre film," against which the innovations of later filmmakers can be measured. Finally, I shall consider the "Zapruder film," which stands at the intersection of the "Blow-Up" theme and a public/political consciousness in the United States that was reflected in and influenced by the films of De Palma, Coppola, Stone, and others.

### *Hitchcock's* Rear Window *(1954)*

The fundamental plot circumstances of Alfred Hitchcock's film are strikingly similar to those of Cortázar's short story. The protagonist (L. B. Jefferies, who is laid up at home with a broken leg) is a photographer who, quite by accident but also thanks to his professional curiosity and powers of observation, discovers a crime. He creates and manipulates photographic images (including the preparation of blowups) in an effort to solve the mystery of the crime. His intervention as observer and photographer forces a confrontation with the agent of the crime, who had supposed that his actions were going unobserved. That confrontation results in the (temporary) victimization of the protagonist (in his struggle with the murderer whom he has revealed, Jefferies falls from his apartment window and breaks his other leg).

Typical of the Hollywood thriller, Hitchcock's film has as its source of narrative tension the search for truth – the truth of the nature of and responsibility for the crime. As in Cortázar's story, this search is both morally motivated and fraught with moral dilemmas, as it involves unauthorized spying into the private lives of others (from his darkened apartment, Jefferies uses binoculars and a telescopic lens to peer into the apartments of his neighbors). Thus, Jefferies, like Cortázar's protagonist, is an unwitting voyeur, a role that is not only morally but also existentially problematical: The voyeur, deficient in his own ability to live, partakes vicariously of the experiences of others.[5] Voyeurism is linked, in turn, with problematical sexuality: Jefferies seems unable to respond to the sexual and matrimonial cues offered by his girlfriend (played, as if to underscore Jefferies's "problem," by the flawlessly beautiful Grace Kelly) in the "real space" of his apartment, while receiving various forms of stimulation from the surveillance of his neighbors in the "fictional spaces" of their apartments, visible to Jefferies as so many movie or television screens.

Jefferies's voyeurism, and the physical circumstances in which it is indulged, have long suggested to critics a fundamental self-reflexivity that makes *Rear Window*, in essence, a film about film – specifically, a film about the experience of film viewing, even as Cortázar's story has been read as a metanarrative about the process of telling a story.[6] To realize that self-reflexive design, both film and story incorporate shifting planes of narrative space and reality. In the case of *Rear Window*, those spaces include Jefferies's apartment, the courtyard that separates his building from those of his neighbors, and the individual spaces of his neighbors' apartments (Belton). These spaces are divided by "screens": Jefferies's window serves as a large movie screen upon which the dramas he observes are panoramically displayed, and the windows of his neighbors serve as miniscreens, each displaying a story that is both autonomous and connected with those surrounding it. Self-reflexivity also suggests, in both film and story, self-inscription on the part of the "author." In *Rear*

*Window* this goes beyond Hitchcock's standard cameo appearance: Jefferies can be read as a surrogate for the director, because he is a photographer whose intervention changes the course of events and because he controls the gaze and interpretation of other viewers – his fellow voyeurs in his apartment as well as the viewers of *Rear Window* itself (Stam, 43–55).

Although fundamentally congruent, Hitchcock's film and Cortázar's story show some striking differences. Prominent among these is the narrative determinacy and sense of closure in *Rear Window:* As the conventions of the Hollywood thriller demand, the crime is solved, the hero/protagonist is vindicated, and the villain is apprehended. Moreover, social order – a return to romantic "normalcy" defined by restrained sexuality within matrimony – is restored in the various minidramas being played out in the apartments of Jefferies's neighbors. Jefferies himself will marry and forsake the voyeuristic habits that, by film's end, seem like a deviant interlude within a normal life. Despite some dark shadings that remain – typical of Hitchcock – the ending establishes an overall sense of a return to order and convention, artistically as well as socially: The norms of the genre are respected, and Hitchcock's exacting control of the director's art never permits the kind of radical questioning of photographic and literary mimesis to which Cortázar's story will lead.

### Cortázar's "Blow-Up" (1959)

Cortázar's story is narrated by an amateur photographer (Roberto Michel) who thwarts the apparent seduction of an adolescent by an older woman by taking their picture, only later to reinterpret the nature of the "crime." The intended agent of the seduction, he believes, is a man sitting in a car, visible in the photograph's background. Michel reaches this conclusion after examining blowups of the photograph and witnessing an apparently hallucinatory animation of those photographic images in a movielike sequence.

The elements of "Blow-Up" that have been mentioned above as congruent with Hitchcock's *Rear Window* are also among the most critically commented upon: the question of moral responsibility, the phenomenon of the voyeur, the problematic sexuality of the protagonist, narrative self-reflexivity, and the story's complex structure with its intersecting planes of narrative space, time, and reality. Critics often note, as well, Cortázar's fictional self-inscription in the story: like Cortázar, Roberto Michel is a professional translator, amateur photographer, and a Parisian of (partial) Latin American origin; moreover, in his highly self-conscious role as narrator he is quintessentially a writer.[7]

However, Cortázar's departures from Hitchcock's precedent – a precedent, it is worth repeating, that cannot be posited as a direct influence – are what he will bequeath to Antonioni and his Hollywood successors. Those departures, in sum, can be characterized as a kind of staged surrender of semantic control. For example, Cortázar's story takes the search for truth beyond the conventions of mystery narrative and explicitly thematicizes it as an unsolvable existential and artistic question. Photography (the "lie" of the captured moment) and film (the "lie" of sequential narrative) serve as emblems for the mendacity of written narrative – indeed, for all forms of mimetic art – and, ultimately, for the breakdown of all ontological quests.

Far from Hitchcock's narrative realism, which is tightly controlled even when he most cleverly plays with space and perspective, Cortázar indulges his surrealist inclinations, especially in the story's final, hallucinatory sequences. The surreal in "Blow-Up" is inseparable from the narrator's aberrant psychological state: The story is the narrative enactment of a mental breakdown, one that is motivated by an apparently fragile psychosexual past, by the solitude in which the narrator exists (unlike Hitchcock's Jefferies, who shares his anxious search with others), by the uncontrolled proliferation of meaning to which the narrator's interpretative quest leads him, and by the sense of permanent and irremediable victimization, within an alien moral framework, which that failed quest engenders. In Roberto Michel's feverish reflections on the autonomy and distorting power of machines (cameras, typewriters, automobiles) there is also a hint of "techno-anxiety" – a theme that will become prominent in De Palma, Coppola, Stone, and other American directors of their generation.

### The "Zapruder film" (1963)

When, on 22 November 1963, Abraham Zapruder shot a home movie of John F. Kennedy's motorcade in Dallas, he unintentionally filmed that president's assassination, producing the most significant and famous of the many still and film images that were recorded by through-the-lens witnesses of the murder in Dealey Plaza. These images have had a complicated history: Some have been lost under mysterious circumstances; those remaining have been exhaustively scrutinized, manipulated, and interpreted, while at the same time serving as physical tokens in an elaborate commerce of journalistic products for mass consumption. All of these images, taken together, represent a turning point in the historical relationship between reportage, photographic mimesis, collective consciousness, and political culture in the United States.

If Cortázar's "Blow-Up" is a well-crafted staging of a surrender of semantic control, Abraham Zapruder's film is a historically real recording of a moment of semantic explosion. Intending to film a presidential motorcade (like royal processions of old, a prearranged, symbolically laden event), Zapruder captured a moment of violence and chaos. Ultimately, what he recorded was a loss of the control of *image* in all senses: Kennedy's political career was determined by the careful management of photographic, film, and television images, which fostered an overall "image" of youth, vitality, and glamour. Kennedy's assassination represented not only a physical act of violence, but also a symbolic act of semantic seizure by his murderer(s): youth destroyed, physical beauty maimed, norms of propriety and privacy violated. (Jacqueline Kennedy's effort to retrieve a bit of her husband's brain from the trunk of the limousine perhaps can be read as a spontaneous and instinctive attempt to regain command of image.) That the assassination was recorded only accidentally adds a level of randomness to what was already an intrusion of the chaotic into the realm of the controlled.

The "Zapruder film" as a photographic image of events is in many ways inseparable from the Zapruder film as a physical artifact. The amateurish, "home movie" look of the film underscores its physicality and distinguishes it from the professional film of movies and television whose mimetic transparency is accepted by viewers as a given. The film's blurriness is part of its meaning, a meaning that resides in its simultaneous ability to disclose and conceal the historical truth of the murder. Moreover, the "Zapruder film" is rarely viewed without some form of visual manipulation; that manipulation obsessively draws attention to its reality as a physical artifact. The artifact, in turn, has had a history that is as symbolic of the loss of semantic control as the events it records, beginning with Abraham Zapruder's surrender of the film to authorities for processing and copying on the day of the assassination. Subsequent charges that the film was tampered with by the FBI or CIA before its return to Zapruder have become a commonplace of conspiracy lore (Marrs, 64–81).

Unlike Jefferies's film in *Rear Window*, but much like Michel's film in "Blow-Up," the "Zapruder film" has proved both infinitely manipulable and infinitely uninterpretable. Indeed, J. Hoberman's characterization of the "Zapruder film" seems to be an unwitting sketch of the kinds of philosophical problematics that critics have explored in Cortázar's story:

The Zapruder footage is . . . a challenge to the ontology of the medium itself. Not just an amazing snuff film and the vulgar modernist antecedent for the "structural" cinema of the late '6os, it was made to be blown up, slowed down, computer enhanced, and overinterpreted until not just the notion of documentary investigation but the laws of physics are subsumed in its seething grain.

To study the Zapruder footage is to enter a world of subatomic particles somewhere beyond the outer limits of photographic representation. (49)

If, in that "subatomic world" (the realm of the blown-up image and of projected psychic terrors) Roberto Michel encounters the man in the car, "a flour-powdered clown or bloodless man," investigators of the Kennedy assassination have discovered "Dog Man" and "Badge Man" (Marrs, 72–81). These alleged assassins, who emerge from behind the fence in blowups of the Grassy Knoll like so many photographic ghosts, are the (barely) visible embodiments of those groups (the CIA, the FBI, the Mafia, Cuban operatives) who, in the American public consciousness, exchange places in the unending variations of conspiracy narratives that constitute a kind of collective nightmare. The indefinitely postponed resolution of that nightmare is especially cruel for a culture obsessed with closure (or, more appropriately in this context, the Happy Ending) in all of its national narratives, especially its mythologized history.

Indeed, the entire Kennedy assassination narrative, of which the "Zapruder film" serves here as an emblem, seems perversely to frustrate certain constants in American culture. One of these, the fascination with and confidence in technology, has been subverted by the failure of forensic medicine, ballistics, film and sound technology, and so on, to resolve the mysteries surrounding the Kennedy case. Photography, specifically, has proved unable to deliver truth (the Zapruder film and its like offering inconclusive evidence at best) while at the same time being effective at obscuring or distorting truth through the photographic doctoring of evidence, as in the allegedly falsified pictures of Lee Harvey Oswald or the possibly altered Zapruder film itself.

The Kennedy assassination and its aftermath constituted the first time in American public consciousness that the "ontology of the medium" of photography intersected in a critical way with a collective sense of history, identity, and national character. It was perhaps inevitable that Cortázar's own exploration of photography's "ontology" should cross paths,

through the intermediate step of Antonioni's film, with America's traumatized obsession with the Kennedy assassination, an obsession that
would be indulged (appropriately, through the medium of film itself) by
directors De Palma, Coppola, Stone, and others.

## Antonioni's Blow-Up (1966)

Michelangelo Antonioni's film, which was "inspired," according to its
credits, by Cortázar's story, concerns a young London photographer who
becomes convinced that he has discovered a murder while examining
blowups of photographs he has taken in a park. His suspicion is confirmed when he returns to the park and discovers a corpse in a grove of
trees. But eventually all evidential traces of the crime, including the photographs, the negatives, and the corpse itself, vanish (as does the photographer himself – literally – in the film's final scene).

Antonioni's *Blow-Up* often has given rise to allegorizing interpretations which, though plausible, are doomed to failure as definitive pronouncements about the film's "meaning." Like Cortázar's story, Antonioni's film lacks the systematized closure of allegory. And like Cortázar,
who countered one critic's interpretation of "Blow Up" with the assertion that he had conceived the story as "essentially, a fantasy" (Chatman,
87), Antonioni denied that his *Blow-Up* was born of a guiding idea,
observing, in the middle of work on the film: "I am not at all sure what I
am in the middle of."[8] Perhaps because of the film's rich purposeless-
ness, its provocative ambiguities, even what *happens* in the film has been
a source of confusion and disagreement among critics.[9] One could say
that the problem of *seeing*, which is a central preoccupation of the film,
as it is of Cortázar's story, is strangely reenacted in the criticism of *Blow-
Up*, the film's emphasis on the issue serving to foreshadow the perceptive
gaps, the overextended critical reach, of the film's commentators.

A good deal of criticism has considered the question of Antonioni's
"fidelity" to Cortázar, perhaps an inevitable concern for a film adapted
from a literary source. The issue played itself out on a more popular level
as well, as Cortázar himself ruefully observed: "Thousands of Latin American readers cried out against the 'betrayal' of a writer whom they appre-
ciated, and I had to spend years defending Michelangelo in interviews
and irate interpolations."[10] On this level, the "fidelity" issue apparently
reflects a North–South or First World–Third World polemic of cultural
politics. But whether in critical journals or the popular press, the issue,
like that of the problem of seeing and interpreting, would also seem to
reflect a central theme of the story and film: translation (the faithful and

accurate reproduction) from language to language, from medium to medium, or from prior event to its subsequent relation. The story and the film, separately and together, have generated a *mise-en-abyme* of critical commentary that seems endlessly to restage, as much as reveal, the epistemological problematics of the texts.

Although extant interviews give ample evidence of Cortázar's impatience with the "fidelity" issue, they give no sense of his assessment of the commercial impact of Antonioni's *Blow-Up* on his literary career. The film not only received enormous critical attention, but enjoyed unprecedented – for a foreign and "art" film – popular success and wide release in the United States (Kauffmann, 70–1). It seems not coincidental that the first English-language publication of *Final del juego* – Paul Blackburn's translation entitled *End of the Game and Other Stories* (including "Blow-Up") – appeared just one year after Antonioni's film. Surely it was no coincidence that the collection was very promptly reissued as *Blow-Up and Other Stories*, with suitably eye-catching cover advertising that made prominent mention of Antonioni. Even Cortázar himself would come to refer to his story as if it had been officially rechristened: "Cuando escribí eso que ahora se llama 'Blow Up' . . ." ["When I wrote that which now is called 'Blow Up' . . ."].[11]

Blackburn's *Blow-Up and Other Stories* brought Cortázar out of academic and into popular circles in the United States, helping to spark the popularization of the "Boom" generation of Latin American novelists in the English-speaking world. Antonioni's film provided the bridge, not only between Cortázar and an American reading public, but also between a European tradition of "high-art" films and American moviegoers and moviemakers. Specifically, Antonioni's *Blow-Up* helped to create a new American awareness of such self-reflexive films as Fellini's *8 1/2* and Bergman's *The Magician* – films about film and filmmaking, in the spirit of Hitchcock's *Rear Window* but without the latter's concessions to Hollywood conventions. These "signature films," suggestive of directorial importance and European cachet, were to serve as a kind of credentializing genre for an ambitious new generation of American directors.

## De Palma's Greetings *(1968)*

*Greetings* was one of Brian De Palma's earliest film efforts and the first to be released commercially. It was a low-budget production that brought its maker attention and money – a success that apparently had more to do with the film's topicality and novelty than with its coherence and production quality. The film concerns three young men, one of whom endeavors to avoid the draft with the help of his friends. In the process, the three have a series of very loosely connected adventures, some of which are sufficiently ribald to have earned the film an X rating – which, along with its offbeat humor and antiwar themes, probably helped to guarantee its surprising box office.[12]

Themes of "specularity" are conspicuous in *Greetings,* suggesting that the young De Palma had already chosen to emulate (but had not mastered) the sophisticated, self-reflexive posture of mature artists like Hitchcock and Antonioni. One of the film's three main characters is himself a filmmaker, whose shooting sessions are more lewdly voyeuristic than the much commented upon ones of Antonioni's fashion photographer. His story intersects with the film's political content in the final scene when the young filmmaker, now a combat photographer in Viet Nam, begins to "direct" a beautiful young Vietnamese peasant in a sequence he is shooting as war reportage. The photographic staging of "reality" in this scene seems to suggest a connection between pornography, voyeuristic violence, and the manipulation of images to pander to audiences' thirst for both – a connection anticipating debates that have burgeoned in the 1980s and 1990s regarding the relationship between the political and media cultures of the United States.

More importantly for the purposes of this essay, De Palma's *Greetings* forges the link between the *Blow-Up* phenomenon and the photographic record of the Kennedy assassination, which by the late 1960s had already spawned a conspiracy genre in print and film.[13] One of De Palma's characters is an assassination buff – actually, an obsessed conspiracy theorist, who by picture's end becomes another victim on the conspirators' hit list. His victimization, resulting in part from insights he has gained by examining photographs of the assassination site, recalls (but does not "cite") that of Cortázar's protagonist. In one scene he asks a female photographer friend to make blowups of his pictures of the Grassy Knoll. Her languid response to his agitated request turns the matter into a kind of artsy in-joke, a measure both of De Palma's cool, allusive style and of the degree to which the thematics and devices of Antonioni's film had become a commonplace: "You're not going to be able to see anything but grain the size of golf balls. Look, I saw *Blow-Up.* I know how this turns out. You can't see anything. It's been blown up so many times . . . ."[14]

### Coppola's The Conversation (1974)

Unlike De Palma's youthful effort, Francis Coppola's *The Conversation* was the work of a mature filmmaker very much in control of his craft; con-

versely to *Greetings,* it was a critical success and a box office disappointment. Prominent among the recognized sources of Coppola's film is
Antonioni's *Blow-Up.* Antonioni had constructed the thematics of his film
around the principal technological element of film: photography. Coppola turned to the secondary element, sound, to explore similar themes.
The protagonist of *The Conversation* is a professional sound man, Harry
Caul, who comes to believe that his surveillance work for a corporation
is part of a murder plot. Endeavoring to intervene, he discovers – too late
– that he has mistaken the villains for the victims and unwittingly aided
the true murderers. In the process, Caul himself becomes a victim of the
sound technology and surveillance practices that are his specialty; the
final scenes show an unhinged Caul destroying his own apartment in an
attempt to discover the bug that he believes the murderers are now using
to monitor him.

The Conversation was released in the year of the Watergate scandal but,
despite its timeliness, was not really a "Watergate film"; Coppola had conceived the screenplay in 1966. Rather, *The Conversation* stands at the same
intersection of Kennedy conspiracy lore and the *Blow-Up* phenomenon
as De Palma's *Greetings.* While lacking the latter's explicit references to
the Kennedy assassination, Coppola's film is marked by that event's aftermath. For one thing, a source for the Harry Caul character was the real-
life expert in electronic surveillance Bernard Spindel, whose story, first
told in the popular press in 1966, involved Kennedy intrigue.[15] More
generally, the issue of the potential, the limits, and the dangers of sound
technology was illustrated in the investigation of the Kennedy murder:
analysis of sound recordings made in Dealey Plaza, such as the famous
"stuck" microphone of the motorcycle policeman that allegedly recorded gunshots, proved as maddeningly inconclusive as the analysis and
manipulation of photographic images of the event. Even more generally,
the film presents the same sense of the potential for victimization by sinister and technologically powerful individuals and institutions, whose
crimes are at least partially recognized but go unpunished, as is found in
the Kennedy conspiracy genre in print and film that arose in the mid-
1960s.

If the photographer characters of Hitchcock, Cortázar, Antonioni, and
De Palma are voyeurs, Caul is an *auditeur,* a role that has similar moral, sexual, and existential implications. Unlike any of his fictional predecessors,
however, Caul is also a professional who is paid for the surveillance of others, and is thus implicated – if not legally, then ethically – in the crimes
that his surveillance facilitates. The moral implications of his actions
therefore go beyond those of his predecessors. He comes to recognize

those implications as his professional detachment from the consequences of his work gives way to an awareness of his role as accomplice to evil, making his ultimate victimization, in turn, more complicated than that of Jefferies, Michel, and the others. Caul's relationship to technology is different as well: he is a "cutting edge" expert in sound technology who nonetheless suffers technoshock, beaten at his own game by other professionals and foiled by the uncanny nature of the medium itself.

True to its genesis as an *auteur* film (one that would establish the artistic "European" credentials of a director known for commercial successes), *The Conversation* is very much a self-reflexive exercise. Critics note its unorthodox, deliberately confusing use of sound, photography, and framing, which draws attention to the film as an artifact and problematizes for the audience the act of observing and perceiving in a way that parallels the experience of the film's protagonist (Chown, 94–7). The lack of closure in the film's plot is another art-film touch; though the protagonist does finally identify the criminals and their motives, more loose plot ends and unanswered questions remain than the American thriller genre would normally allow. Moreover, the truly evil characters go unpunished, while the at best ambiguously guilty Caul is the real victim; the film denies a restoration of justice and moral equilibrium. *The Conversation*'s simultaneous closure and nonclosure, its vacillation between the conventions of the European art film (*Blow-Up*) and the American genre film (*Rear Window*), is, in the opinion of Dennis Turner, a kind of ultimate self-reflexive maneuver that "raises the problems of boundary and textual authority which are suggested within its own diegesis" (9).

More importantly for the "genealogy" that this essay traces, the simultaneous closure and nonclosure in *The Conversation* is analogous to that of the conspiracy genre itself. Closure in the film is actually *exposure:* The true culprits and their motives are revealed, paralleling the journalistic exposé of conspiracy literature; in both, official versions of the *histoire*/history are discredited. Nonclosure in the film, as in conspiracy literature, means the irreconciliation of details of the "plot," the postponement or blocking of justice, a resulting permanent state of moral disequilibrium. *The Conversation* seems to recognize that the conspiracy genre which it echoes ultimately depends on holding closure and nonclosure in a poised tension: Complete "provability" would signal the demise of the genre; total "unprovability" would move the genre toward novelistic fiction, depriving it of its own voyeuristic allure: the pleasure of the exposé, the stimulation of scandal, the thrill of contemplating (even while identifying with) the victim, the satisfaction of outrage.

## Cortázar's "Apocalypse at Solentiname" (1977)

Cortázar's story is a semiautobiographical narrative with a fictional twist. The narrator, the details of whose life largely match those of Cortázar, visits Ernesto Cardenal's community in Solentiname, Nicaragua, sometime during the waning years of the Somoza regime (as Cortázar himself did in 1976). While there, he photographs some idyllic, naïf paintings done by residents of the community to "help things along." Upon his return to Paris, he has the slides of his trip developed, finding, to his horror, that the images of the paintings have been replaced by images of politically motivated atrocities in Latin America. When his companion (Claudine) views the slides, however, she sees only the naif paintings; the story ends with no resolution or explanation of the disparity in what the two have seen.

In "Apocalypse at Solentiname," Cortázar's references to his own life and experience, and to other historically real people, are explicit. Far from being a clever, high-art touch (like Coppola's cameo as director of his own movie in *Apocalypse Now*), Cortázar's self-inscription within this work of fiction signals a serious existential inquiry, an enactment of the issues of his own life and work (more in the tradition of Fellini in *8 1/2*, but with a powerful political dimension). The course of that inquiry is charted in the story's opening paragraph, in what appears at first reading to be an autobiographical touch that is tangential to the story. The narrator describes a press conference that he endures upon his arrival in San José, Costa Rica:

It was one of those hot spells and to make things even worse it all got started right away, a press conference with the usual business, why don't you live in your own country, why was *Blow-Up* so different from your short story, do you think a writer must be involved? With things going like that I can see that my final interview will be at the gates of hell and there're sure to be the same questions, and if by chance it's chez St. Peter it won't be any different: don't you think that you're writing over the heads of the people down there? (119–20)

Besides being an amusingly accurate version of the sorts of questions that in fact recur with wearisome frequency in Cortázar interviews, the fictional press conference questions capture the larger polemics that informed Cortázar's career and haunted (judging by the textual evidence of interviews and essays) his own sense of identity. The questions, interestingly, are all marked by a form of separation or division: Cortázar's self-imposed exile from Argentina, Antonioni's departures from Cortázar's story, the debate over political engagement or disengagement among writers, and the related question of the need for stylistic accessibility among politically committed writers. The questions thus anticipate the existential problematics of the larger story, which relate to a sense of a divided self.

These problematics are explored through a literary palimpsest: "Blow-Up" is always present just beneath the textual surface of "Apocalypse at Solentiname," in many senses.[16] Besides the explicit allusion in the interview question, certain plot circumstances point toward the earlier story. The narrator, for example, marvels at a bit of 1970s photographic technology, when his hosts take group pictures using the first of the Polaroid cameras whose photographs developed instantly, outside of the camera; he muses aloud what would happen if the image of "Napoleon on horseback" were to emerge from a family photo. This, of course, anticipates the climax of the story, which, like "Blow-Up," offers a fantastic and terrifying photographic vision that departs from the "reality" of what was actually photographed (the disparity of vision divided between two people rather than occurring within the undecided consciousness of a solitary narrator). In that vision, political crimes are revealed, their unidentifiable agents relegated to dim backgrounds.

One of the victims of these crimes is named: Roque Dalton, the slain Salvadoran poet, described as "the fellow [*un muchacho*] with a long face and a lock of hair falling down over his dark forehead . . . , one hand half-raised, the other probably in his pants pocket" (*A Change of Light*, 126). In his horror, the narrator wishes to "save" the victim from the act of murder that the photograph portrays by "pressing the button" of the projector, even as the photographic act in "Blow-Up" was regarded by the narrator as a possible salvation of another *muchacho*, who was "sticking his hands into his pockets, taking them out immediately, one after the other, running his fingers through his hair" (*Blow-Up and Other Stories*, 118–19). Ultimately, both of these two innocents – one an inexperienced adolescent, the other a martyred intellectual in the leftist struggle in Central America – escape the redemptive impulse of the narrator. In both cases, the ultimate reality of the crime remains obscure, and the moral imperative (for salvation, for justice) that is so passionately felt by the narrator remains unfulfilled. The reader, moreover, is left with an unclosed text in each case: The narrative end of "Blow-Up" dissolves into ambiguous and overlapping frames of photographic and "real" reality, whereas the conclusion of "Apocalypse at Solentiname" offers two irreconcilably different visions (one idyllic, the other apocalyptic, but which one is hallucinatory?) of Latin American reality.

Like the films by De Palma, Coppola, and Stone discussed earlier, "Apocalypse at Solentiname" stands at the intersection of the "Blow-Up" tradition and the world of political crime – specifically, unsolved political murders. The photographic plot device, like the camera used by photojournalists, offers the possibility of an exposé of the political reality of Latin America. The use of the fantastic is both in the surrealist tradition of the earlier Cortázar and easily allegorized in a new political context: The violence of Latin American reality is too horrible to be real. The narrator's slide show is also a call to political consciousness, a declaration of a moral imperative. Interestingly, the actual blowup device is not used in "Apocalypse at Solentiname": The frustrated ontological quest, metaphorized in the enlargement of images that reveal less as they reveal more, is not the issue. The problem of seeing and interpreting, rather, is divided between people: the newly aware narrator, who sees the horrible, versus the complacent Claudine, who sees only the picturesque, the idyllic, and the consumable.

Yet, lest the story fall too easily into a facile allegory about political awareness, the narrator clearly problematizes his own existential situation, in ways that seem to reflect that of Cortázar himself (or rather, the textual construct whom we know as "Cortázar"). The narrator's divided self is vividly evoked in the descriptions of his very different lives in Latin America and Europe. Moreover, the divided self is portrayed in the very enunciative act, as in the following passage:

It was pleasant thinking that everything would be revealed to me again little by little, after the paintings from Solentiname I would go though the box with the Cuban photographs, but why the paintings first, why the professional deformation, art before life, and why not, the one said to the other in their eternal unresolvable fraternal and rancorous dialogue . . . ? (124)

This creation of a fictional divided self, presumably reflective of Cortázar's own, brings the story full circle to the questions posed by his fictional interviewers at the outset. The story's denouement seems to suggest that those questions cannot be dismissed as so many tiresome clichés. What, indeed, are the political obligations of the Latin American intellectual? Are they to expose the truth, as the story itself does? If so, what existential posture should accompany the act of truth telling? Are the bourgeois luxuries of a Parisian existence irreconcilable with the political commitment of a leftist Latin American writer?

Those questions remain unanswered, or rather, they are recognized as active questions – a kind of productive self-doubt – as they are, in a sense, in Cortázar's famous "Letter to Roberto Fernández Retamar."[17] The stylistic question, however, is answered decisively – again, as in Cortázar's "Letter" and in other essays and interviews – by the very textual nature of the story. Its recourse to the fantastic, its narrative indeterminacy, its adherence to the polyvalent and the difficult, and its corresponding denial of realism and allegory, all square with Cortázar's passionate defense of stylistic liberty – indeed, his belief that literary liberation is a complement to political struggle. In this sense, "Apocalypse at Solentiname" can be read as a grand, self-referential metaphor for Cortázar's problematized political conversion, and for his tolerance of (or is it an insistence on the necessity for?) the coexistence of political conviction and existential self-questioning.

### De Palma's Blow Out (1981)

More than ten years after *Greetings,* during which period he experimented continually with Hitchcockian techniques and themes of voyeurism and specularity, Brian De Palma returned explicitly to the "Blow-Up" theme with *Blow Out*.[18] The film concerns a sound man (Jack Terri), a collaborator on low-budget porno/slasher films, who inadvertently makes an audio recording of the fatal car accident of a presidential hopeful. That recording, followed by his rescue of a young woman from the submerged automobile the victim was driving, leads Terri to the belief that the accident was in reality an assassination: not a tire blowout, but a tire shoot-out.[19] By joining his audio recording with another witness's photographs of the event, Terri produces evidence for his theory – evidence that proves impossible to bring to light because of the cover-ups effected by both the victim's aides and his murderers. Terri and the young woman become involved in postassassination intrigues that lead to their silencing: Terri, by fear, cynicism, and despondency; the young woman, by her murder at the hands of the assassin.

*Blow Out* serves as a virtual catalogue of themes and effects in the Hitchcock film lexicon and the Antonioni *Blow-Up* tradition. Terri is a voyeur *and* an auditeur. Technology (photographic and sound) is both thematicized in the plot and conspicuously and self-consciously employed by the film itself. Technology is linked with the existential situation of the protagonist, a situation marked by solitude and moral ambiguity, with hints of problematic sexuality.[20] In his quest for truth, he is frustrated and ultimately victimized by conspiracies beyond his ken and by the traps set by the very technology that is his professional forte. Moreover, Terri is both implicated in and thwarted by an exploitative media culture (the culture of pornography, marketed violence, sensationalized journalism). Finally, enough self-reflexive and self-inscriptive hints are present to imply an identification between Terri and De Palma himself.[21]

Interestingly, *Blow Out* "cites" three real or presumed historical conspiracies: the John F. Kennedy assassination, the Edward Kennedy Chappaquiddick incident, and Watergate (Bliss, 100). The story recounts the assassination of a liberal, Irish American politician, an event that is accidentally recorded on film and audio tape. The film is only seen by the public in separate still images in news magazines, as was the "Zapruder film" years before it was released for public viewing. Terri combines those still images with the recorded sounds of the murder, as did Kennedy assassination investigators, and challenges the official version of the event, just as many challenged the Warren Commission Report. Terri's silencing recalls the fate – according to conspiracy lore – of many witnesses of the Kennedy assassination. The Chappaquiddick incident is suggested by the accident, in that the candidate's car careens off a road into a river (the drowning victim is the candidate himself, not his female companion), and the candidate's aides endeavor to "kill" the story of his sexual indiscretions. Finally, Watergate is evoked by details of the conspiracy, some election-year "dirty tricks" that have gotten out of control.

Like Coppola's *The Conversation,* De Palma's *Blow Out* challenges the conventions of the Hollywood thriller in its unorthodox mix of closure and nonclosure. As in a certain variety of the thriller genre, the reality of the crime and of the conspiracy behind it is disclosed to the audience; the narrative tension, then, derives from the protagonist's struggle to discover what the audience already knows, from his efforts to convince others to believe the truth, from his competition with the criminal, and from the threat the latter poses. These tensions are resolved only partially: the protagonist never does gain full knowledge of the assassination conspiracy, nor is he successful in overcoming the cover-up. He both wins and loses the competition with the criminal: He kills him at the end, but only after the young woman – a largely innocent character and a potential love interest – has been murdered. Justice, then, is only marginally triumphant; on the largest scale – the national, the political – it is not served.

The resulting portrait of an unjust and corrupt America is communicated through the most transparent and closed of narrative devices: allegory. In the film's final scenes, Terri chases the murderer, who has abducted the young woman and is dragging her through the middle of a fireworks display that concludes "Liberty Day" in Philadelphia. Amid frenzied crowds, a giant replica of the Liberty Bell, gaudy swaths of red, white, and blue, and against a background of exploding rockets and an enormous American flag, Terri kills the man who has already killed the young woman; he then embraces her in a pose that suggests, in the apt phrase of Michael Bliss, "a tragic political pietà" (114). The death of the innocent love interest suggests the death of American idealism, as patriotic icons are amassed in a kind of holocaustic crescendo. Such a broad use of visual symbolism is complemented by technical flourishes which, as throughout the film, clearly articulate rather than problematize the message – a departure from the discursive precedent of Cortázar, Antonioni, and Coppola, and a return, perhaps, to the narrative style of Hitchcock, De Palma's acknowledged master.

De Palma's allegory of a fallen America corresponds with a stance of political cynicism, one that is signaled early on in the film's telescoping of Kennedy references: If JFK was the heroic martyr slain by sinister forces, his brother was the fallen hero capable of cover-ups of his own; both left and right are corrupt. At the end, Jack Terri's actions and demeanor embody the film's overall cynicism: He listens obsessively to the recordings of his female friend's final moments (he had "wired" her for protection, to no avail), ending with cries of "Oh, God, God, Jack!" (chillingly evocative of Dealey Plaza on 22 November 1963) and a scream. Back at work in what appears to be an alcohol- or drug-induced daze, he dubs those "realistic" screams into the sound track of the porno slasher film he is collaborating on. *Blow Out* thus ends with what is perhaps a self-reflexive metaphor for De Palma's own insertion of American cultural "reality" into his film – a reality that is horrible but, when transmuted into fiction, marketable to a society eager to be entertained and willing to consume, in the process, its own most bitter images of itself.

## Stone's JFK (1991)

Oliver Stone's *JFK* recreates the story of New Orleans District Attorney Jim Garrison's investigation of the Kennedy assassination and his failed prosecution of businessman Clay Shaw for conspiracy in the crime, in the late 1960s. Through this story, Stone elaborates a complicated assassination conspiracy theory and illustrates it through extensive use of narrative flashback combining historical film footage with reenactments of documented or imagined events surrounding the crime and its aftermath. The conclusion – that Kennedy was eliminated in a vast, right-wing coup d'état because of his desire to end the Cold War, remove troops from Viet Nam, and advance other liberal positions – earned the film considerable notoriety in the popular press even before its release.

*JFK* bears inevitable traces of the intersection of the conspiracy-genre film with the "Blow-Up" tradition. It is a piece of virtuoso filmmaking, as complicated and well-crafted as any of the technically self-conscious films that followed in Antonioni's wake. Like other films in the tradition, it uses that virtuosity to create an effect that one critic of *JFK* has called the "intimation of the uncanny" (Denby, 50), the sense that sinister forces are behind and in control of the apparent randomness of events – an effect very much in the spirit of Cortázar's seminal story. The unsuccessful quest of the protagonist, which is to persuade others that his vision is not one of paranoia but of truth, also recalls other films of the tradition. The quest, in turn, implies a political posture, as in Cortázar's "Apocalypse at Solentiname" and De Palma's *Blow Out*. Through the self-inscription of the author – in this case, the much noted identification of Stone with his character Garrison – the film's politics become strongly identifiable with those of its fictionally embodied creator, as in the precedents established by Cortázar and De Palma.

However, *JFK* is far from being a self-reflexive meditation on the art of filmmaking and the "ontology of the medium." Stone was reproached for his manipulations of film technique to advance his conspiracy theory, especially the photographic simulacra – reenactments of events, imitation newsreel, fabricated "home movie" footage – that diminish the viewer's ability to distinguish the fictional or speculative from the historical. Such devices constitute a powerful and confident exploitation of the medium's potential, without the kind of ironic or self-critical distance that had characterized the tradition from Antonioni to De Palma. The film's apparent lack of concern or compunction about its own manipulativeness is itself an irony, as many have pointed out, given the charges of distortion or fabrication of photographic evidence that have always been a cornerstone of Kennedy conspiracy theories, and to which the conspiracy investigators in the film constantly allude.[22]

Furthermore, unlike its predecessors in the "Blow-Up" line, *JFK* is a film of closure, revelation, and semantic fullness. The film's "intimations of the uncanny" emerge, ultimately, into the clear light of the knowable, as Garrison unravels the tangled skein of the conspiracy in his long courtroom summation speech at the film's end. Nothing is left unexplained; the photographic ghosts on the Grassy Knoll are embodied and ascribed identities, motives, and a modus operandi. Even the "Zapruder film," a copy of which Stone purchased for use in the film, is "resemanticized" as it is replayed and explicated; it is placed within a context in which all visual details are accounted for, all appearances have a foundation in history and reality, and all revealed horrors are fathomable. The rending of

national myths that the Zapruder film recorded is, in effect, reversed in
*JFK*, as a new "countermyth" – the phrase is Stone's[23] – is fashioned, one
that is politically provocative but morally familiar and comforting.

The moral dimension of that myth is developed, in part, by the film's
characterizations. Critics point to Stone's recreation of Jim Garrison as
an archetypal American hero: a modest and quiet family man, traditional
in his morals, persevering in his convictions, and courageous in his individual crusade against evil institutions. The Garrison character stands in
contrast to the broadly stylized portraits of the story's kinky villains. Garrison is also made to parallel the film's remythologized images of
Kennedy – images that were largely self-created and prevailed until the
revisionist version of his life which emerged decades after his death. Garrison's characterization is consolidated by intertextual film references as
well, from the casting of Kevin Costner (well-known for all-American
hero roles) to the often observed "Mr. Smith Goes to Washington" quality of his courtroom speech (Hoberman, 49). In his role as one who
shows and explicates evidence, as the narrator of the story behind the
story, Garrison can also be regarded as Stone's alter ego, a heroic persona
that contrasts with the evanescent, self-loathing, or self-interrogating
alter egos of Cortázar, Antonioni, Coppola, and De Palma.

### Conclusion

Most of the important themes and narrative strategies of "Blow-Up" were
effectively translated into the film world, and to a new generation of
American filmmakers, by Antonioni's version of Cortázar's story. De
Palma, Coppola, Stone, and others recontextualized those themes and
strategies in terms of the Hollywood generic conventions from which, as
commercial filmmakers, they never completely escaped, and in the light
of social and political circumstances that were generationally and culturally specific. For these directors, the near side of the "Antonioni bridge"
was, most importantly, a political space. Cortázar's themes of surveillance
and privacy, conspiracy, technological anxiety, criminality, the moral
obligation of the observer, and so on, had by necessity strong political
connotations in an America that, following the Kennedy assassination,
emerged into a troubled middle age. Phenomena like the "Zapruder
film," which in its very nature was an illustration of Cortázar's exploration of the ontology of the photographic medium, also inevitably
politicized and nationalized the "Blow-Up" tradition.

Some of the recontextualizations effected by De Palma, Coppola,

Stone, and others have been especially effective as social commentary: The victimization of Roberto Michel (to give just one example) by the allied traps of human conspiracy, mimetic technology, and social isolation has been forcefully transferred by those directors into larger social contexts; indeed, they have represented that victimization on a collective scale, in an America fragmented and traumatized both by specific events and by the overall character of the modern (and postmodern) condition. In this sense, these filmmakers have ranged beyond the concerns of Cortázar and Antonioni to illustrate social phenomena that continue to evolve in troubling ways. De Palma, especially, seems aware of the changing role of photographic, film, and, most recently, video and computer technology in all levels of social discourse. One example would be his citation of the Zapruder film in *Blow Out,* which seems to recognize in it a precursor of the "home video" phenomenon in American culture, with its as yet unfathomable implications for the definition of public and private space, access to and dissemination of information, and negotiation of power between individuals and institutions – a phenomenon dramatically exemplified by the Rodney King affair.[24]

Yet, despite the timeliness of Cortázar's legacy for a generation of directors who are politically and socially aware, conscious of the power and weirdness of technology, and anxious to be avant-garde and artful, not all the elements of Cortázar's story have survived the crossing into American film/pop culture with their integrity intact. Cortázar's self-reflexive narrative posture, for example, was transformed by Antonioni into film language that remained, on some levels, too arcane for the young generation of American directors who imitated it as a kind of European manner. That manner was useful for credentializing purposes but devoid, in their versions, of existential profundity – with the possible exception of Coppola, whose *The Conversation* seems to employ such an enunciative stance with an awareness of its larger implications. One can also question the degree to which the directors in question have been constructive and effectual in their political rewritings of "Blow-Up"; the films surveyed in this essay seem to illustrate what Ryan and Kellner have observed in the American conspiracy film genre in general: a failure to articulate a radical political critique (95–105). For all their tone of protest, disenchantment, cynicism, or outrage, these films are populist and commercially palatable, in terms of their swerve to narrative closure (most notably in *Blow-Out* and *JFK*), their conventional morality (*JFK*), and especially in their insistent portrayal of political evil as aberrant and conspiracy-driven rather than systemic and structural.

On this last point, Cortázar's own evolution serves as an enlightening contrast. Antonioni's *Blow-Up* was also a bridge from Cortázar to Cortázar; in "Apocalypse at Solentiname," the author uses his story, as filtered through Antonioni and refracted through the world of the cultural marketplace, as a measure of his change and his constancy as a man and as a writer. He turns his good-natured irritation with the Antonioni question into an ultimately serious and self-reflexive gesture, adding a final layer of metanarrativity to the already multilayered "Blow-Up" phenomenon. In so doing he declares the integrity of his radical (and radically self-questioning) political posture. His awareness of the political potential of unclosed narrative and of the self-reflexive and self-interrogatory narrative act is, in the final analysis, what separates him from his American progeny and what makes him, for them, an unknown and unknowable forebear.[25]

### Notes

1. In *Cortázar por Cortázar,* 122–3; my translation.
2. First published in *Las armas secretas* (1959). The present essay cites from Blackburn's translation.
3. Mahieu traces the history of film versions of borrowings from Cortázar's works, mostly in the Spanish-speaking world.
4. Originally published as "Apocalipsis de Solentiname" in the collection *Alguien que anda por ahí.* This essay cites from the English version, published in *A Change of Light and Other Stories.*
5. Other films that have returned to the theme of voyeurism, if not with Hitchcock's artistry, include the British film *Peeping Tom* (1960), De Palma's *Body Double* (1984), and the 1993 film version of Ira Levin's novel *Sliver.*
6. Critics cite Douchet as the pioneer in this interpretation of the film.
7. The Cortázar bibliography is so vast that to attempt to choose the most significant critical pieces on these standard themes is next to impossible. However, the articles by Matas, Gutiérrez, Chatman, Schiminovich, López de Martínez, and Pérez can serve as representative samples.
8. Cited by Huss, 11.
9. This is discussed by Peavler and Grossvogel in their respective articles.
10. In the *Diacritics* interview, 40.
11. *Cortázar por Cortázar,* 17; my translation.
12. For a survey of this now little-known film, see Malmfelt's review and references in the books by Bliss and MacKinnon.
13. Among the important films in that genre are *Rush to Judgment* (a 1967 documentary), *Executive Action* (a 1973 semidocumentary that anticipates Stone's *JFK* in its depiction of a right-wing conspiracy to eliminate President Kennedy), *The Parallax View* (a 1974 fictional film based loosely on both Kennedy assassinations), and *Winter Kills* (a 1979 parody/satire that draws on Kennedy assassination references).

14. The "in-joke" nature of the blow-up device is also evident in Mel Brooks's *High Anxiety* (1977), a Hitchcock parody. In one scene, a blowup of a surveillance photograph reveals nothing more terrifying than the protagonist's nervousness (he suffers from acrophobia) in a glass-walled elevator.

15. For a complete summary of the history of Coppola's involvement with the project and his various "sources," see Chown, chap. 5.

16. Munoz, Sosnowski, and Tittler have each considered the relationship between the two stories, and their readings collectively have informed mine.

17. "Carta a Roberto Fernández Retamar," elsewhere published under the title "Acerca de la situación del intelectual latinoamericano."

18. De Palma's continued interest in these themes is evident in his *Body Double* of 1984.

19. Thus De Palma's title, though an allusion to Antonioni's film, has a specific plot justification. The appropriation of the "Blow-" prefix in film titles has been reprised in the 1991 political satire *Blowback* and the 1994 action film *Blown Away*.

20. See Wood, 155–61, on Terri's sexuality and the larger sexual issues that are discernible in the film.

21. Pauline Kael's very favorable review of the film was based on this presumed identification.

22. Hoberman's summary of the issue, which countless critics and reviewers touched on, is concise and eloquent.

23. Cited by Hoberman, 49.

24. For a survey of these issues and of the scholarly literature that deals with them, see Berko.

25. Stam (13–17) surveys the issues surrounding "the political valence of reflexivity" in film and literature.

## References

Belton, John. "The Space of *Rear Window*." In *Hitchcock's Rereleased Films,* ed. Walter Raubicheck and Walter Srebnick, 76–94. Detroit: Wayne State University Press, 1991.

Berko, Lili. "Surveying the Surveilled: Video, Space, and Subjectivity." *Quarterly Review of Film and Video* 14, nos. 1–2 (1992): 61–91.

Bliss, Michael. *Brian de Palma*. Filmmakers 6. Metuchen, NJ: The Scarecrow Press, 1983.

*Blow Out*. Dir. Brian De Palma. Filmways Pictures, 1981.

*Blow-Up*. Dir. Michelangelo Antonioni. Metro-Goldwyn-Mayer, 1966.

Chatman, Seymour. "The Rhetoric of Difficult Fiction: Cortázar's 'Blow-Up.'" *Poetics Today* 1, no. 4 (1980): 23–57.

Chown, Jeffrey. *Hollywood Auteur: Francis Coppola*. New York: Praeger Publishers, 1988.

*The Conversation*. Dir. Francis Ford Coppola. Paramount Pictures, 1974.

Cortázar, Julio. *Blow-Up and Other Stories*. Trans. Paul Blackburn. New York: Random House, 1967.

"Carta a Roberto Fernández Retamar." *Casa de Las Américas* 8, no. 45 (1967): 5–12.

*A Change of Light and Other Stories.* Trans. Gregory Rabassa. London: Harvill Press, 1984.

*Cortázar por Cortázar.* With Evelyn Picon Garfield. Mexico City: Universidad Veracruzana, 1977.

Interview. With Lucille Kerr et al. *Diacritics* 4, no. 4 (1974): 35–40.

Denby, David. Review of *JFK. New York*, 6 January 1992, 50.

Douchet, Jean. "Hitch et son public." *Cahiers du Cinéma* 113 (1960): 7–15.

*Greetings.* Dir. Brian De Palma. Sigma III, 1968.

Grossvogel, David I. "Blow-Up: The Forms of an Esthetic Itinerary." *Diacritics* 2, no. 3 (1972): 49–54.

Gutiérrez Mouat, Ricardo. "'Las babas del diablo': Exorcismo, traducción, voyeurismo." In *Los ochenta mundos de Cortázar: Ensayos,* ed. Fernando Burgos, 37–46. Madrid: EDI-6, 1987.

Hoberman, J. Review of *JFK. Village Voice,* 31 December 1991, 49.

Huss, Roy, trans. "Antonioni in the English Style: A Day on the Set." From *Cahiers du Cinéma* 186 (1967): 13–15. In *Focus on "Blow-Up,"* ed. Roy Huss, 7–12. Englewood Cliffs, NJ: Prentice-Hall, 1971.

*JFK.* Dir. Oliver Stone. Warner Brothers, 1991.

Kael, Pauline. "Portrait of the Artist as a Young Gadgeteer" (review of *Blow Out*). *The New Yorker,* 27 July 1981, 74–9.

Kauffmann, Stanley. "A Year with *Blow-Up:* Some Notes." In *Focus on "Blow-Up,"* ed. Roy Huss, 70–7. Englewood Cliffs, NJ: Prentice-Hall, 1971.

López de Martínez, Adelaida. "'Las babas del diablo': Teoría y práctica del cuento." *Hispania* 67, no. 4 (1984): 567–76.

MacKinnon, Kenneth. *Misogyny in the Movies: The De Palma Question.* London and Toronto: Associated University Presses, 1990.

Mahieu, José A. "Cortázar en cine." *Cuadernos Hispanoamericanos* 364–6 (1980): 640–6.

Malmfelt, A. D. Review of *Greetings. Film Society Review* 4 (1969): 37–41.

Marrs, Jim. *Crossfire: The Plot That Killed Kennedy.* New York: Carroll & Graf Publishers, 1989.

Matas, Julio. "El contexto moral en algunos cuentos de Julio Cortázar." *Revista Iberoamericana* 39 (1973): 593–609.

Muñoz, Willy O. "Julio Cortázar: Vértices de una figura comprometida." *Hispanic Journal* 8, no. 1 (1986): 135–45.

Peavler, Terry J. "Blow-Up: A Reconsideration of Antonioni's Infidelity to Cortázar." *PMLA* 94 (1979): 887–93.

Pérez, Genaro J. "Auto-Referential Elements in 'Blow-Up' and 'The Gates of Heaven.'" *The Review of Contemporary Fiction* 3, no. 3 (1983): 48–51.

*Rear Window.* Dir. Alfred Hitchcock. Paramount Pictures, 1954.

Ryan, Michael, and Douglass Kellner. *Camera Politica: The Politics and Ideology of Contemporary Hollywood Film.* Bloomington: Indiana University Press, 1988.

Schiminovich, Flora H. "Cortázar y el cuento en uno de sus cuentos." *Nueva Narrativa Hispanoamericana* 1, no. 2 (1971): 97–104.

Sosnowski, Saul. "Imágenes del deseo: El testigo ante su mutación: 'Las babas del diablo' y 'Apocalipsis de Solentiname.'" *Inti: Revista de Literatura Hispánica* 10–1 (1979–80): 93–8.

Stam, Robert. *Reflexivity in Film and Literature from Don Quixote to Jean-Luc Godard.* Ann Arbor, MI: UMI Research Press, 1985.

Tittler, Jonathan. "Los dos Solentinames de Cortázar." In *Los ochenta mundos de Cortázar: Ensayos,* ed. Fernando Burgos, 111–17, Madrid: EDI-6, 1987.

Turner, Dennis. "The Subject of *The Conversation.*" *Cinema Journal* 24, no. 4 (1985): 4–22.

Wood, Robin. *Hollywood from Vietnam to Reagan.* New York: Columbia University Press, 1986.

# PART FOUR
The Ethics of Reading

# 10

## Pursuing a Perfect Present

### Doris Sommer

From his opening lines in Julio Cortázar's "The Pursuer" (1959), the narrator seems uneasy.[1] Bruno is a jazz critic, respected among Parisian publishers and academics but surprisingly out of phase from the very beginning of his story.[2] By contrast, the disarmingly lucid character here is a drug-dependent saxophonist who stands in for Charlie Parker. Any jazz buff would recognize him from the biographical dates and details that follow, and maybe even from the title and our first glimpse of a self-destructive and arrogant "Johnny Carter"; but Cortázar makes sure we get the reference from his dedication to Parker in memoriam. The narrating critic, as I said, shows signs of awkwardness even before Johnny greets him sardonically, "Faithful old buddy Bruno, regular as bad breath" (161).[3] Not that Bruno deserves Johnny's distasteful reception, as if faithfulness were any reason for embarrassment. On the contrary, Bruno assumes no responsibility for Johnny's bad mood. Why should he, when the loyal friend had rushed to the musician's cheap hotel room to rescue him – once again – from the childish irresponsibility that only artists get away with?

This time Johnny had forgotten his saxophone under the seat of a subway car and Bruno has offered to replace it. The rescuer's condescending concern obviously grates on the black musician, who seems helpless, sweating, and shivering after some forbidden drug-induced high. Patronized and misprized, Johnny surely knows the self-serving motives for solicitude, and he probably dismisses Bruno's genuine concern for the man wasting his talent and his life, just as Charlie Parker dismissed his own friends and fans.[4] Bruno's objection to heroin means, for Johnny, a determination to cancel the trips that take him away from work. Johnny's work is, after all, the necessary condition for Bruno's success. "I'm thinking of the music being lost, the dozens of sides Johnny would be able to cut, leaving that presence, that astonishing step forward where he had it over any other musician" (167).[5] The poor "savage monkey" of a musician is not only the object of Bruno's own, casually racist dismissals (see 258, 263, 288, 291, 299; English, 164, 174, 179, 199); he is also the sub-

ject of the critic's authoritative biography. Johnny plays the alto sax as
"only a god can play" (251; 163), and he continues to be the capital for
Bruno's critical purchase. But Johnny is precarious capital, because – as
Bruno frets toward the end – he could publicly contradict the interpreter, or simply leave him behind in the wake of musical and personal
mischief.

Bruno has good reason to fret, because the new jazzmen of the 1940s
and early 1950s were notorious for psychologically harassing those who
couldn't keep up: other musicians as well as a public still avid for the
musical Uncle Toms who played the sensual sounds of "hot" music.[6]
Louis Armstrong was probably the most visible target, and his characteristic courtesy to other jazzmen cracked with the boppers: "They want to
carve everyone else because they're full of malice, and all they want to do
is show you up," he complained. "So you get all them weird chords which
don't mean nothing . . . and you got no melody to remember and no
beat to dance to."[7] Sometimes literally turning its back on the audience,
"cool" jazz refused to pander. Instead of tortured and passionate, repeat-
able songs, cool "bebop" delivered an oblique sense of melody, a deliberate exploration of unsuspected harmonies and rhythms. Bruno fancies
himself a "hipster" on the inside of innovation, but he can feel the chill
of being left out. (*"And furthermore, cool doesn't mean, even by accident ever,
what you've written,"* Johnny would accuse him) (208; 300). And Bruno
worries about a possible professional shaming.

Honestamente, ¿qué me importa su vida? Lo único que me inquieta es
que se deje llevar por esa conducta que no soy capaz de seguir (digamos que
no quiero seguir) y acabe desmintiendo las conclusiones de mi libro. Que
deje caer por ahí que mis afirmaciones son falsas, que su música es otra cosa.
(303–4)

[To be honest, what does his life matter to me? The only thing that both-
ers me is that if he continues to let himself go on living as he has been, a style
I'm not capable of following (let's say I don't want to follow it), he'll end up
by making lies out of the conclusions I've reached in my book. He might let
it drop somewhere that my statements are wrong, that his music's something
else.] (211)

That "something else" haunts Bruno when he's in Johnny's company.
Brooding about getting it all wrong (Johnny, his music, his biography),
Bruno knows the pain of writing it anyway. He also knows, and tells us
early on, that his pathetic insufficiency is its own paradoxical license to
narrate. Because he admits his own shortcomings, Bruno can become

strangely trustworthy as a critic of what continues to elude him. (Were it not for this paradox, how could any reader dare to comment on this story by Cortázar, on his pursuits and accomplishments?)

Soy un crítico de *jazz* lo bastante sensible como para comprender mis limitaciones, y me doy cuenta de que lo que estoy pensando está por debajo del plano donde el pobre Johnny trata de avanzar con sus frases truncadas, sus suspiros, sus súbitas rabias y sus llantos. A él le importa un bledo que yo lo crea genial, y nunca se ha envanecido de que su música esté mucho más allá de la que tocan sus compañeros. Pienso melancólicamente que él está al principio de su saxo mientras yo vivo obligado a conformarme con el final. El es la boca y yo la oreja, por no decir que él es la boca y yo . . . (256)

[I'm sensitive enough a jazz critic when it comes to understanding my limitations, and I realize that what I'm thinking is on a lower level than where poor Johnny is trying to move forward with his decapitated sentences, his sighs, his impatient angers and his tears. He gives a damn where I think everything ought to go easy, and he's never come on smug that his music is much farther out than his contemporaries are playing. It drags me to think that he's at the beginning of his sax-work, and I'm going along and have to stick it out to the end. He's the mouth and I'm the ear, so as not to say he's the mouth and I'm the . . . ] (167)

Self-awareness, though, does not mean that Bruno is resigned to the aesthetic and intellectual asymmetry. The limitations that he confesses, together with Johnny's relentlessly searching talk, evidently make the critic nervous. The very next thing Johnny says, in fact, sounds like a reproach: "Bruno, maybe someday you'll be able to write. . . . Not for me, understand, what the hell does it matter to me?" (167).[8] Bruno feels diminished in Johnny's presence, both because he has trouble following the musician's verbal improvisations and because he may be serving as Johnny's instrument to be played on and with. "[A]fter the wonder of it's gone you get an irritation, and for me at least it feels as though Johnny's been pulling my leg" (173).[9] In either case, Bruno can't wait to leave the hotel room so that Johnny's troubling text can safely unravel into commonplaces. "I smile the best I can, understanding fuzzily that he's right, but what he suspects and the hunch I have about what he suspects are going to be deleted as soon as I'm in the street and've gotten back into my every day life" (173).[10]

The layered relationship that Cortázar manages to portray in this initial scene would be admirable enough: Bruno's vexed reverence for the "childish" genius who makes the mature critic feel stupid; Johnny's reluc-

tant respect for the interpreter who gets more right than it is safe to
acknowledge, and who listens well enough to keep Johnny talking. (In
fact, experimental jazz was indebted to European, even academic, influences.)[11] But the story is admirable beyond the probing dialogue and
reflection, just beyond, in the subtly disquieting performance of the narrative passages that frame the encounter. From the first lines, as I said,
while the narrator still casts himself as blameless and forbearing before
acknowledging any uneasiness at the level of story, his plight is *felt* in the
grammar.

To be precise, Bruno's nervousness comes out in his obsessive recourse to the present perfect tense. The very term *present perfect* is oxymoronic, unstable, dislocating, with one foot in the past and the other in
the present. Its function is logically pivotal, providing a point of departure from one component tense to the other. But Bruno's compound
tense doesn't resolve itself into either the past or the present; instead it
stays deadlocked and dizzying in its own repeated contradiction. Fourteen present perfect verbs cluster on the first full page of text ("Dédée
me ha llamado . . . yo he ido . . . Me ha bastado . . . he encontrado . . . ha
dicho . . . he sacado . . . no he querido . . . he preguntado . . . se ha le-
vantado y ha apagado . . . nos hemos reconocido . . . ha sacado . . . he
sentido . . ha dicho . . . Me ha alegrado").

Dissonant, almost shrill from repetition, the present perfect tense
becomes a structural feature of Bruno's writing. It is as if the writing
refused to fit into time, the conventional grammatical time that opposes
past to present in neat, mutually exclusive categories. The present perfect scrambles categories. It straddles between excess and inadequacy,
too much time and too little. Does a present perfect action spill over
from past to present, an exorbitance and difference carried in a single
composite tense? Or does the action fit nowhere, already exiled from the
past and not quite surviving into the present? The specific problem for
Bruno is that Johnny is unstable, exorbitant as the subject of a definitive
biography. He is still alive, and willful, too present and palpable to be the
manageable material of an informative story. Alive, he is not really perfect, a term which I take here in the grammatical sense of finished, past.
Only at the end of Bruno's long struggle in the disturbingly present perfect of Johnny's life, after sixty-three closely written pages, does the biographer finally put a full stop to his work in simple, perfect, grammar.
Johnny dies, Bruno reports with some relief and no less bad faith, "as he
really is, a poor sonofabitch with barely mediocre intelligence" (218).[12]

And the story achieves the finality of a simple past tense that can be superseded by the repose and plenitude of a perfectly simple present.

Todo esto coincidió con la aparición de la segunda edición de mi libro, pero por suerte tuve timpo de incorporar una nota necrológica redactada a toda máquina, y una fotografía del entierro donde se veía a muchos *jazzmen* famosos. En esa forma la biografía quedó, por decirlo así, completa. Quizá no esté bien que yo diga esto, pero como es natural me sitúo en un plano meramente estético. Ya hablan de una nueva traducción, creo que al sueco o al noruego. Mi mujer está encantada con la noticia. (313)

[All this happened at the same time that the second edition of my book was published, but luckily I had time to incorporate an obituary note edited under full steam and inserted, along with a newsphoto of the funeral in which many famous jazzmen were identifiable. In that format the biography remained, so to speak, intact and finished. Perhaps it's not right that I say this, but naturally I was speaking from a merely aesthetic point of view. They're already talking of a new translation, into Swedish or Norwegian, I think. My wife is delighted at the news.] (220)

Presumably the verbs were always simple in the biography, even in the first edition, but now there are comforting grounds for simplicity. Real death, mercifully for Bruno, has stabilized the virtual loss that biography effects into loss pure and simple. The very genre that presumes to preserve a life defaces it, as Paul De Man argues so poignantly, because biography petrifies living movement into a monument, spirit into letter.[13] Here the hardening takes the form of fixing an unstable present perfect tense into a solidly perfect past. Until that final page, though, Johnny's vitality has been outstripping Bruno's best biographical efforts to control it. The biographer would reduce the complexity of his subject's relationships to an orderly report of information. The violence of that project should be clear. It collapses the obliging and ensnaring discourse of *sociability* into the unencumbered, antiseptic language of *knowledge*, to use Emannuel Levinas's terms.[14] In the place of a social subject who makes claims on his interlocutors, Bruno prefers the unfettered objective hero, a cluster of data available for bloodless exchanges among music mavins.

But Bruno cannot seem to package the narrative interlude we are reading now, the story that comes between the official editions of Johnny's life. Bruno's writing in "The Pursuer" doesn't cooperate with marketing demands. As if to call attention to his performance in an anxious present perfect tense, the narrative voice pauses after a first page.

The writing is, in fact, so apparently clumsy that Paul Blackburn's overly graceful English translation refuses to respect the redundant awkwardness. The English version presumes to correct Cortázar's purposefully unpleasant Spanish with the predictable elegance of variety that good taste dictates. For example, the first two Spanish verbs, which set the dissonant tone and timing for Bruno's nervous style, are fixed in the translation into easily chronologized past perfect conjugations: "Dedée had called me . . . and I'd gone." Johnny, we know, reviles conventional "good taste"; and perhaps surprisingly, respectable Bruno seems incapable of practicing it.

The attention-getting pause after that first narrative page is a short dialogue about timing, the very feature that has presented a problem. Bruno begins with a conventional comment about how long it had been since the friends had seen one another. That triggers Johnny's objection to Bruno's penchant for putting everything into orderly, linear time. The irony, of course, is that the page we have just seen, but that Johnny has not, can hardly keep things straight. And Bruno's messy compound tense continues to narrate in the frame of the dialogue. "'We haven't seen one another for a while,' I [*have*] said to Johnny. 'It's been a month at least.' 'You got nothin' to do but tell time,' he [*has*] answered in a bad mood. 'The first, the two the three, the twenty one. You, you put a number on everything'" (162; my insertions and emphasis).[15]

Johnny's objection is to counting, to marking time in foreseeable sequences. Were his emphasis on time, understood differently, it would point to his own obsession as well. "Johnny . . . kept on referring to time, a subject which is a preoccupation of his ever since I've known him. I've seen very few men as occupied as he is with everything having to do with time" (164).[16] Among those rare obsessives is the narrator Bruno himself. Johnny noted as much, but too impatiently, perhaps because he is not reading the text before us. In it Bruno's discordant performance in the present perfect is unmistakably doubled. Though it seems to comment cooly on the confusing temporality of the jazz musician, the narrator's timing is in fact contaminated by Johnny's own experiments with music. This slippage between musical timing and verbal tenses works in both directions; this is particularly plain when Johnny's drive to get beyond convention finds textual representation in oxymoronic verbs. Consider the way he forces the present progressive or the simple past to perform in the future. "I am playing this tomorrow," Bruno remembers him complain during a rehearsal years earlier. "I already played this tomorrow, it's horrible, Miles, I already played this tomorrow" (164).[17]

And Bruno himself will play an extended variation, when he takes a break from the present perfect and narrates the recent past (or the present?) in a consistent future tense (201–4; 293–5).

By making his agonists share a preoccupation with time, Cortázar is evidently deconstructing the difference between Bruno's intellectual work and Johnny's artistic genius. Bruno should logically be talking about artistic challenges; instead he performs them. And Johnny should be pursuing his speculations through performances, musical rather than verbal; yet he talks far more than he plays. Like Charlie Parker's critics – who acknowledge his superior intelligence and technical appreciation for his own work – Bruno is careful to let Johnny talk, always quoting rather than reporting his textual riffs.[18] This slippery difference between art and critique has at times, of course, been taken to be a more stable opposition. It was, for instance, fundamental to a fascist aesthetics that distinguished radically between two types of writers: the pedantic Schriftsteller and the inspired Dichter. The opposition is unhinged by Cortázar's own variegated virtuosity, combining inspiration and intellection as a continual challenge to his own critics. Readers usually develop along with Cortázar's experimental writing, but more slowly.

His accomplishment in "The Pursuer," it would seem, both depends on and overrides a naive reading that would simply oppose Bruno to Johnny. To appreciate the deconstructive turn is also to acknowledge its polarized pretext as a simple reading that would make the title refer only to Johnny. He "was no victim, not persecuted as everyone thought, as I'd even insisted upon in my biography of him . . . Johnny pursues and is not pursued" (196).[19] Only this disingenuous interpretation could mistake Johnny as the sole medium of the story's almost mad metaphysical desire to beat down the doors of arbitrary limits. Only willful simplicity could demote Bruno to the prosaic condensation of everything Johnny resists. It would draw a stark contrast between the castrating conventionality of Bruno's language and the liberating trespasses of Johnny's music.

A conclusion, logically, would be that Cortázar is celebrating the superiority of extralinguistic and nonintellectual communication. This is not the only story where nonliterary arts seem to compensate Cortázar for the limitations of his medium. (See "Apocalypse at Solentiname," in which viewing his own slides of naive Nicaraguan paintings shocks the narrator into finally seeing Somoza's official terror; "Return Trip Tango," where the recursive rhythm of urban music provides the logic of human disencounters; and "Graffiti," where an academic painter wakes up to political repression through an amorous dialogue of public drawings.) The examples come readily to mind, and Cortázar's borrowings from the visual and performing arts are already the topic of important studies.[20] But the borrowings should not obscure the obvious fact that Cortázar's own pursuit is rendered in the apparently disdained medium of literature. In other words, a simple reading that would diminish the value of Bruno's probing literary styles in order to exalt the spontaneity of experimental music misses the charm of this story: "The Pursuer" manages to accomplish those winning experiments through writing. Even Johnny's putative superiority is, after all, an effect of his own evasive words and of Bruno's tortuous, tense-troubled, responses. Bruno's haunted memory "insists and insists on Johnny's words, his stories" (178; 265).

This irony – about outperforming writing through writing – might make a nice point in a deconstructive reading, a generalizable or abstract point that could follow from the personalized ironies about Bruno's unstable difference from Johnny. And if we cared to circle back in order to insist on the virtual collapse of differences between the cautious Schriftsteller and the daring Dichter, we could develop the point about Johnny's capacity for intellectual speculation being more than equal to Bruno's. Johnny does more than merely quote lines from Dylan Thomas; he glosses them. "O make me a mask," the line that frames the story from Cortázar's epigraph to the coda on Johnny's words (220; 313), is an opportunity for the jazzman to extrapolate on the general arbitrariness of signs. His own life, for example, could not possibly be contained in Bruno's biography; it is not even in the records (212; 304). And his face, to take an even more intimate example, could not possibly be an adequate representation of Johnny himself. Instead it is a mask that makes recognition both possible and impossible; it is someone else, to be caught by surprise as he stares from the glass, menacing to pass for and replace the person looking in.[21] Tirelessly driven, Johnny develops the mystery by wondering about words as such, the way they stick to things and overcome them with the connecting slime that passes for meaning.[22]

Imagínate que te estás viendo a ti mismo; eso tan sólo basta para quedarse frío durante media hora. Realmente ese tipo no soy yo . . . lo agarré de sorpresa, de refilón y supe que no era yo. . . . No son las palabras, son lo que está en las palabras, esa especie de cola de pegar, esa baba. Y la baba viene y te tapa, y te convence de que el del espejo eres tú. (282)

[Imagine that you're looking at yourself; that alone is enough to freeze you up for half an hour. In reality, this guy's not me . . . I took it by surprise, obliquely, and I knew it wasn't me. . . . No, not words, but what's in the words, a kind of glue, that slime. And the slime comes and covers you and convinces you that that's you in the mirror. (192)

His speculations range in apparent disorder, disorder itself being one theme in his obsession with "elastic" time. Even more than an obsession, more than simply a problem to harass him the way it does Bruno, the variability of time for Johnny is an invitation to study and to speculate. "I [have] read some things about all that, Bruno. It's weird, and really awfully complicated . . . [sic] I think the music helps, you know. Not to understand, because the truth is I don't understand anything" (165).[23] His own reflections sound distinctly Bergsonian, about the variable durée of experience. Sometimes, Johnny muses, a suitcase, like a song, will hold more and sometimes less. Other times it is packed so full that the contents seem limitless. "The best is when you realize you can put a whole store full of suits and shoes in there, in that suitcase, hundreds and hundreds of suits, like I get into the music when I'm blowing sometimes. Music, and what I'm thinking about when I ride the metro" (168).[24] With this breathless transition, the speculation about elasticity continues with the subway as a vehicle for musical compression: The minute-long ride from one stop to another is so crammed with lovingly detailed reveries that the trip seems impossibly concise (172–3; 260–1). "Bruno, if I could only live all the time like in those moments, or like when I'm playing and the time changes then too . . . " (173).[25] Timing was always Charlie Parker's musical frontier, too. "Charlie Parker's idea of rhythm involves breaking time up. It might be said that it is based on half beats. No other soloist attaches so much importance to short notes (eighth notes in quick tempos, sixteenths in slow)," writes André Hodeir early enough for Cortázar to have read it. Hodeir's Hommes et problèmes du jazz was published in the same place and year as Bruno's biography (Paris, 1954), to become a standard work for other jazz historians. At about the same time, jazz pianist Jay McShann was saying that Parker "played everything offbeat. He had it in his head long before he could put it together."[26] And none of his contemporaries ever caught up to him in pursuit of polyrhythms, the very pulse of the new music.[27] As the period's giant of jazz (along with Gillespie), Parker pioneered a variety of styles that would develop into the opposing "hot" and "cool" trends that lesser musicians would choose between.[28] They appropriated pieces of Parker, mostly his experiments with melody and harmony. But no one overtook over his talent for timing, not even his most admiring students, like the pianist Hampton Hawes. "It was Bird's conception that . . . made me realize how important meter and time is in jazz . . . I began experimenting, taking liberties with time, or letting a couple of beats go by to make the beat stand out, not just play on top of it all the time."[29]

To develop a reading of deconstructed oppositions would be to include a counterpoint to our artist's critical acuity. And Bruno the critic has in fact been showing himself to be an unconventional artist. We have already heard him play with the dissonant "chord tensions" (one of Charlie Parker's performative signatures) of an unstable tense. Now we might add that Bruno is also given to the kind of cramming, overpacking, and overloading so characteristic of bebop and of Johnny's particular speculations about music and time. And just to make sure that we get the connection, Bruno thematizes his own performance as he comments on another hanger-on whose language is also "contaminated" (217; 310) by jazz: "When the marquesa started yakking you wondered if Dizzy's style hadn't glued up her diction, it was such an interminable series of variations in the most unexpected registers . . ." (178).[30] Bruno stretches and pads his own story, especially through the long middle section, where linear writing breaks down under the weight of worry. Telling asides erupt through spaces that are visually represented as barely constraining parentheses. In those unpredicted spaces, extradiegetic writing plays with and against Bruno's simpler themes. Crouching inside the breaches and ready to outshout the line of continuity (like Johnny crouches, "lying in ambush") (211; 303) are pieces of dangerously supplemental information, Bruno's reflexive musings, and his wonder at what he admits to misinterpreting. He squeezes words into his paragraphs like bebop squeezes notes into a melody. It squeezes so hard that the new music verges on exploding the familiar line; melody is not entirely overwhelmed, but it is continually commented on, challenged, critically caressed.[31] And Bruno sees his own project ready to burst from the pressure of overwriting: "(I swear I don't know how to write all this)" (210), he confesses in one parenthetical riff.[32]

Readers who notice this visual aid to Cortázar's trespassing from music to manuscript may be surprised – as I was – to know that it may well be borrowed from a jazz critic writing about Parker, perhaps the very critic who inspired Bruno. André Hodeir writes that Parker played "in parentheses." That is, he suggested as much music as he actually played; "his phrase frequently includes notes that are not played but merely suggested. . . . Thus, anyone who writes down a Parker chorus is obliged to include, *in parentheses* [my emphasis], notes that have hardly been played at all."[33] Hodeir's own page then visibly breaks up into parenthetical asides, as if consciously imitating the master. Whether or not Cortázar was imitating too, whether he took a cue for improvisation from jazz criticism, he certainly played stunning variations. Usually they are doubled solos (between Bruno's nonstop narrative and his preoccupied parentheses), but at least one inspired adaptation sets competitive voices in counterpoint. Regular print and italics alternate and crescendo in a debate about Bruno's book, between an ever more anxious biographer and his progressively angrier hero:

—Faltan cosas, Bruno—dice Johhny. . . .
—Las que te habrás olvidado de decirme—contesté—bastante picado. Este mono salvaje es capaz d . . . (habrá que hablar con Delaunay, sería lamentable que una declaración imprudente malograra un sano esfuerzo crítico que. . . . *Por ejemplo, el vestido rojo de Lan*—está diciendo Johnny. Y en todo caso aprovechar las novedades de esta noche para incorporarlas a una nueva edición; no estaría mal. *Tenía como un olor a perro*—está diciendo Johnny—*y es lo único que vale en ese disco.* Sí, escuchar atentamente y proceder con rapidez, porque en manos de otras gentes estos posibles desmentidos podrían tener consecuencias lamentables. *Y la urna del medio, la más grande, llena de un polvo casi azul*—está diciendo Johnny—*y tan parecida a una polvera que tenía mi hermana.* Mientras no pase de las alucinaciones, lo peor sería que desmintiera las ideas de fondo, el sistema estético que tantos elogios. . . . *Y además el* cool *no es ni por casualidad lo que has escrito*—está diciendo Johnny. Atención.) (300)

["There're things missing, Bruno," Johnny says. . . .
"The things that you've forgotten to tell me," I answer, reasonably annoyed. This uncivilized monkey is capable of . . . (I would have to speak with Delaunay, it would be regrettable if an imprudent statement about a sane, forceful criticism that. . . . *For example, Lan's red dress,* Johnny is saying. And in any case take advantage of the enlightening details from this evening to put into a new edition; that wouldn't be bad. *It stank like an old washrag,* Johnny's saying, *and that's the only value on the record.* Yes, listen closely and proceed rapidly, because in other people's hands any possible contradiction might have terrible consequences. *And the urn in the middle, full of dust that's almost blue,* Johnny is saying, *and very close to the color of a compact my sister had once.* As long as he wasn't going into hallucinations, the worst that could happen would be that he might contradict the basic ideas, the aesthetic system so many people have praised. . . . *And furthermore, cool doesn't mean, even by accident ever, what you've written,* Johnny is saying. Attention.)] (208)

One result of all this overwriting is a very long short story. The tale seems compact – a conversation in Johnny's hotel room, a get-together at the

marquesa's place, a drink and more talk just before Johnny dies – but the
narrative is tellingly stretched beyond the capacity of more conventional
stories. Cortázar almost always writes them within twenty pages. More
than doubling that length by adding variations, speculations, reveries,
and repetitions is the kind of experimental performance that brings
Bruno close to bebop.

The analogy between modern music and modern writing is redun-
dantly clear. Even so, Cortázar takes few risks with his readers' interpretive skill. He informs us, outright, that Johnny's jazz is part of a general
postwar culture exploding with artistic experiments. "This is not the
place to be a jazz critic, and anyone who's interested can read my book
on Johnny and the new postwar style, but I can say that forty-eight – let's
say until fifty – was like an explosion in music . . . " (176).[34] The image of
exploding standard forms, the following reference to an ever greater and
more avid public, and the timing in the late 1940s and early 1950s, are
unmistakable allusions to the Latin American literary "boom" that
Cortázar helped to detonate. So is the geographical displacement that
made American jazz flourish in Paris, the same haven that attracted the
most influential new Spanish American novelists – Carlos Fuentes, Mario
Vargas Llosa, and Cortázar himself, among others. As a late and
supremely self-ironizing wave of modernist experiments, boom writing
distinguished itself from the kind of expository prose for which Bruno's
biography stands. The genre of biography in Cortázar's Argentina, had,
in fact, been extolled by the great nation builder Domingo F. Sarmiento.
For him and for generations of practical and productive disciples, biography was the most effective guide to personal and political development.[35] And Bruno's book about the bebop artist who "turned the page"
(177; 266) on music history might well have fit the mold of celebrating
exemplary men in a mimetic effort to become one.

Cortázar is presumably offering a critique of this self-improving genre
by replacing biography with a story that tracks the troubled afterthoughts
about the very possibility of writing a life. But he may be even more self-
promoting than simply preferring his own type of experimental prose to
the biographical developmentalism that stays beyond the scene of writing like some guilty pretext for the drama. Cortázar may also be object-
ing to some of his own interpreters who have tried to tidy up his really
unpredictable production into a linear story of development.[36] Both they
and Bruno the biographer tend to lose focus on the mystery pursued, on
the nonchronological play that, ironically, can make artistic history. Con-

ceivably, the story is meant to leave Cortázar's critics in the dust raised by his own superior flair for speculative interpretation and by his endless pursuit of forms that describe desire without controlling it.

Without denying the possibility of Cortázar's self-promotion or self-defense, and far from discarding the deconstructive reading that I have been describing, I want to argue a different point here. It sidesteps immediate self-interest and goes beyond the kind of deconstruction that heaps glaring ironies onto inconsistent oppositions in order to level the feeble differences between Bruno's project and Johnny's performance. The story, I would boldly point out, is not merely about the ultimate naiveté of binary oppositions. It is also – and most powerfully – about a refusal to overcome difference. The agonists resist the leveling effect and remain in murderous tension with one another. Johnny refuses to be contained in Bruno's smug prose; and Bruno strains to be free of Johnny, of the self-doubts and complexity he inflicts. I am saying, in other words, that the "naive" interpretation that a familiar version of deconstruction would override survives the sophisticated assault, in a more responsible deconstructive practice. This survival is most palpable, as I will repeat, in the diegetic passages and at the level of grammar. Whereas a standard deconstructive reading (more De Manian than Derridean) would focus on Bruno's bebop style, on the futility of keeping oppositional categories clear, the "agonistic" emphasis I prefer to give this story keeps an eye on the energy invested in safeguarding the oppositions. The differences between the agonists are evidently not essential, not organic. But their very fragility, their almost arbitrary constructedness, makes the characters whose identity depends on them nervous enough to insist on distinctions.

The fact that Bruno and Johnny overlap as personae and performances is no happy liberation from the tensions of difference; rather it is a threat to the difference that gives each character his specificity, his life. "([M]aybe I'm a little afraid of Johnny, this angel who's like my brother, this brother who's like my angel)" (174; 263). To override that respectful distance between self and other, a distance that provides the ground for dynamic social relationships, is to risk reducing sociability to solipsism. Closing up distances and coming perilously close to the other threatens to overtake him or her in a gesture of an ontological appropriation that Levinas calls "totality."[37] Both Bruno and Johnny threaten one another in this way. Each implicates the other in the deadlock of ethical engagement.

Bruno cannot help but perfect his living subject into an inanimate object of discourse. That is the cost of writing a life. Mikhail Bakhtin almost benignly called the process "consummation" in an early philosophical essay titled "Author and Hero in Aesthetic Activity." It is an especially suggestive piece for reading Bruno's relationship to Johnny.[38] Consummation, for Bakhtin, describes the process whereby an author contextualizes and completes his hero from a necessarily exterior vantage point; for example, from Bruno's perspective on Johnny. Critics, Bruno protests after feeling especially stupid, are more necessary than they sometimes think, "because the creators . . . are incapable of extrapolating the dialectical consequences of their work, of postulating the fundamentals and the transcendency of what they're writing down or improvising" (208–9).[39] To hear this almost funny, hollow, and impersonal academic jargon after Johnny has just complained about being left out of Bruno's biography is to get Johnny's point. Bruno has had to fictionalize his friend, to flatten and substitute him, in order to celebrate him. We are already remarking the culpability of completing a character. And Bakhtin is explicit, at points, about the violence inherent in the process, although the thrust of his sometimes rambling essay is to define a properly ethical engagement between authors who respect their heroes' qualified autonomy even as the writers help to confer it. The violent surplus of establishing pleasing contours for a hero, whose interior sense of himself cannot appreciate his own outline, is that to confer coherence on a character is, necessarily, to finish him.

Artistic vision presents us with the *whole* hero, measured in full and added up in every detail; there must be no secrets for us in the hero with respect to meaning; our faith and hope must be silent. From the very outset, we must experience all of him, deal with the whole of him: in respect to meaning, he must be dead for us, formally dead.

In this sense, we could say that death is the form of the aesthetic consummation of an individual.[40]

Cortázar's fans may remember his own repeated explorations of the murderous price authors pay for congealing incoherent lives into perfected fictions. In fact, much, if not most, of Cortázar's writing is driven ahead of the danger posed by fixing and finishing. He will resist perfection, characteristically, by deforming his grammar, with "shifty" pronouns as well as oxymoronic verbs.[41] Perhaps the most dramatic example of the danger is, predictably, a story that succumbs to it. "We Love Glenda So Much" (1981) is practically a parable about deadly perfectibility. That story ends once Glenda's fans conspire to kill her in order to polish the movie-star image that stabilizes their devotion. The very last lines draw an unmistakable parallel with another necessary sacrifice to cultish heroism. "We loved Glenda so much that we would offer her one last inviolable perfection. On the untouchable heights to which we had raised her in exaltation, we would save her from the fall, her faithful could go on adoring her without any decrease; one does not come down from a cross alive."[42] Sacrifice and deification also menace Bakhtin's essay to describe the dynamic between hero and author. But his efforts run directly into the paradoxical possibility that the hero can be redeemed by the author's finishing work. Love runs the risk of fixing, and killing, the beloved; but it also promises to raise him or her to another more perfect plane.

It is only love (as an active approach to another human being) that unites an inner life (a *subiectum*'s own object-directedness in living his life) as experienced from outside with the value of the body as experienced from outside and, in so doing, constitutes a unitary and unique human being as an aesthetic phenomenon. (82–3)

[T]he enrichment in this case is formal, transfigurative in character – it transposes the recipient of the gift to a new plane of existence. And what is transposed to a new plane, moreover, is not the material, not an object, but a *subiectum* – the hero. It is only in relation to the hero that aesthetic obligation (the aesthetic 'ought') as well as aesthetic love and the gift bestowed by such love are possible. (90)

Some pages earlier, Bakhtin had spelled out the fundamentally Christian and paradoxical nature of this consummating and redemptive love. In that passage, Bakhtin might have capitalized the word *Author* because he casts himself as one possible creation. The mystery of redeeming a life through death can be read here as one result of Christ's synthetic embrace of traditions, a synthesis that allows for slippages from one plane to another.

In Christ we find a synthesis of unique depth, the synthesis of *ethical solipsism* (man's infinite severity toward himself . . . ) with *ethical-aesthetic kindness* toward the other. For the first time, there appeared an infinitely deepened *I-for-myself* . . . one of boundless kindness toward the other. . . . [Thanks to Christ,] God is no longer defined essentially as the voice of my conscience . . . God is now the heavenly father who is *over me* and can be merciful to me and justify me where I, from within myself, cannot be merciful to myself and cannot justify myself. . . . What I must be for the other, God is for me. What the other surmounts and repudiates within himself as an unworthy given, I accept in him and that with loving mercy as the other's cherished flesh. (56)

To become "the other's cherished flesh," it is a phrase passionate enough to send chills through readers of "Glenda," where passion achieves its sacrificial meaning and the heroine's fans (short for fanatics) become living shrines to her memory. By the time he wrote this story, Cortázar was himself a venerated superstar, or a venerable monument as vulnerable to his carping critics as Glenda was to her fans. "As always, why don't you live in your country, why was *Blow-Up* so different from your story, don't you think writers should be committed? And . . . chez Saint Peter there'll be no difference, don't you think that down below you used to write too hermetically for regular people to understand?"[43] "Glenda," therefore, may be a cautionary tale about loving the beloved to death. But such a reading would diminish the meaning of love, shrink it into simple, cannibalistic, appropriation. Glenda's fanatics could not possibly have loved her, Cortázar is probably saying, not in the generous and tolerant sense that Bakhtin gives the word. No one among the "faithful" could have justified Glenda in her imperfections, forgiven her for that which she could not forgive herself. Therefore, no one could have consummated the character with the pleasing coherence achieved only outside one's own intolerant "ethical (or esthetic) solipsism."

Bakhtin's idea of redemptive love is obviously inimical to the ritual cannibalism of Glenda's celebrants. In the least case, their cannibalism digests away the tension between interiority and exteriority that makes writing possible. The expression of their love means the end of Glenda, as a character and as a narrative. Even an autobiographer, Bakhtin observes, needs to define a tension between author and hero in order to write himself (151). And beyond the aesthetic need to keep them apart, there is an ethical imperative for the author to maintain, or regain, a respectful distance from his hero: The distance allows the hero's fullness to come into focus (26). "What's hard is to circle about him and not lose your distance," Bruno reminds himself, "like a good satellite, like a good critic" (197).[44] But despite Bakhtin's own cautions about overtaking or being overtaken by the other, despite repeated warnings against the undifferentiating empathy that offers cheap rushes of feeling and shirks the labor required for consummation (64, 81, 88), his essay seems so steeped in the paradox of redemption through death that even his supremely reflexive and careful kind of loving nudges the argument toward the foot of a cross. An author's loving justification hardly allows for struggle; instead it would seem to stop the hero, to perform for him by substituting his development for an external and more pleasingly coherent perspective.

Maybe there is no help for approaching the cross. Writing, even or especially writing with love, tends to flesh out characters, to finish them off and then to finish narrating. Therefore, to read from the ending, at the point of closure, is almost inevitably to read the violence loosed on life when it is stabilized as a story. But more specific and interesting observations are to be made before the inevitable endings, during the engagement between author and hero, sometimes, that is, between characters cast in those roles. The particular process of consummation, rather than its mere fact, gives a narrative its specificity. And Bakhtin himself would later sharpen his critical focus on the almost open-ended dynamic he called dialogism, so characteristic of modernity, rather than on the consummate promise of salvation as the end of writing. Consider how different Glenda's fans are from Johnny's biographer. Their refusal to engage her is a brutal narrative shortcut, a dime-store deification, whereas Bruno's vulnerability to Johnny keeps the hero, their conversations, and therefore the narrative alive for many, many, pages. The temptation to crucify Johnny is there for Bruno too, but it is openly and self-critically there. So, besides being an unavoidable trap, temptation is also a goad for more writing: "Basically we're a bunch of egotists," Bruno admits in this rehearsal of Glenda's demise; "under the pretext of watching out for Johnny what we're doing is protecting our idea of him, . . . to reflect the brilliance from the statue we've erected among us all and defend it till the last gasp" (182).[45] Later on, Bruno will even imagine the others looking at him looking at Johnny, as if Bruno were "climbing up on the altar to tug Christ down from his cross" (204).[46] The first to reproach him was Johnny himself, and to the extent that they struggle against one another, author and hero survive the violence. The story flows between them, through the fissures of Bruno's fictional but still functional authority. Compared to Glenda's fans and to privileged narrators who stay in business by being willfully stupid (like the one who keeps missing the connections in *Cecilia Valdés* and like Bartleby's boss in Melville's story), Bruno seems almost defenseless.

Yet he menaces Johnny by the very fact of taking his life down, of getting it right. And Johnny reciprocates by dismissing Bruno's capacity to understand him. Why, he practically demands of Bruno, don't you leave biographical logic alone and do as I do, pursue the inarticulable energy behind art, even in the uncooperative medium of writing: "Bruno, maybe someday you'll be able to write . . ." (167). Each makes unsatisfiable demands on the other; yet each resists those demands and remains himself. It is the resistance that safeguards their vexed, but dynamic, sociability. The agonists depend on one another in their differences, and they know it. Bruno needs the unfettered genius as the featured subject of an

academic career and the catalyst for his own probing performance, while
Johnny needs Bruno's sensible attentions in order to survive. He also
needs the critic's trained ear to elicit more music and more talk. "You
ought to have been happy I put on that act with you," Johnny tells him a
few days after the scene in the hotel room. "I don't do that with anybody,
believe me. It just shows how much I appreciate you. We have to go some-
place soon where we can talk . . ." (181).[47]

But Johnny usually prefers not to admit his entrapment; and refusal
suggests the bad faith of a man who declines any real engagement with
another. "I understand nothing" (165; 254), he protests to the critic who
is supposed to understand. Johnny objects that any text would betray him,
that any meaning assigned to him would be a falsification. "Right away you
translate it into your filthy language" (213; 305). The filth, the slime that
makes language work also makes Bruno's book "like a mirror" (207; 300),
as falsifying and substitutive as a mirror. Bruno apparently gets it wrong
even when he modestly writes that Johnny's real biography is in the
records. The point is that the biography cannot be written, or made right,
because Johnny's life is driven by inarticulable desire. "And if I myself
didn't know how to blow it like it should be, blow what I really am . . . you
dig, they can't ask you for miracles, Bruno" (212).[48] But Bruno tries to
content himself with less than miracles, as he translates Johnny's objection to being left out of his own biography with a literary critical commonplace: "Basically, the only thing he said was that no one can know anything about anyone, big deal. That's the basic assumption of any
biography, then it takes off, what the hell."[49]

Of course his dismissal of the problem doesn't make it go away. Right
before Johnny dies, and just as the biography was going into its second edition, Bruno indulges in self-critical plans for rewriting. "To be honest
within the limits permitted by the profession, I wondered whether it
would not be necessary to show the personality of my subject in another
light" (217; 310). But he controls himself. Another light might promote
a "literary infection," Bruno's colleagues worry, and weaken the points
about Johnny's music, "at least as all of us understood it" (218; 310).
Whether the infection is *of* literature (Bruno's biography), or *by* literature (Johnny's poetic version of finally ineffable experience) seems purposefully ambiguous. In any case, Bruno closes the prophylactic cover of
his book against any possible disease. It is a characteristically self-preserv-
ing move.

For all his repeated admissions of intellectual and spiritual inferiority,
Bruno usually braces himself against Johnny. To be in Johnny's company is to lose composure, to become a misfit in time. The parallels with

Johnny's experiments (present perfects, future for the past, and paren-thetical riffs) are problems for Bruno the character, as opposed to oppor-tunities for Cortázar the writer. Bruno's problem would perhaps not be so profound if his *resentiment* were not so obviously driven by jealousy along with self-defensiveness. Less guilty of provocative bad faith than Johnny's conversation, Bruno's private writing seems brutally self-reflective: "I envy Johnny, that Johnny on the other side, even though nobody knows exactly what that is, the other side. . . . I envy Johnny and at the same time I get sore as hell watching him destroy himself, misusing his gifts" (180).[50] And the solution for problem-solving Bruno is to finish Johnny, to make him perfect and stable in a finite past. "[M]aybe basically I want Johnny to wind up all at once like a nova that explodes into a thousand pieces and turns astronomers into idiots for a whole week, and then one can go off to sleep and tomorrow is another day" (180).[51] Thirty pages later the murderous wish for release recurs: "Sure, there are moments when I wish he were already dead" (210). Then Bruno undercuts the wish by worrying if release is even possible.

Pero cómo resignarse a que Johnny se muera llevándose lo que no quiere decirme esta noche, que desde la muerte siga cazando, siga salido (yo ya no sé cómo escribir todo esto) aunque me valga la paz, la cátedra, esa autoridad que dan las tesis incontrovertidas y los entierros bien capitaneados. (302)

[(H)ow can we resign ourselves to the fact that Johnny would die carrying with him what he doesn't want to tell me tonight, that from death he'd con-tinue hunting, would continue flipping out (I swear I don't know how to write all this) though his death would mean peace to me, prestige, the status incontrovertibly bestowed upon one by unbeatable theses and efficiently arranged funerals.] (210)

But relief and repose finally do come. The last sentences, over Johnny's consummately finite body, rescue Bruno from the mire of deconstructive contaminations and tangled tenses. Whatever subtle com-plications may haunt the biographer after his hero's death, the writing shows symptoms of release. Bruno has straightened out his verbs; he has disaggregated past from present, disengaged himself from the present perfection that Johnny pursued. Finally, Bruno frees himself from Johnny, after "sticking it out to the end" (167; 256). He releases his grip on the unmanageable genius who has dragged him through relentlessly self-reflexive writing. Now tension abates. The energizing if tortuous pre-sent perfect tense slackens and breaks down into either a haltingly sim-ple past or a comfortingly stable present. And the supplementary paren-thetical riffs evacuate the text, now hell-bent on setting itself straight.

Only now, in the deadly timing of his verbs and in the cause-and-effect continuity of the necrological notes, does Bruno show some bad faith. He shows it clearly in the mildly embarrassed reflection that follows his relief at Johnny's death. More than relieved, Bruno actually seems happy about the lucky timing of Johnny's funeral because it produced pictures for the improved biography. The book "remained, so to speak, intact and finished. Perhaps it's not right that I say this," Bruno interjects almost contritely, "but naturally I was speaking from a merely aesthetic point of view" (220; 313). Merely aesthetic is what Johnny's life becomes for Bruno once the hero gets the finishing touches that fix him in a satisfying story. Therefore, the embarrassed aside is hardly exculpating. Instead, it belies an unhappy conscience. Although Bruno manages to strike a kind of happy note in the last paragraph, he knows that the note is drowning out much richer music. He holds that easy note long enough to stop everything else, as if to say that counterpuntal melodies no longer matter, as if dissonance were now merely cacophony, a problem to be solved. Again, it is Bruno's grammar that plays so convincingly. Whatever information we may or may not get about Bruno's will to survive, that will is *felt* through his newly orthodox verbal conjugations. Willfully simple, Bruno evokes here the purposefully deaf narrators of *Cecilia Valdés* and "Bartleby," self-serving narrators who defend their privilege by defending against understanding. All Bruno wants to know, as he gets on with his life, is what fits into the disaggregated, perfectly simple past and present tenses that end Johnny's story. The hero died, and the book is finished.

*Notes*

I am indebted to Adam Zachary Newton for conversations about Bakhtin and Bruno as this essay developed.

1. Julio Cortázar, "El perseguidor," *Las armas secretas* (Buenos Aires: Sudamericana, 1959), 249–313. For convenience, I have avoided redundancy (for bilingual readers) and eliminated incomprehensibility (for the English reader) by quoting Cortázar in the Notes, and the English version—sometimes adjusted to capture Cortázar's style—in the text. See "The Pursuer," trans. Paul Blackburn, in *Blow Up and Other Stories* (New York: Collier Books, 1985), 161–220. If two page numbers appear in parentheses, the first refers to the translation, the second to the Spanish. Nevertheless, where longer passages are easily identified and skipped in one language or the other, I include the Spanish original.

2. Could Bruno be "the brilliant André Hodeir," quoted by Marshall W. Stearns about Charlie Parker? It seems plausible, given the respect Hodeir's book commanded in the year of publication (a year before Parker's death) and his characterization of Parker as "the most perfect example" of the jazzman:

"*L'oeuvre de ce genial improvisateur est l'expression la plus parfaite du jazz moderne,*"
*Hommes et problèmes du jazz* (Paris, 1954), 128. American edition: *Jazz: Its Evolution and Essence*, trans. David Noakes (New York: Grove Press, 1956). See Stearns, *The Story of Jazz* (New York: Oxford University Press, 1956), 227. Stearns concurs: "The giant of giants was saxophonist Charlie Parker" (227).

　　But a retrospective view questions Parker's ascendancy over Gillespie. "Today Parker is given the lion's share of the credit for inventing the harmonic changes bop brought to jazz, but on the evidence of the records it seems clear enough that Gillespie was making the same discoveries on his own, possibly in advance of Parker." See James Lincoln Collier, *The Making of Jazz: A Comprehensive History* (Boston: Houghton Mifflin Company, 1978), 350.

3.　—"El compañero Bruno es fiel como el mal aliento" (149).

4.　For one of many examples, see Collier, 356–7. "Parker . . . was already (1944) exhibiting the personality problems from which he suffered. He missed jobs; slept through others. . . . [W]here Charlie Parker wasted his talent on the *pursuit* of the moment, Gillespie managed his career with intelligence and skill" (my emphasis). Collier begins the chapter "Charlie Parker: An Erratic Bird in Flight" (362–76) by calling him a "sociopath . . . who managed in a relatively short time to destroy his career, every relationship important to him, and finally himself," largely through drugs and the arrogance that required that his every desire be fulfilled immediately (363).

5.　"Pienso en la música que se está perdiendo, en las docenas de grabaciones donde Johnny podría seguir dejando esa presencia, ese adelanto asombroso que tiene sobre cualquier otro músico" (255).

6.　Stearns, 221. "Public interest in bop didn't last long – the musicians themselves seemed to go out of their way to discourage it – and the threat in bop soon became more psychological than economic. But the young and formerly admiring bop musician did not hesitate to tell the old-timer: 'If you don't dig these new sounds, man, you're real square.' In fact, he made a point of doing so – in a variety of ways – and many older musicians felt this hostility keenly. The revolt in bop was frequently revolting. . . . The switch from 'hot' to 'cool' as the epithet of highest praise goes deeper. . . he refused to play the stereotype role of Negro entertainer, which he rightly associated with Uncle Tomism. He then proceeded to play the most revolutionary jazz with an appearance of utter boredom, rejecting his audience entirely."

　　In his review of the militant journalism that accompanied the "bebop" revolution, Martin Williams points out that the battle was pitched between those who claimed that bop had blasted everything else out of the field and those who claimed it was a passing aberration. See his introductory note to Ross Russel's 1948–9 articles in *The Record Changer*. See *The Art of Jazz: Ragtime to Be-bop*, ed. Martin Williams (New York: Da Capo Press, 1980; reprint of 1959 Oxford University ed.), 185.

7.　"Bop Will Kill Business unless It Kills Itself First," *Down Beat*, April 7, 1948, 2.

8.　"Bruno, si un día lo pudieras escribir. . . . No por mí, entiendes, a mí qué me importa" (256).

9. "[D]espués de la maravilla nace la irritación, y a mí por lo menos me pasa que siento como si Johnny me hubiera estado tomando el pelo" (262).

10. "Sonrío lo mejor que puedo, comprendiendo vagamente que tiene razón, pero que lo que él sospecha y lo que yo presiento de su sospecha se va a borrar como siempre apenas esté en la calle y me meta en mi vida de todos los días" (262).

11. Collier, 351: "The ideas of Parker and Gillespie were not so very novel from an academic viewpoint, and would have come into jazz anyway. By the 1940s conservatory-trained musicians were beginning to enter jazz, and they were bringing with them similar ideas worked out by master composers in the previous century. Indeed, it may not be coincidental that Hawkins's 'Body and Soul,' virtually an exercise in chromatic chord movement, had become, late in 1939, one of the biggest jazz hits of the period. But Parker and Gillespie set about building a whole music around this concept, and, perhaps more important, they had the courage to insist that they were right." Parker, like Johnny, was reluctant to admit debts of gratitude and respect, even to mentor musicians (Collier, 365). See also Stearns, 218, 224.

12. "como lo que era en el fondo: un pobre diablo de inteligencia apenas mediocre . . ." (311).

13. Paul de Man, "Autobiography as Defacement," *Modern Language Notes* 94 (1979): 919–30.

14. Emmanuel Levinas, *Ethics and Infinity: Conversations with Philippe Nemo,* trans. Richard A. Cohen (Pittsburgh, PA: Duquesne University Press, 1985). "Knowledge has always been interpreted as assimilation. Even the most surprising discoveries end by being absorbed, comprehended, with all that there is of 'prehending' in 'comprehending.' The most audacious and remote knowledge does not put us in communion with the truly other; it does not take the place of sociality; it is still and always a solitude. . . . Sociality will be a way of escaping being otherwise than through knowledge" (60–1).

15. —Hace rato que no nos veíamos—*le he dicho* a Johnny—. Un mes por lo menos.
—Tú no haces más que contar el tiempo—*me ha contestado* de mal humor. El primero, el dos, el tres, el veintiuno. A todo le pones un número, tú (250); (my emphasis).

16. "Johnny . . . sequía haciendo alusiones al tiempo, un tema que le preocupa desde que lo conozco. He visto pocos hombres tan preocupados por todo lo que se refiere al tiempo" (252).

17. "Esto lo estoy tocando mañana. . . . Esto ya lo toqué mañana, es horrible, Miles, esto ya lo toqué mañana" (253).

18. "I'd been getting bored with the stereotyped changes that were being used all the time . . . and I kept thinking there's bound to be something else. I could hear it sometimes but I couldn't play it.
"Well, that night, I was working over *Cherokee,* and, as I did, I found that by using the higher intervals of a chord as a melody line and backing them with appropriately related changes, I could play the thing I'd been hearing. I came alive." Quoted in Nat Shapiro and Nat Hentoff, *Hear Me Talkin' to Ya* (New York: Rinehart & Company, 1955), 340.

19. "no es víctima, no perseguido, sino perseguidor" (287).

20. See, e.g., Lois Parkinson Zamora, "Movement and Stasis, Film and Photo: Temporal Structures in the Recent Fiction of Julio Cortázar," *The Review of Contemporary Fiction* 3, no. 3 (Elmwood Park, IL: Fall 1983): 51–64.

21. The suggestion of Lacan's essay on "The Mirror Stage . . ." is so strong here, it makes one wonder if Cortázar had read the piece or heard it referred to in a later seminar. In that essay, representations likely to cause paranoia in the onlooker, who suspects that the coherent image knows more about him than he does himself.

    The scene also evokes "Author and Hero in Aesthetic Activity," by Mikhail Bakhtin, although Cortázar almost certainly did not know this piece.

    > The mirror can do no more than provide the material for self-objectification, and even that not in its pure form. Indeed, our position before a mirror is always somewhat spurious, for since we lack any approach to ourselves from outside, in this case, as in the other, we project ourselves into a peculiarly indeterminate possible other, with whose help we then try to find an axiological position in relation to ourselves . . . I am not alone when I look at myself in the mirror: I am possessed by someone else's soul. More than that. At times, this other soul may gain body to the point where it attains a certain self-sufficiency. Vexation and a certain resentment, with which our dissatisfaction about our own exterior may combine, give body to this other – the possible author of our own exterior. Distrust of him, hatred, a desire to annihilate him become possible.

    From *Art and Answerability: Early Philosophical Essays by M.M. Bakhtin,* ed. Michael Holquist and Vadim Liapunov (Austin: University of Texas Press, 1990), 32–3.

22. That slime or "drool" is the same stuff that obsesses the photographer in "Las babas del diablo."

23. "He leído algunas cosas sobre todo eso, Bruno. Es muy raro, y en realidad tan difícil. . . . [*sic*] Yo creo que la música ayuda, sabes. No a entender, porque en realidad no entiendo nada" (254).

24. "Lo mejor es cuando te das cuenta de que puedes meter una tienda entera en la valija, cientos y cientos de trajes, como yo meto la música en el tiempo cuando estoy tocando a veces. La música y lo que pienso cuando viajo en el *métro*" (257).

25. "Bruno, si yo pudiera solamente vivir como en esos momentos, o como cuando estoy tocando y también el tiempo cambia . . ." (262).

26. Jay McShann, quoted in Robert Reisner, *Bird: The Legend of Charlie Parker* (New York: Da Capo Press, 1962); Collier, 353.

27. Ross Russell, "Bebop," in *The Art of Jazz: Ragtime to Be-bop,* ed. Martin Williams (New York: Da Capo Press, 1980; reprint of 1959 Oxford University ed.), 186–214. "Perhaps the most controversial aspect of bebop jazz is its rhythmic organization. Bebop rhythmics, or better polyrythmics, are so revolutionary that they have been largely misunderstood and, since no jazz can exist without a solid beat, the new style has been suspect among many uninformed listeners" (189).

Miles Davis has this telling memory of Parker revolutionizing the rhythm section: "Like we'd be playing the blues, and Bird would start on the 11th bar, and as the rhythm sections stayed where they were and Bird played where he was, it sounded as if the rhythm section was on one and three instead of two and four. Everytime that would happen, Max used to scream at Duke not to follow Bird but to stay where he was. Then eventually, it came around as Bird had planned and we were together again." Davis adds that Parker's "turning the rhythm section around" so frustrated him that for a while he would quit the group every night. Miles Davis, quoted in *Metronome* (June 1955), 25; Stearns, 231–2.

28. Hodeir writes that Parker was the real leader of the bebop movement. Like Armstrong around 1930, Parker got jazz out of a rut. *Jazz: Its Evolution and Essence,* 101. Later the standard attribution was to Parker and Gillespie. Their contributions, and the differences of personal style between them, are put succinctly by Leonard Feather, whose early *Inside Bebop* became required reading for other jazz historians. In *The Pleasures of Jazz* (New York: Horizon Press, 1976, 21), he writes, "the emergence of bebop, a new and enduring genre, was primarily the creation of Charlie Parker – whose pleasures during his appearances took several forms: odd quotes during an improvised solo, caustic comments to an apathetic or uncomprehending audience – and of Dizzy Gillespie, whose fame as a comedian has often enhanced the undimmed grandeur of his musical contribution."

Keeping Gillespie in view tempers more romantic and self-destructive assumptions about great music, such as the one Robert Reisner repeats in "I Remember Bird," *Bird: The Legend of Charlie Parker* (New York: Da Capo, 1962), 11–27, 19. "Bird was neurotic, but the great strides in the arts are not made by happy, well-adjusted people. Art is a form of sublimation and is created by neurotics and compulsion-ridden people, not by the happy, nine-to-five, family man." This brings to mind some of Spike Lee's reasons for making *Mo Better Blues,* his memorial to musical family men, including his own father.

29. From the liner to "Hampton Hawes Trio," Contemporary Records LP C3505, quoted by Lester Koenig (26 August 1955) (Stearns, 228). Hodeir had already made the point: "It is clear that he [Parker] created a school.... But, as we shall see, the new generation has not completely assimilated his acquisitions, particularly in the field of rhythm" (*Jazz,* 104).

30. "Cuando la marquesa echa a hablar uno se pregunta si el estilo de Dizzy no se le ha pegado al idioma, pues es una serie interminable de variaciones en los registros más inesperados . . ." (268).

31. André Hodeir describes Charlie Parker as a musical magician, "making appear and then disappear scraps of a melody that should have been rendered in full, hiding them up his sleeve." "The Genius of Art Tatum," *The Art of Jazz: Ragtime to Be-bop,* ed. Martin Williams (New York: Da Capo Press, 1980; reprint of 1959 Oxford University ed.), 173–80, 175.

32. "([Y]o ya no sé cómo escribir todo esto)" 302.

33. Hodeir, *Jazz,* 108.

34. "Este no es el momento de hacer crítica de *jazz*, y los interesados pueden leer mi libro sobre Johnny y el nuevo estilo de la posguerra, pero bien puedo decir que el cuarenta y ocho – digamos hasta el cincuenta – fue como una explosión de la música . . . " (266).

 Stearns starts his chapter on "Bop" (218–42) by calling it a revolution from within, no longer traceable to musical waves from the South: "For 'bop' was a sudden eruption within jazz, a fast but logical complication of melody, harmony, and rhythm" (218). As for dates, Stearns writes that World War II did a lot to break down the color line between black and white music: "by 1947–8, eager patrons formed queues around the block waiting to enter the Royal Roost, 'The Metropolitan Bopera House,' on Broadway" (219–20).

35. Domingo Faustino Sarmiento: "Biography is the most original kind of book that South America can produce in our times, and the best material we can offer history" (*Recuerdos de provincia* [1850], in the appendix on biography).

36. I find Jaime Alazraki unconvincing, for example, when he applauds Cortázar's fiction as having matured from an obsessive focus on plot to "more concentrated on characters, more vital and less dependent on plot"; but his partiality to character development is consistent with his appreciation for Cortázar's mastery as a writer of fiction. See his "From *Bestiary* to *Glenda*: Pushing the Short Story to Its Utmost Limits," in *The Review of Contemporary Fiction* 3, no. 3 (Elmwood Park, IL: Fall 1983): 94–9. Cortázar, of course, kept mastery at enough distance to incite innovation. He always feared writing too easily or too well. Even if Alazraki is not wrong about the initial shift of focus, it is only one shift; and Cortázar is a moving target for his readers.

37. His *Totality and Infinity* is an extended critique of the tradition of Western philosophy, a fundamentally ontological tradition that moves out in appropriative concentric circles from the subject. In its stead, Levinas appeals for an ethics based in the other, the locutor who preexists the subject and constructs him as a necessary listener. Only an appreciation for the radical and unassimilable alterity, and primordialness, of the other can ground ethical relations.

38. I thank Adam Zachary Newton for the general turn of this argument to the question of ethical engagement, and specifically for pointing out the relevance of Bakhtin for Cortázar. He develops his own reading in chapter 2 of his masterful *Narrative Ethics: Readers and Fiction in Each Other's Hands,* forthcoming from Harvard University Press. Newton's focus is on the duration of the enabling engagement between author and hero.

39. "Que los críticos son mucho más necesarios de lo que yo mismo estoy dispuesto a reconocer . . . porque los creadores, desde el inventor de la múscia hasta Johnny . . . , son incapaces de extraer las consecuencias dialécticas de su obra, postular los fundamentos y la trascendencia de lo que están escribiendo o improvisando" (300–1).

40. Bakhtin, 131.

41. See my "A Nowhere for Us: The Promising Pronouns of Cortázar's 'Utopian' Stories," *Dispositio* (Ann Arbor, 1986). Also printed in *Discurso Literario* 4, no. 1 (Stillwater, OK): 231–63. My focus is on his experiments with the very

components of literary and common language – that is, on the arbitrarily produced linguistic signs which he shows to be constructed, changeable, flexible, and as unstable as the world they allegedly represent.

42. Julio Cortázar, *We Love Glenda So Much and Other Stories,* trans. Gregory Rabassa (New York: Alfred A. Knopf, 1983), 16. For the original, see *Queremos tanto a Glenda:* "Queríamos tanto a Glenda que le ofreceríamos una última perfección inviolable. En la altura intangible donde la haíamos exaltado, la perservaríamos de la caída, sus fieles podrían seguir adorándola sin mengua; no se baja vivo de una cruz" (28).

43. "Apocalypse at Solentiname," in *We Love Glenda So Much,* 119–20. "Lo de siempre, por qué no vivís en tu patria, qué pasó que *Blow-Up* era tan distinto de tu cuento, te parece que el escritor tiene que estar comprometido? A esta altura de las cosas ya sé que la Ultima entrevista me la harán en las puertas del infierno y seguro que serán las mismas preguntas, y si por caso es chez San Pedro la cosa no va a cambiar, a usted no le parece que allá abajo escribía demasiado hermético para el pueblo?" "Apocalipsis de Solentiname," *Alguién que anda por ahí* (Madrid: Ediciones Alfaguara, 1977), 95.

44. "Lo difícil es girar en torno a él sin perder la distancia, como un buen satélite, un buen crítico" (288).

45. "En el fondo somos una banda de egoístas, so pretexto de cuidar a Johnny lo qu hacemos es salvar nuestra idea de él . . . sacarle brillo a la estatua que hemos erigido entre todos y defenderla cueste lo que cueste" (272).

46. "que se trepara a un altar y tironeara de Cristo para sacarlo de la cruz" (296).

47. "Deberías sentirte contento de que me haya portado así contigo; no lo hago con nadie, créeme. Es una muestra de cómo te aprecio. Tenemos que ir juntos a algún sitio para hablar . . ." (271).

48. "Y si yo mismo no he sabido tocar como debía, tocar lo que soy de veras . . . ya ves que no se te pueden pedir milagros, Bruno" (304).

49. "En el fondo lo único que ha dicho es que nadie sabe nada de nada, y no es una novedad. Toda biografía da eso por supuesto y sigue adelante, qué diablos" (304–5).

50. "envidio a Johnny, a ese Johnny del otro lado, sin que nadie sepa qué es exactamente ese otro lado. . . . Envidio a Johnny y al mismo tiempo me da rabia que se esté destruyendo por el mal empleo de sus dones . . ." (269–70).

51. "y quizá en el fondo quisiera que Johnny acabara de una vez, como una estrella que se rompe en mil pedazos y deja idiotas a los astrónomos durante una semana, y después uno se va a dormir y mañana es otro día" (270).

# 11

## "Press Clippings" and Cortázar's Ethics of Writing

### Aníbal González

Call me no longer Naomi, call me Mara, for the Almighty
has dealt bitterly with me.
I went away full, but the Lord has brought me back empty.

—Ruth, 1:20–21

Evil, therefore, if we examine it closely, is not only the
dream of the wicked: it is to some extent the dream of
Good.

—Georges Bataille, *La Littérature et le mal*

There was something that made comment impossible in
his narrative, or perhaps in himself. . . .

—Joseph Conrad, "The Secret Sharer"

Since the late nineteenth century, specifically after naturalism and symbolism in Europe and *modernismo* in Spanish America, it has been assumed that literature is written, in Nietzsche's phrase, "beyond good and evil." In fact, this thesis was advanced mostly by literary critics who wished to distance themselves from the fruitless moralizing of much nineteenth-century criticism (which, in Hispanic letters, reached its nadir in the work of Marcelino Menéndez y Pelayo) rather than by the fiction writers themselves, whose texts continued to display ethical concerns about the act of writing and the relationship between writer and society.[1] Until recently, such concerns were usually mediated by ideology: Ideologies, whether from the left or the right, tended to dictate the writers' relation to their society and to their work. We are now witnessing the emergence in Spanish American literature of an "ethics of writing" as a more encompassing phenomenon, one imbued, above all, with a critical, philosophical spirit. Instead of a catalogue of moral injunctions about the writers' responsibility to society (as one finds in nineteenth-century literary criticism as well as in twentieth-century Marxist criticism), the contemporary ethics of writ-

ing is an attempt by the writers themselves to figure out the moral implications of their work. Instead of commandments and principles, this
ethics of writing formulates questions – questions for which there are no
simple, dogmatic answers, such as: What does it mean to be a writer in
countries where the vast majority of the population is illiterate? Does fiction writing tend to be complicitous with the sources of social and political oppression or is it, on the contrary, an inherently subversive, antiau-
thoritarian activity? Can one truly write "beyond good and evil" or does all
fiction contain implicit moral judgments?

Like many of his counterparts in the Spanish American narrative
"boom," Julio Cortázar attempts to answer some of these questions in his
work of the 1970s and early 1980s. Novels such as *A Manual for Manuel*
(1973), short stories like "Apocalypse at Solentiname" (1977) and "Press
Clippings" (1981), and poems such as "Policrítica a la hora de los chacales" (1971), among others, evidence concerns with the nature of authority and authorship, with the writer's civic duties as an intellectual,
and, in general, a questioning of the role of the writer in the power relationships that are at work in literary texts. I have dealt elsewhere at some
length with this phenomenon in works by other boom authors such as
Carpentier (*The Harp and the Shadow,* 1979), García Márquez (*Chronicle
of a Death Foretold,* 1981), and Vargas Llosa (*The War of the End of the World,*
1981), and in younger authors such as Elena Poniatowska (*Massacre in
Mexico,* 1971).[2] However, unlike these writers' more distanced and ironic
stance, in Cortázar the search for an ethics of writing is frequently presented as a gut-wrenching, intimate experience, similar in scope and
intensity to a religious conversion. A conveniently brief but richly suggestive example is his late short story, "Press Clippings," collected in *We
Love Glenda So Much and Other Stories* (1981).

Regarded by some of his critics as one of Cortázar's most disturbing
stories in a realistic and political vein, "Press Clippings" has also been
seen as "the culmination of his overtly political writing, which began with
'Reunión' in *Todos los fuegos el fuego*" (Boldy, 126; see also Peavler, 93).[3]
There are, as we shall see, significant parallels (as well as differences)
between this story and "Meeting" ("Reunión," 1966). One salient difference is that "Press Clippings" has a female protagonist and first-person
narrator who is also an author figure. This is something of a departure in
Cortázar's oeuvre and clearly indicates his intention of bringing into this
story issues of gender in society and literature.

Briefly, "Press Clippings" is the first-person narrative of Noemí, an
Argentine woman and successful author living in Paris, who is asked by a

fellow countryman, a sculptor who has done a series of works on the subject of violence, to write a text to accompany a collection of photographs of the works. They meet in his apartment in a seedy neighborhood, and while Noemí studies the sculptures she shows the artist a press clipping that is an open letter written by an Argentine woman living in Mexico, denouncing how the woman's oldest daughter, along with the woman's husband and other close relatives, were kidnapped and murdered by the military junta. Noemí and the sculptor discuss their anguish and feelings of impotence over the facts contained in the clipping. Noemí agrees to write the text about the sculptures, and goes out into the street to take a taxi. On her way to the taxi stand, she comes upon a little girl crying alone in the street. "My papa is doing things to my mama," the girl tells Noemí, and reaching out, practically pulls the writer into a labyrinthine courtyard and toward a shack where Noemí comes upon a dreadful scene: The father has tied the mother to a bedstead and is torturing her by burning her nude body systematically with a lighted cigarette. Following an uncontrollable impulse, Noemí knocks the man unconscious with a stool, unties the woman, and then helps to tie the man to the bedstead. Without exchanging a word with the woman, Noemí, an intellectual who abhors violence, helps her torture the man.

Noemí returns to her apartment in a daze, drinks several glasses of vodka, and passes out. That afternoon, she writes down her experience, which will be the text to accompany the sculptor's works. She then phones the sculptor and, without giving him a chance to interrupt, tells him her story. Several days later, the sculptor sends Noemí a letter with a press clipping from the tabloid *France-Soir* recounting the story of a crime that happened in Marseille, presumably a few days before, in which a man had been tied to a bed and tortured to death. The man's mistress, the clipping says, is a suspect in the crime, and the couple's little girl has been reported missing. The part of the clipping describing the exact details of the man's torture is missing, but the photographs show the shack where Noemí had been. Noemí rushes back to the sculptor's neighborhood, trying in vain to locate the place where, in defiance of space and time, she had had her experience. However, she does find the little girl, and is told by a concièrge that the girl had been found lost in the street and that a social worker would come to get her. Before leaving, Noemí asks the little girl what her last name is, then in a café she writes down the ending to her text on the back of the sculptor's letter, and goes to slip it under his door, "so that the text accompanying his sculptures would be complete" ("Press Clippings," 96).

The complexities in this intense and gloomy story are evident from the beginning, when, after the title, an author's note diffidently advises us: "Although I don't think it's really necessary to say so, the first clipping is real and the second one imaginary" (81). The story is indeed constructed, in a typically Cortazarian fashion, following a series of polar oppositions that are later collapsed: reality/imagination, past/present, literature/journalism, male/female, France/Argentina, Paris/Marseille, and so on. In terms of its structure, binarism and a *mise en abyme* effect also prevail. "Press Clippings" contains two sets of stories, one placed inside the other. The first set comprises the story "Press Clippings," in *We Love Glenda So Much and Other Stories,* written by Julio Cortázar, and the text Noemí writes to accompany the sculptor's works, which is contained in "Press Clippings" and is essentially coextensive with it. The second set includes the two press clippings, each of which presides over one-half of the narrative: the Argentine mother's press clipping in the first half; and the clipping from *France-Soir* in the second half. Cortázar's choice of a female first-person narrator also places the question of narrative authority within a *mise en abyme:* Do we read the story as if it were written by Noemí? or by Cortázar writing as Noemí? or by Cortázar writing as Cortázar writing as Noemí?[4]

As my analysis of the story will show, the principal rhetorical device used by Cortázar to coordinate his use of binary elements and the *mise en abyme* is the chiasmus. This figure, as Richard A. Lanham explains, names "the ABBA pattern of mirror inversion" (Lanham, 33). A well-known instance is a quote from Knute Rockne: "When the going gets tough, the tough get going" (ibid.). Lanham observes that chiasmus "seems to set up a natural dynamics that draws the parts [of the construction] closer together, as if the second element wanted to flip over and back over the first, condensing the assertion back toward the compression of *Oxymoron* and *Pun*" (ibid.). Chiasmus may also be seen as a figure that tends to create indifferentiation, as it "seems to exhaust the possibilities of argument, as when Samuel Johnson destroyed an aspiring author with, 'Your manuscript is both good and original; but the part that is good is not original, and the part that is original is not good'" (ibid.).

Several notable similarities between this story and Cortázar's earlier experiment in politically committed fiction in "Meeting" should be pointed out: Both stories take real-world, historically verifiable events and documents as their point of departure (Che Guevara's *Pasajes de la guerra revolucionaria* [1963] and a 1978 press clipping from the Mexican daily *El País*), and both make use of religious allusions and figural allegory to structure their narrative.[5] Also, like "Meeting," this story can be regarded as the account of an experience so extreme and life-changing as to constitute a "conversion." "Meeting" is the allegorical account of Cortázar's political conversion to Cuban-style Marxism through the first-person retelling of Che Guevara's first guerrilla experiences in Cuba in 1959. Written in the (rather naive) hope of harmonizing revolutionary fervor with the elitist values inherent in literary discourse, "Meeting" succeeds, as I have argued elsewhere, not because it achieves such congruence, but because it artistically distorts and censors the texts by Che Guevara on which it is based ("Revolución y alegoría," 104–5, 109). "Press Clippings," which may be read as a critical rewriting of "Meeting," is the record of an equally radical, though less hopeful, change in Cortázar's outlook. Far more pessimistically and skeptically than in his previous fiction, Cortázar comes face-to-face in this story with the "heart of darkness" that lies at the core of literature.

Journalism is clearly an important element in this context, as it serves to spark the narrative's ethical interrogations. Although the first press clipping does not, properly speaking, belong to any genre of journalism – it is, as I have already indicated, an open letter, written in the style of an affidavit or legal deposition – it is nevertheless disseminated through the newspapers. The clipping's use of legal discourse further heightens its journalistic impact: It is an immediate, direct appeal for justice, and its language therefore carries a powerful performative element. It is not merely a piece of journalistic reporting, but an action carried out by a victim of violence seeking redress. Not unexpectedly, when Noemí and the sculptor read it, the clipping makes them painfully aware of the futility of their own activities to stop the violence:

> "You can see, all this is worth nothing," the sculptor said, sweeping his arm through the air. "Worth nothing, Noemí, I've spent months making this shit, you write books, that woman denounces atrocities, we attend congresses and round tables to protest, we almost come to believe that things are changing, and then all you need is two minutes of reading to understand the truth again, to—" (85)

Noemí responds in a reasonable and worldly-wise fashion to the sculptor's passionate exclamations, reminding him that writing and making art are what they do best, and that their relative weakness and marginality "will never be any reason to be silent" (86). She regards the sculptor's expressions of anguish as a form of "autotorture," and in fact is pleased that the man's works are "at the same time naive and subtle, in any case without any sense of dread or sentimental exaggeration" (82). She is leery of any sort of sensationalism or directness in representing the subject of torture and is sophisticated enough to realize that she herself feels an "obscure pleasure" when evoking images of torture (83).

The second half of the story, which begins when Noemí leaves the sculptor's apartment, is controlled – fittingly, as it turns out – by a hidden journalistic subtext: the crime story in *France-Soir*, which Noemí unknowingly and mysteriously reenacts. This section of the narrative is a descent into darkness, literally and metaphorically: the darkness of the passageways that lead from a street in Paris to a shack in Marseille and the darkness of Noemí's unconscious, which yearns to pay back the torturers in their own coin, in a version of talionic justice like the Old Testament's "an eye for an eye, a tooth for a tooth." (There are other, more direct links with the Bible in the story, as will be seen shortly.) For now, suffice it to note that this section's discourse combines, in a volatile mix, sensationalist journalism with psychoanalysis.

But, why journalism? Why not deal more directly with the question of art and violence, or art and crime, as in De Quincey's *On Murder Considered as One of the Fine Arts* (1827) or, to mention a more recent example, Patrick Süsskind's *Perfume* (1985)? Journalistic discourse, as I have pointed out in a recent study, appears in many works of contemporary Latin American narrative as a marker for ethical inquiry, specifically for what I have called an ethics of writing (González, *Journalism,* 109–11). In literary works up to the nineteenth century, religious discourse was predominant whenever ethical issues were raised; in twentieth-century Latin American narrative, however, it is frequently the figure of the journalist who confronts moral questions and agonizes over them, and in a language that is predominantly secular and philosophical rather than religious. The reasons for this journalism–ethics linkage in Latin American literature are complex,[6] but in general they have to do with that literature's constant return to its own discursive roots and to the historical importance of journalism as one of the founding discourses of Latin American writing. In "Press Clippings," furthermore, the artist characters are confronted by journalism with a transcription of reality unhampered by the norms of artistic and literary taste and decorum as Noemí and the sculptor understand them. The first clipping's performative use of language, and the second's sensationalistic rhetoric, are both able to name what the sculptures and Noemí's own text (as she foresees it at the story's beginning) repress or elide in the name of "good taste" or intellectual sophistication. By dealing openly with violence and crime, the press clippings expose literature's hypocritical denial of its links with evil.

Although this story's ethical inquiries are secular in nature, religious discourse still fulfills an auxiliary function in the text. Cortázar has seen fit to insert it obliquely by the allusion, in his choice of the protagonist's name, to the biblical story of Ruth. The allusion to the Book of Ruth in Noemí's name reinforces the theme of male–female relations in the story, but it also brings into play a figural allegorical framework derived from biblical exegesis similar to the one Cortázar uses in "Meeting."

"Noemí" is the Spanish version of Naomi, who was Ruth's mother-in-law. Though not an unusual name in Spanish-speaking countries, where it is used by Christians as well as Jews, it nevertheless also suggests a figural link between the protagonist and the Argentine mother of the first clipping, who is Jewish.[7] The biblical Naomi, it should be recalled, was an Israelite woman who had gone with her husband and two sons to live abroad in the country of Moab. Her husband and sons die, and she is left alone with her Moabite daughters-in-law, Orpah and Ruth. When she decides to return to her native land, she tells her daughters-in-law to go back to their families, reminding them that they no longer have any obligation toward her, but Ruth is determined to remain: "Where you lodge, I will lodge; your people shall be my people, and your God my God" (Ruth 1:16). The latter verse is a reminder that the story of Ruth, as Bible commentators have remarked, entails profound personal transformations:

In what amounts to a change of identity, from Moabite to Israelite (for there was as yet no formal procedure or even the theoretical possibility for religious conversion), Ruth adopts the people and God of Naomi. Religion was bound up with ethnicity in biblical times; each people had its land and its gods (cf. Mic. 4:5), so that to change religion meant to change nationality. (*Harper's Bible Commentary*, 263)

The mutual loyalty between Ruth and Naomi throughout the story is seen in the rabbinical tradition as an example of *chesed*, "loyalty or faithfulness born of a sense of caring and commitment" (*Harper's Bible Commentary*, 262). The story of Ruth also develops the theme of family continuity. The males in Naomi's family, who might be expected to perpetuate their family, disappear at the beginning of the story, and it falls to the women, an elderly widow and a non-Israelite, to achieve the continuity of the family through Ruth's marriage to Boaz (ibid.).

Noemí and the Argentine mother stand in a figural allegorical relationship to the biblical Naomi. Like her, both Noemí and the Argentine mother have no husband (in Noemí's case, because she is unmarried), and both seem to be women in their middle age or past it.[8] Like Naomi at the beginning of the Book of Ruth (1:20–1), Noemí clearly harbors a great bitterness (in her case, about her country's situation), and one may surmise that the Argentine mother harbors similar feelings, as her experience of losing her husband and daughters parallels that of the biblical Naomi. Furthermore, like Naomi, both women display *chesed* – loyalty and solidarity – although Noemí does so in an unexpectedly evil fashion, when she helps the tortured woman to turn the tables on her torturer. In contrast, the Argentine mother is closer to the instance of Naomi, because she petitions international organizations like the United Nations, the OAS, and Amnesty International for help in her plight; that is, she acts within a legal framework, as Naomi does to help her daughter-in-law Ruth at a time when Israel is under the rule of the judges (Ruth 1:1).

The figural allegory of Naomi, the Argentine mother, and Noemí clearly breaks down during the scene of violence in which Noemí is an active participant. This is the point when a chiasmatic reversal occurs in the narrative, a mirrorlike inversion of both the story of Naomi and that of the Argentine mother. This section may be read as Noemí's dream or fantasy of wish fulfillment in which, by assuming the male's agressive role, she ends up displaying the same dark impulses as the male power-figures.[9] The question of gender comes shockingly to the fore in this section. Unlike the powerless women in the Book of Ruth and in the first press clipping, who must appeal to a higher – and masculine – authority for aid, Noemí takes violent action to defend the tortured woman and, in a gesture that connotes not only solidarity with the victim but a distrust of the male-dominated system of justice, helps her to get even in the same brutal way as a male might do.

Despite its rather graphic realism, the atmosphere in this section of the story is oneiric, suggesting a symbolic rather than a literal reading. Earlier, the narrator had indicated a latent desire for wish fulfillment, when she recalled a religious anecdote about the conversion of King Clovis:

I remembered something I'd read when I was a girl, in Augustin Thierry, perhaps, a story about how a saint, God knows what his name was, had converted Clovis and his nation to Christianity and was describing the scourging and crucifixion of Jesus, and the king rose up on his throne, shaking his spear and shouting: "Oh, if only I could have been there with my Franks!" – the miracle of an impossible wish, the same impotent rage of the sculptor, lost in his reading. (87)

As well as prefiguring the story's narrative strategy (the use of wish fulfillment), the anecdote foregrounds the ambiguous use of the representation of violence in religious and, by extension, narrative discourse.

King Clovis's naive reaction to the story of Christ's crucifixion uncovers the violent subtext on which the narrative depends even as it symbolically supresses it: Hearing the story, Clovis did not see the cross as a Christian symbol of redemption but as an instrument of torture on which Jesus was being unjustly punished.

Like Clovis, Noemí literalizes in the account of her experience elements from a symbolic system – in her case, the Freudian "primal scene." The little girl's complaint ("My papa is doing things to my mama") rings with a psychosexual double entendre, suggesting a link with Noemí's unconscious, but also with her literary work: Earlier, Noemí has told the sculptor, "I've been writing a story where I talk, no less, about the psycho-log-i-cal problems of a girl at the moment of puberty" (87). It should be stressed that, in the end, this process of literalization and wish fulfillment does not uncover Noemí's unconscious so much as it does the hidden impulses behind the production of a literary text, in this case, the text to accompany the sculptures about violence. Cortázar's focus in this story, I would argue, is resolutely fixed on the gray no-man's-land (so to speak) between literature and psychoanalysis. Thus, the "primal scene" Noemí witnesses is not quite that of the sexual act between the father and the mother, but yet another symbolization. Although sexual implications are still present in this scene (in the symbolic equation of sex with violence and death common to many cultures), in this instance, like Jesus' crucifixion, the torture of the woman by the man clearly stands also for something else: writing. The connection with writing is brought out through a series of conventional symbolic equivalencies between the sexual act and the act of writing: The lighted cigarette is the penis/pen, the woman's body "burned from the stomach to the neck" ("Press Clippings," 91–2) is the page, the "purple or red splotches that went up to the thigh and the sex to the breasts" (92) are a form of somatic writing.[10]

As a whole, the tableau that Noemí interrupts suggests an equation between sexuality, violence, and writing in a context of transgression – a view that has much in common with that of the French writer Georges Bataille in *Literature and Evil* (1957). In his work, Bataille, who sees literature as the product of an unconscious human desire to exceed all boundaries (whether legal, religious, or cultural), offers a Nietzschean "hypermorality" as a position *au dessus de la melée*, as it were, from which to judge literature ethically (Bataille, 8). Provocatively, to be sure, Bataille writes as if the question of evil in literature were already settled: "Literature is not innocent. It is guilty and should admit itself so" (8a). Cortázar, on the other hand, seeks to go beyond Bataille's rather

detached "hypermorality" toward a more personal and critical view of literature's links with evil. Cortázar wishes to show instead that there is no
fixed, exterior place from which one can safely pass judgment: Just as the
distinctions between male and female, inside and outside, reader and
writer, torturer and victim, are blurred in the story, so the possibility of
rendering an objective moral judgment about events becomes more difficult, if not impossible – even as the need to do so becomes more urgent.

In "Press Clippings," Cortázar creates a referential *mise en abyme* in
which "literature" and "reality" (as both are symbolized in multiple ways
in the story) continually reflect and interpenetrate each other at various
levels, in a back-and-forth movement that ends in indifferentiation: We
have already remarked how Noemí's story stands in a figural allegorical
and chiasmatic relation to both Naomi's (in the Book of Ruth) and to
that of the Argentine mother; and how, by "gendering" (to use a fash-
ionable verb) the narrator, by making his narrator female, Cortázar
encourages an abysmatic reading of his authorial pronouncements in
the story (how do we separate Noemí's utterances from those of Cortázar,
or from Cortázar writing as Noemí, etc.?). Even when Noemí supposedly
comes face-to-face with the grimmest reality in the second half of the
story, literature creeps in. Noemí's actions, as said before, are obvious
wish fulfillments; but their improbable, conventionally fictional nature is
further underscored by the narrator's reference to books and films. After
she has struck the man with a stool, she finds a knife and cuts the
woman's bonds: "What came afterward I could have seen in a movie or
read in a book, I was there as if not being there, but I was there with an
agility and an intent that in a very brief time – if it happened in time – led
me to find a knife on the table, cut the bonds that held the woman" (92).

In another wish-fulfilling reversal, Noemí and the woman then tie up
the still-unconscious man to the bed and proceed to torture him as he
had tortured the woman. The narrator refuses to offer the exact details
of the man's torture, save by an indirect – and terrifying – reference to a
story by Jack London ("Lost Face," 1910), suggesting that the man's fate
is different from what he inflicted upon the woman (93).[11] But is this
really so? The allusions to the Jack London story suggest a scene not of
maenadic frenzy, but of carefully deliberate dismemberment:

now that I have to remember it and have to write it, my cursed state and my
harsh memory bring me something else indescribably lived but not seen, a
passage from a story by Jack London where a trapper in the north struggles
to win a clean death while beside him, turned into a bloody thing that still

holds a glimmer of consciousness, his comrade in adventures howls and twists, tortured by women of the tribe who horribly prolong his life in spasms and shrieks, killing him without killing him, exquisitely refined in each new variant, never described but there, like us there, never described and doing what we must, what we had to do. (93)

The passage suggests that the man is subjected to a process of indifferentiation – he is turned, like London's character, "into a bloody thing" – which appears to be the opposite of what the woman suffered: I have already remarked that the cigarette burns on her body evoke a form of somatic writing, and as such they are connected to differentiation. But it can be argued that what we have here is another chiasmus, "an ABBA pattern of mirror inversion," and that in fact the fates of both the man and the woman are equivalent.

The way in which Jack London's story is alluded to becomes in itself a clearer indication of what happened to the man. Unwilling to repeat in writing the horror in which she participated, Noemí takes recourse to literature in order to avoid describing, while strongly suggesting, what took place. Not surprisingly, given the story's pervasive use of the *mise en abyme,* the passage from London alluded to here also performs the same act of elision by allusion. In "Lost Face," the narrator refers to the torture thus:

So that thing before him was Big Ivan – Big Ivan the giant, the man without nerves, the man of iron, the Cossack turned freebooter of the seas, who was as phlegmatic as an ox, with a nervous system so low that what was pain to ordinary men was scarcely a tickle to him. Well, well, trust these Nulato Indians to find Big Ivan's nerves and trace them to the roots of his quivering soul. They were certainly doing it. It was inconceivable that a man could suffer so much and yet live. Big Ivan was paying for his low order of nerves. Already he had lasted twice as long as any of the others. (5)

As Noemí says, in London's tale the torture "by the women of the tribe" is "never described but there" ("Press Clippings," 93). Comparing this reference to Jack London with one in "Meeting," one sees that in the latter story London is mentioned indirectly through an edited quote from Che Guevara's *Pasajes de la guerra revolucionaria* that serves as the story's epigraph: "I remembered an old story by Jack London, where the protagonist, resting against the trunk of a tree, prepares to end his life with dignity" (*Todos los fuegos el fuego,* 67). As I show in my essay on this story, Cortázar reads this quote as a convergence between life and fiction, as well as an allegory of death and resurrection, although in fact there is no

precise correspondence between Che's circumstances (a guerrilla skirmish in a Cuban forest) and those of Jack London's fictional hero: As
Che himself indicates in a phrase that Cortázar chose to cut, "the protagonist . . . prepares to end his life with dignity, *knowing that he is doomed
to die of the cold in the frozen zones of Alaska*" (quoted in González, "Revolución y alegoría," 104–5; my italics).[12] In "Press Clippings," on the other
hand, the allusion to London opens up a vertiginous *mise en abyme* of elisions, cuts, or "clippings": A paraphrase, it is itself already a "clipping," a
piece cut from London's text; furthermore, in its content, the passage
avoids describing directly the way the trapper dies (another elision),
although it strongly suggests that this occurs through some variant of the
proverbial "death of a thousand cuts," which is yet another grim
metaphor for writing.

Commenting astutely on *Hopscotch* (*Rayuela,* 1963) in his essay "Del
yin al yang (Sobre Sade, Bataille, Marmori, Cortázar y Elizondo)," the
late Severo Sarduy focuses on chapter 14 of the novel, the episode in
which Wong, a Chinese who is a marginal character in the novel, shows
the members of the Serpent's Club a portfolio of photographs of the
Leng T'che, the "death of a thousand cuts," which he is using for a book
on Chinese art, because "In China," as Wong explains, "one has a different concept of art" (*Rayuela,* 70). Sarduy remarks that Wong symbolizes
in the novel an alternative to the Western metaphysics of presence and to
the yearning for totality that predominates in Cortázar's ideology in *Hopscotch.* Wong and his photographs emblematize the discontinuous, fragmentary nature of literary language, and its links with death and emptiness. However, Sarduy points out, Cortázar's text does not fully develop
these implications, perhaps because they are too unsettling to the search
for wholeness thematized in the novel (*Escrito sobre un cuerpo,* 24–7). Both
the man and the woman in "Press Clippings," therefore, attempt to
destroy each other through a mutilation that is emblematic of writing.
There is no symbolic death and resurrection here, no possibility of allegorically "healing" the break between the text and its meaning: A
panorama of "cuts" or "clippings" extends as far as the eye can see.

"Press Clippings" proposes a view of writing as a cutting or mutilation
very similar to Jacques Derrida's notion of "textual grafting":

One ought to explore systematically not only what appears to be a simple etymological coincidence uniting the graft and the graph (both from *graphion:*
writing implement, stylus), but also the analogy between the forms of textual
grafting and so-called vegetal grafting, or even, and more commonly today,
animal grafting. It would not be enough to compose an encyclopedic cata

logue of grafts . . . ; one must elaborate a systematic treatise on the textual graft. Among other things, this would help us understand the functioning of footnotes, for example, or epigraphs, and in what way, to the one who knows how to read, these are sometimes more important than the so-called principal or capital text.(*Dissemination*, 202–3)

Could it be by chance that the scene of torture in the second press clipping, in which Noemí uncannily (vicariously?) participates, takes place in a shack next to "a vegetable patch with low wire fences that marked off planted sections, there was enough light to see the skimpy mastic trees, the poles that supported climbing plants, rags to scare off the birds" (90) and with "a vague entrance full of old furniture and garden tools" (91)? Cortázar's use of chiasmus not only negates the possibility of any allegorical interpretation that would give his story a sense of wholeness and transcendent meaning, but it also makes visible the story's dependence on cuts or elisions at every level: from that of writing (as a systematic spacing of signs as well as an operation involving textual grafts), to the structural (the story's binary divisions), to the thematic (the sculptor's works and the instances of torture and mutilation described in the text). Noemí's disjointed thoughts, while self-reflexively harking back to the story's overall theme of cutting or dividing, show that she has witnessed a terrifying truth about herself, not only as a human being, but as a writer: "How could I know how long it lasted, how could I understand that I too, I too even though I thought I was on the right side, I too, how could I accept that I too there on the other side from the cut-off hands and the common graves, I too on the other side from the girls tortured and shot that same Christmas night . . ." (93).

The psychoanalytic element in the story helps explain the delayed appearance of the second press clipping, the one from *France-Soir,* as an instance of *Nachträglichkeit,* or deferred action. As Jonathan Culler summarizes it, this is "a paradoxical situation that Freud frequently encounters in his case studies, in which the determining event in a neurosis never occurs as such, is never present as an event, but is constructed afterward by what can only be described as a textual mechanism of the unconscious" (*On Deconstruction,* 163). Arguably, the event that precipitates the deferred action is the encounter with the little girl, which causes Noemí to construct a fantasy in which she acts out her neuroses; what is uncanny about the fantasy is that it is built out of elements from another clipping, one that Noemí had not previously mentioned (although she never denies having seen it before). The story leaves open the possibility, however, that Noemí might have learned about the events in Marseille from the little girl herself, who was the (presumably runaway) daughter of the couple in *France-Soir,* and that what we have read is Noemí's conflation of the little girl's account with her own wish-fulfilling fantasy.

In the end, it matters little. Clearly, there are two opposite ways to read this story: a "fantastic" one, which discounts the story's political and documentary elements (the first clipping) by subsuming everything into fiction; and a "realist" or "symbolic" one, in which the whole second half of the story (after Noemí leaves the sculptor's home) would be Noemí's fictional response to the first clipping, a narrative-within-the-narrative, and thus subject to a "symbolic" rather than a literal interpretation. This reading, however, is based on assumptions that are not fully and unequivocally supported by the text (that the story as a whole, or a large part of it, is a fiction penned by Noemí and therefore attests only to her "state of mind") and essentially acts to suppress the "fantastic" reading. Both readings conflict with each other and do violence to the text. I have been pursuing the latter, more "symbolic" reading, mainly because it has allowed me to focus on the story's many self-reflexive aspects, including the question of the narrator's gender, but it clearly breaks down when I try to explain, in a non-"fantastic" way, the chain of events of the story's second half. The preliminary authorial statement that one of the clippings is real and the other imaginary (81), further muddies the waters by first strictly delimiting two domains – "reality" and "imagination" – and then suggesting that, save for the first clipping, which has been "grafted" into it, the story as a whole belongs to the "imaginary" domain. Nevertheless, even this apparently authoritative statement is subject to fictionalization, and more ruthless readers who want to opt for the "fantastic" view might choose to do this, if they were willing to consider the powerfully performative first clipping to be purely fictional as well – an option that goes to the heart of the ethical issues raised by the story, as will be seen shortly.

The ethical questions in "Press Clippings," however, focus first not on the reader but on the figure of the author. In a curiously perverse (chiasmatic?) version of his old theory of the "lector cómplice" (*Rayuela,* 453–4), Cortázar posits in this story a theory of an "autor cómplice," an "author-accomplice," not of the reader, but of the torturers, the criminals, and any other entity that uses violence as a means to control others. The writer's craft is a sublimated version of the mechanisms of aggression used by those in power and those who wish to have power. To write is to cut, to wound, to hack away at something that is (or seems to be) alive: language, words, texts. Even if texts are viewed as already "dead bodies" or "epitaphs," writing is still a macabre affair, a form of necromancy or necrophilia.

Considering that all of Cortázar's novels after *Hopscotch* have fragmented, collage-like structures in which "expendable chapters" (that are
often quotes taken from newspapers and magazines, as in *Hopscotch*) or
outright press clippings (as in *A Manual for Manuel*) play a significant
role, then "Press Clippings" clearly implies a broad and anguished reappraisal by Cortázar of a large portion of his own oeuvre. And Cortázar,
unlike Bataille, seems to find no reassurance in a view of literature as a
form of desire and transgression. "Press Clippings" marks a point of crisis in Cortázar's work, a crisis that had been haunting that work at least
since chapter 14 in *Hopscotch,* where Wong displays the photographs of
the Leng T'che. The source of those photographs, as Severo Sarduy
points out, is Bataille's *Les Larmes d'Eros* (1961; *Escrito sobre un cuerpo,* 16,
24–5); "Press Clippings" would thus be merely the latest episode in a
long-standing and tense "dialogue" between Cortázar and Bataille's
texts. Sarduy also remarks on the narrative distance with which Cortázar
approaches this subject, and on the *"perturbation"* (Sarduy's italics)
Wong's presence brings into *Hopscotch* (*Escrito sobre un cuerpo,* 25, 27).
Cortázar continued to tiptoe around the subject of literature and evil in
texts such as "Suspect Relations" (in *Around the Day in Eighty Worlds,*
1967), which can be considered a tepid gloss on De Quincey's *On Murder Considered as One of the Fine Arts,* and in such novels and stories as *Manual for Manuel* and "Apocalypse at Solentiname," which, in their search
for ideological solutions, are still merely rough drafts of "Press Clippings." Of course, Cortázar's stories have often featured characters who
confront evil and perversity, or who are themselves monstrous;[13] but in
"Press Clippings" the terms of the equation (literature, politics, violence)
are fully present and clearly laid out, the ethical questioning is deeper,
and the sense of crisis is unequivocal.

The discomfort this story generates in both author and readers is
directly traceable to the grafting of the first press clipping, that of the
Argentine mother. This powerful text unsettles the story and critical
readings of it, making them seem superfluous, if not downright immoral.
Bringing legal discourse into play, and evoking notions of justice and
morality at their most fundamental level, the first press clipping uses ethical discourse as a shield and as a weapon to further its cause.

The clipping's ultimate effect is to make the critical reader feel like an
accomplice to the crimes it denounces. It achieves this first through its
testimonial nature, which asserts the text's absolute truthfulness and
almost literally rubricates it in blood. In general, testimonial narratives
are profoundly ethical, in that their stories are built around moral imper-
atives; one of these is *Thou shalt not lie.* (From the reader's standpoint,

this particular imperative translates as *Thou shalt not doubt*.) Despite their frequent claims to objectivity, moralism is pervasive in testimonial narratives, since, like melodrama (to which many of these texts recur), they always deal with fundamental polar oppositions: truth *versus* falsehood, justice *versus* injustice, society *versus* the individual (Brooks, 4). With the best intentions, these texts often manipulate their readers' emotions, forcing them to judge or be judged, to accept the narrative at face value or risk moral opprobrium. Testimonial narratives impose upon the reader the burden of making a moral choice, partly because they make ethically unacceptable the option of reading them as fiction.

The clipping's second strategy is the use of the performative, which shifts the clipping's textual dimension to the level of an act. A text such as the first clipping addresses itself to the readers, asking, almost demanding, that they do something. But what? Certainly, art or literature is not what first springs to mind. For the artists – Noemí, the sculptor, or Cortázar himself – the clipping poses an almost existentialist dilemma of how to react without betraying their personal identity, of which literature (in Noemí's and Cortázar's case) forms an inseparable part. Cortázar's life and work, in particular, despite his ludic inclinations, were always characterized by his desire to be true to his vocation as a writer, as his sometimes strained but always close relationship with the Cuban Revolution attests: To the demands by the Marxist and *fidelista* hard-liners that he deal with subjects such as revolution and oppression in Latin America and elsewhere, Cortázar replied that he would do so, but "in my own way" ("Policrítica," 128). In interviews, Cortázar insisted on "the horror I feel toward anyone who is an 'engaged writer' and nothing else. In general, I've never known a good writer who was engaged to the point that everything he wrote was subsumed in his engagement, without freedom to write other things. ( . . . ) I could never accept engagement as obedience to an exclusive duty to deal with ideological matters" (Prego, 131–2; my translation).

Speaking about *A Manual for Manuel*, Cortázar states that in that novel he tried to "achieve a convergence of contemporary history . . . with pure literature. . . . That extremely difficult balance between an ideological and a literary content . . . is for me one of the most passionately interesting problems in contemporary literature" (Prego, 133; my translation). The Argentine mother's clipping, however, does not allow for any such "balance." It is an imperative text, which demands that the reader give an ethically unambiguous reply to its appeal. But is a literary reply ethical? In "Press Clippings," Cortázar addresses the question of how to react ethically *as a writer* to acts of violence and evil, only to discover that literature itself is violent. Like the torturers and their dictatorial masters, literature is impassive and heartless, not given (in Noemí's phrase) to "sentimental exaggeration." In the end, Cortázar appears to agree with Bataille's dictum that "Literature is not innocent." But he does so grudgingly and with profound anguish, as this notion runs counter to Cortázar's publicly stated view of literature as ludic, childlike, and therefore innocent.[14] At the story's end, in a last twist of figuralism and chiasmus, the orphaned little girl becomes a figure for the Argentine mother and for Noemí herself. A witness to the horrors of the second clipping, the little girl, her innocence lost, is to be picked up by a "social worker" ("Press Clippings," 96), swallowed up by society. The best literature can do, it seems, is to "graft" the Argentine mother's clipping onto its own textual body and pass it on to the reader, along with the ethical dilemma it poses.

## Notes

1. My layman's understanding of ethics is heavily indebted to a group of current books that attempt to link ethics with literature, some of which seek to expand on Jacques Derrida's rather cryptic statement in *Signéponge/Signsponge:* "the ethical instance is at work in the body of literature" ("l'instance éthique travaille la littérature au corps"; 52–3). Among those which I have found most useful – although they often differ widely among themselves in approach – are: Geoffrey Galt Harpham's *Getting It Right: Language, Literature, and Ethics* (1992); J. Hillis Miller's *The Ethics of Reading: Kant, De Man, Eliot, Trollope, James, and Benjamin* (1987) and *Versions of Pygmalion* (1990); and Adam Zachary Newton's *Narrative Ethics* (1995). Harpham, whose synthesis of the current problematics of ethics and literature I find persuasive, cautions that "ethics is not properly understood as an ultimately coherent set of concepts, rules, or principles – that it ought not even be considered a truly distinct discourse – but rather that it is best conceived as a factor of 'imperativity' immanent in, but not confined to, the practices of language, analysis, narrative, and creation" (5). Harpham nevertheless identifies certain recurrent traits in discourses dealing with ethics (such as works by contemporary thinkers as diverse as Cavell, Derrida, Foucault, and Levinas) or where it plays a visible role (as in the narratives of Joseph Conrad): A fundamental one is the concern with the Other, particularly with "an otherness that remains other, that resists assimilation" (6). In his view, "the appearance of the other marks an 'ethical moment' even in discourses not obviously concerned with ethics" (7). Glossing a passage from Paul De Man's *Allegories of Reading* (1979), J. Hillis Miller observes that the ethics of language requires that language be referential (i.e., that it speak of something other than itself), even if that same referential impulse leads it (inevitably, according to De Man), into confusion, error, or falsehood (Miller, 46). In its discursive form, ethics does not escape the same contradiction: It has to be referential, which in its case implies passing judgment, formulating commandments,

and making promises about good and evil; but at the same time it happens that such judgments, commandments, or promises cannot be evaluated as to their truthfulness outside the domain of language. Commandments like "Thou shalt not kill," "Thou shalt not lie," or "Thou shalt not commit adultery," for example, are neither true nor false: They simply *are*. Ethical discourse is tautological; it is impossible to verify with reference to any rule or example outside itself (Miller, 49–50). In this, it resembles fiction, since it can be argued that the "falsehood" of any work of fiction can always be recovered as a "truth" on another level. At a strictly referential level, for instance, Góngora's *Fábula de Polifemo y Galatea* (1613) is false, but this is not necessarily the case at a symbolic or an allegorical level. Commandments are also like fictions in that, although they refer to real-world situations in which specific individuals may be involved, they greatly over simplify and generalize these situations.

2. In Chapter 6 of my book *Journalism and the Development of Spanish American Narrative,* I comment extensively on works by García Márquez, Poniatowska, and Vargas Llosa. On Carpentier, see my essay "Etica y teatralidad: *El Retablo de las Maravillas de Cervantes y El arpa y la sombra* de Alejo Carpentier."

3. Other recent essays that comment on "Press Clippings" are Susana Reisz de Rivarola's "Política y ficción fantástica" and Maurice Hemingway and Frank McQuade's "The Writer and Politics in Four Stories by Julio Cortázar." Unlike Boldy and Peavler, these critics view "Press Clippings" as a story that attempts to reconcile the fantastic with the political.

4. The quandary is similar to that in Borges's short story "Averroes' Search," when, in the final paragraph, the narrator notes: "I felt that Averroes, wanting to imagine what drama is without ever knowing what a theatre is, was no less absurd than I, wanting to imagine Averroes with nothing but a few drams of Renan, Lane, and Asín Palacios. In the last page, I felt that my narrative was a symbol of the man I was while I was writing it, and that in order to write that narrative I had to be that man, and that to be that man I had to have written that narrative, and so until infinity" (*El Aleph,* 101). All translations are mine, save where otherwise indicated.

5. See my essay "Revolución y alegoría en 'Reunión' de Julio Cortázar," 96–109. The most complete treatment of figural allegory is still Erich Auerbach's classic essay, "Figura." In it, he defines figural allegory as "the interpretation of one worldly event through another; the first signifies the second, the second fulfills the first. Both remain historical events; yet both, looked at in this way, have something provisional and incomplete about them; they point to one another and both point to something in the future, something still to come, which will be the actual, real, and definitive event" (58).

6. For a more detailed explanation, see González, *Journalism,* 109–11.

7. Her maiden name, Laura Beatriz Bonaparte, suggests that (like the biblical Ruth) she is not of Jewish origin, but she is married to Santiago Bruchstein, who is insulted by the military as "a Jew bastard" ("Press Clippings," 86).

8. Noemí's acquaintance with the sculptor dates back twenty years; "Press Clippings," 81.

9. Inquiring about the origin of the wishes that incite dream-wishes, Freud remarks (in a passage that is highly suggestive in terms of "Press Clippings"): "I readily admit that a wishful impulse originating in the conscious will *contribute* to the instigation of a dream, but it will probably not do more than that. The dream would not materialize if the preconscious wish did not succeed in finding reinforcement from elsewhere. . . . From the unconscious, in fact. *My supposition is that a conscious wish can only become a dream-instigator if it succeeds in awakening an unconscious wish with the same tenor and in obtaining reinforcement from it.* . . . These wishes in our unconscious, ever on the alert and, so to say, immortal, remind one of the legendary Titans, weighed down since primaeval ages by the massive bulk of the mountains which were once hurled upon them by the victorious gods and which are still shaken from time to time by the convulsion of their limbs. But these wishes, held under repression, are themselves of infantile origin, as we are taught by the psychological research into the neuroses. I would propose, therefore, to set aside the assertion . . . that the place of origin of dream-wishes is a matter of indifference and replace it by another one to the following effect: *a wish which is represented in a dream must be an infantile one"* (*The Interpretation of Dreams,* 591–2; Freud's emphasis).

10. See Susan Gubar's overview of sexual/textual metaphors and women's writing in "'The Blank Page' and the Issues of Women's Creativity," 244–7.

11. In London's "Lost Face," an exiled Polish patriot, Subienkow, who had joined with Russian fur trappers in Alaska in the early 1800s, faces certain death by torture at the hands of an Indian tribe. As he hears and watches his comrade, Big Ivan, being tortured by the women of the tribe (in the passage alluded to in Cortázar's story), he devises a way to achieve a quick, clean death at the hand of his enemies. Subienkow, who regards himself as "a dreamer, a poet, and an artist" ("Lost Face," 4), uses his wits to trick the chief into beheading him, thus depriving the tribe of the pleasure of torturing him. The narrator makes it clear that Subienkow is no pure, unsullied hero. Despite his cultivated background and his noble dream of an independent Poland, he too had killed innocent people: the traveler in Siberia whose papers he stole (7,8), and, of course, numerous Indians (7). "It had been nothing but savagery" (7) is a phrase that recurs like a leitmotiv throughout "Lost Face." Interestingly, this is a story that also caught Jorge Luis Borges's attention. Borges translated it into Spanish and included it in an anthology he edited of short stories by London, *Las muertes concéntricas* (1979). It is likely, however, that Cortázar read the story in the original English long before Borges's translation appeared.

12. The story Che had in mind is probably London's "To Build a Fire."

13. As Roberto González Echevarría remarks about the myth of the Minotaur in Cortázar's early play, *Los reyes* (1949): "The confrontation of the monster and the hero constitutes the primal scene in Cortázar's mythology of writing: a hegemonic struggle for the center, which resolves itself in a mutual cancellation and in the superimposition of beginnings and ends. . . . This primal scene appears with remarkable consistency in Cortázar's writing. I do not mean simply that there are monsters, labyrinths, and heroes, but rather that

the scene in which a monster and a hero kill each other, cancel each other's claim to the center of the labyrinth, occurs with great frequency, particularly in texts where the nature of writing seems to be more obviously in question" (*The Voice of the Masters*, 102, 103).

14. "Ever since I began writing . . . ," Cortázar has said, "the notion of the ludic was profoundly meshed, confused, with the notion of literature. For me, a literature without ludic elements is boring, the kind of literature I don't read, a dull literature, like socialist realism, for example" (Prego, 136–7). See also, González Bermejo, 103–12, and Picón Garfield's comments on games and the "man-child" in Cortázar's works in *¿Es Julio Cortázar un surrealista?* 189–99.

## References

Auerbach, Erich. "Figura." In *Scenes from the Drama of European Literature*, 11–78. Minneapolis: University of Minnesota Press, 1984.

Bataille, Georges. *La Littérature et le mal*. Paris: Gallimard, 1957.

Boldy, Steven. "Julio Cortázar (26 August 1914–12 February 1984)." In *Dictionary of Literary Biography: Volume 113, Modern Latin American Fiction Writers, First Series*, 119–33. Detroit: Bruccoli Clark Layman, 1992.

Borges, Jorge Luis. *El Aleph*. Buenos Aires: Emecé, 1972.

Brooks, Peter. *The Melodramatic Imagination: Balzac, Henry James, Melodrama, and the Mode of Excess*. New York: Columbia University Press, 1984.

Conrad, Joseph. "The Secret Sharer." In *The Portable Conrad*, ed. Morton Dauwen Zabel. New York: Viking Press, 1968.

Cortázar, Julio. "Policrítica a la hora de los chacales." In Carlos Fuentes, "Documentos. El caso Padilla." *Libre* 1 (September–November 1971): 126–30.

"Press Clippings." In *We Love Glenda So Much and Other Tales*, trans. Gregory Rabassa, 81–96. New York: Knopf, 1983.

*Rayuela*. Buenos Aires: Sudamericana, 1972.

*Todos los fuegos el fuego*. Buenos Aires: Sudamericana, 1972.

Culler, Jonathan. *On Deconstruction: Theory and Criticism after Structuralism*. Ithaca, NY: Cornell University Press, 1982.

De Man, Paul. *Allegories of Reading*. New Haven, CT: Yale University Press, 1979.

Derrida, Jacques. *Dissemination*. Trans. Barbara Johnson. Chicago: University of Chicago Press, 1981.

*Signéponge/Signsponge*. Trans. Richard Rand. New York: Columbia University Press, 1984.

Freud, Sigmund. *The Interpretation of Dreams*. New York: Avon Books, 1965.

González, Aníbal. "Etica y teatralidad: *El Retablo de las Maravillas* de Cervantes y *El arpa y la sombra* de Alejo Carpentier." *La Torre (Nueva Epoca). Revista de la Universidad de Puerto Rico* 27–8 (1993): 485–502.

*Journalism and the Development of Spanish American Narrative*. Cambridge University Press, 1993.

"Revolución y alegoría en 'Reunión' de Julio Cortázar." In *Los ochenta mundos de Cortázar: Ensayos*, ed. Fernando Burgos, 93–109. Madrid: Edi-6, 1987.

González Bermejo, Ernesto. *Revelaciones de un cronopio: Conversaciones con Cortázar.* Montevideo: Ediciones de la Banda Oriental, 1986.

González Echevarría, Roberto. *The Voice of the Masters: Writing and Authority in Modern Latin American Literature.* Austin: University of Texas Press, 1985.

Gubar, Susan. "'The Blank Page' and the Issues of Women's Creativity." *Critical Inquiry: Writing and Sexual Difference* 8 (Winter 1981): 243–63.

*Harper's Bible Commentary.* San Francisco: Harper & Row, 1988.

Harpham, Geoffrey Galt. *Getting It Right: Language, Literature, and Ethics.* Chicago: University of Chicago Press, 1992.

Hemingway, Maurice, and Frank McQuade. "The Writer and Politics in Four Stories by Julio Cortázar." *Revista Canadiense de Estudios Hispánicos* 13 (Fall 1988): 49–65.

Lanham, Richard A. *A Handlist of Rhetorical Terms.* 2d ed. Berkeley: University of California Press, 1991.

London, Jack. *Las muertes concéntricas.* Ed. and trans. Jorge Luis Borges and Nora Dottori. Buenos Aires: Ediciones Librería de la Ciudad/Franco María Ricci Editore, 1979.

"Lost Face." In *Lost Face.* New York: Macmillan Co., 1910.

Miller, J. Hillis. *The Ethics of Reading: Kant, De Man, Eliot, Trollope, James, and Benjamin.* New York: Columbia University Press, 1987.

*Versions of Pygmalion.* Cambridge, MA: Harvard University Press, 1990.

*The New Oxford Annotated Bible.* New York: Oxford University Press, 1991.

Newton, Adam Zachary. *Narrative Ethics.* Cambridge, MA: Harvard University Press, 1995.

Peavler, Terry J. *Julio Cortázar.* Twayne World Authors Series 816. Boston: Twayne Publishers, 1990.

Picón Garfield, Evelyn. *¿Es Julio Cortázar un surrealista?* Madrid: Gredos, 1975.

Prego, Omar. *La fascinación de las palabras: Conversaciones con Julio Cortázar.* Barcelona: Muchnik Editores, 1985.

Reisz de Rivarola, Susana. "Política y ficción fantástica." *Inti: Revista de Literatura Hispánica* 22–3 (1985–6): 217–30.

Sarduy, Severo. *Escrito sobre un cuerpo.* Buenos Aires: Sudamericana, 1969.

# Index